SEARCHING GOD
IN THE MEDIA MARKET

Convergence of Theology and Media

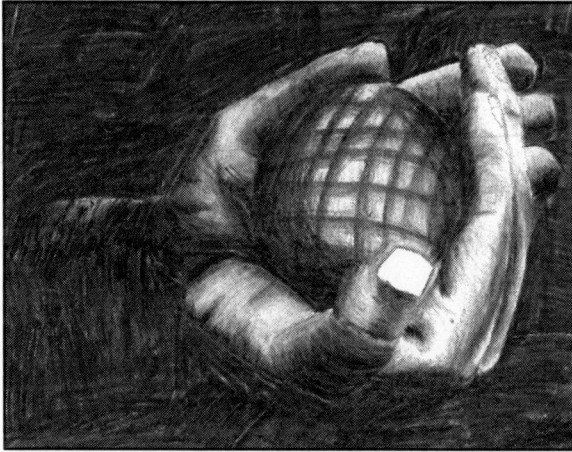

John Joshva Raja

PublishAmerica
Baltimore

First printing

PublishAmerica has allowed this work to remain exactly as the author intended, verbatim, without editorial input.

Softcover 9781462613021
PUBLISHED BY PUBLISHAMERICA, LLLP
www.publishamerica.com
Baltimore

Printed in the United States of America

Contents

Introduction

Media towers were taller than the towers of the churches and thereby symbolically replaced the power of influencing public faith, values and attitude to much extent. Institutions such as churches, schools and families had once been dominant sources of providing meanings of life and of God [Goethals, 1990] but today the media compete with these as dominant sources of meanings and provide a market of meanings from which people buy and borrow meanings that satisfy them in their changing contexts. The changing contexts demand people to search for meanings of God and of life. Among the competing social, cultural and political institutions, media has taken the central role in communicating these meanings to the public and enabling them to share through them as well. Engaging in such search for meanings of life and of God, led media to play the role of a pastor, theologian, prophet and educator in public and private lives of people. When the audience construct and negotiate their meanings of God and of life there begins the dialogue between theology and media.

This book is an attempt to provide a space for dialogue between theology and media from new directions and especially dialogue between perspectives from the South and North. It is difficult to address all the issues and questions related to this area within so slim a book and so inevitably some choices had to be made. This book will focus on those issues that are often neglected by the media scholars in relation to religion and also by theological scholars in relation to media such as imagination, entertainment, representation, freedom and alternatives. The media have created irreversible contexts where many new questions arise for theological thinking and studies. The primary principle of this book is to show that theologians have to take media seriously in their contextualising hermeneutics and particularly in addressing some question being raised by people after their encounter with media. Hermeneutics involves developing meanings of those narratives about God and about life in the universe. These meanings were once provided by the church, family and school which were the main social institutions. Today people develop their own religious and life oriented meanings from different media and from other sources that are available to them. In this market of meanings, a few questions arise: How are Christian meanings shared? What kind of meanings that the people can choose? How can the church use those means and methods to effectively communicate their own meanings? What are the impacts some of these mediated meanings make? What are the alternative ways of communicating Christian meanings? How can we educate Congregation to select the meanings that are relevant to them? In what ways can we listen to some of the serious questions raised to our faith by media? This book will not try to answer these questions but will certainly engage with these questions using examples and cases from different media.

My question is how imagination, aesthetic elements, representation, contemporary audio visuals and interactive characteristics of the media provide a hermeneutic framework within which audience finding their own meanings of God and of life. The word media can also include a wide range of means and methods of communication from a tract to television and also from newspapers to the internet. In this book, I have selected only those media that have changed the context of religious thinking or are popular in the public arena such as films, television, newspapers, and Internet and community media. The purpose of this book is to mainly highlight the changing trends of the people's search for meanings of God and of life in which media personnel engage, by displaying a wide range of theological narratives for the public.

The question of imagination in the public display of religious text today has to be taken seriously by theologians. Frequently, people use imagination to develop new or old imageries of faith to search for meanings that are relevant to their context. My first chapter will deal with the role of imagination in the interaction between media and theology. Films such as *The Da Vinci Code* (2006) and *The Passion of the Christ* (2004) differ in the construction of plot and in the imaginative presentation of the story. The story in *The Passion of the Christ* Film exaggerates the suffering of Jesus before and during crucifixion. The story follows the New Testament stories to much extent. In this sense it follows the accepted version of the Biblical passion narratives. The director also uses contemporary audio and video effects on the display and agony of the suffering. The imagination of the audience is influenced by such extraordinary visual and audio effects.

The way Jesus gets up after flogging is similar to a world wrestling Federation fighter getting up for another round of fight. The role of imagination in such embellished film stories in order to bring the story alive but exaggerated to fit into the contemporary film viewing audience whereby it provides a new hermeneutics using aesthetic elements, imagination and film art to relate story to meet both the expectations of the contemporary audience and also thus remain the public domain as a popular but controversial movie.

In the film *The Da Vinci* Code the story does not follow the New Testament narratives about Jesus though it discusses about the secret code of the art that describes about the last supper of Jesus with his disciples. In this way the hermeneutic role of imagination is different from that of other films that follow the New Testament stories closely. Though the story of Da Vinci provides an entirely different narrative to imagine, this story too provides a public display of Christian tradition, images and stories which are somewhat deviant from that of the New Testament stories or traditional stories. In this sense both films being taken as examples provide a challenge for theologians to think about the role of imagination and the use of contemporary images in doing hermeneutics of the Biblical and traditional stories. Rather than neglecting these stories as a mere non-historical and pure entertainment stories, those who are involved in doing hermeneutics need to look at them and possibly identify the hermeneutic methods and explore whether a systematic theological method for interpreting gospel stories to the public audience today. These films interpret and challenge the meanings that arise out of the biblical stories in a new way that may contribute to the faith and worldview of the audience.

The relationship between revelation, imagination and imageries/ images has not been systematically studied in the visuals of the modern media, particularly in films. McIntyre's book on *Theology and Imagination, (1987)* is a good book but it does not consider the Eastern perspectives where the imaginary visual world and the real world often converge and are often considered the same in the mind of the audience. This will be discussed in the first chapter. Scholars such as Gordon Kaufmann, David Tracy and Sally McFague have discussed the role of imagination in relation to theology but in relation to media and theology, such discussions have yet to happen. The imaginary world that is created by the media provides a wide range of meanings of faith enabling the audience to search for their own meanings and choose them according to their own interest. Theology has to take very seriously the public role of imagination and its relationship to the faith that is displayed in the public. This chapter will discuss the role of imagination in the interaction between media and theology, particularly how imagination plays in the meaning making process of the audience from the text.

The second chapter will deal with the role of entertainment in the interaction between theology and media. It will look at the way tele-gurus play gods in television's various channels. They tend to fix narratives, God and their version of the gospel and package and sell it in the media market. These tele-gurus with their commercial theologies try to entertain, promise and exploit the audience's economic, psychological and physical weakness. The beauty and other elements of entertainment using the technologies and skills of television camera persons attract, popularize and sell the packaged gospel to the public through the media. Such tele-gurus popularize tele-gods to the public through miracles and performance and thus create a public space for themselves. This provides a challenge for theological studies by raising questions about the role of entertainment and leisure in theology. Many scholars such as Stewart Hoover, Peter Horsfield and others have studied tele-evangelists in the United States and have contributed to this area. This chapter will focus not only on the tele-evangelists but also the tele-gurus such as Nameologists (luck with names), Numerologists (prediction with birthdates), Astrologists, Signaterologists (changing future with signature) and Vastuologists (house square and luck calculations). These tele-gurus with their different 'logism' present a great challenge to theological thinking. This will be discussed in this chapter with a special emphasis on theology of religious entertainment and religious leisure.

My third chapter deals with the misrepresentation of various sections of the minorities such as religious and ethnic minorities, women, differently-able persons and HIV infected individuals. This raises a new issue in the area of theology of mission to the public. In displaying not only the minorities but also 'the other', mass media professionals seem to have used a kind of dualistic approach in which the outsider or the other is often shown with a negative or a stereotypical connotation to their character or culture. They use different colours, images and words to reflect and reiterate the known stereotypical concepts about the other that the audience also share. In this way old imageries and their meanings such as darkness and blackness converge with meanings of social evil and negative roles in the stories. This often creates articulate ignorance about 'the other' and provides a misrepresentation in the public. In order to respond to the issues of freedom of expression, culture of ignorance, culture of confrontation and violence, one needs to theologically respond to the issues of 'misrepresentation' and 'less representation'. Some newspapers particularly popularize negative images about other communities and other persons within the communities. To some extent such repeated stereotypical images in the public create a culture of ignorance in the mind set of the majority and creates a lot of tension within families, communities and nations. Such ignorance between communities often leads to confrontation and violence.

In such a context theology needs to be challenged in order to address the issue of community representation and thus to remove the ignorance among communities and to establish relationship

9

and understanding among them. The questions of 'other' and the stereotypical imageries in the media and theology will also be raised in this chapter. In this context, I will refer to Huntington's thesis of the 'Clash of Civilizations' and the review of this thesis by Edward Said. The search for meanings of 'other' and the deconstruction of stereotypical images are part of the ongoing process of every community. Through this process, media personal and audience interact to find their own and relevant meanings.

The fourth chapter will deal with the internet and theology. According to the Lycos[1] search engine, the second most searched subject on the internet, besides sex, is God. It is a challenge for theologians to recognize and engage in such searches for meanings of God and of life in the media along with the audience.

The internet provides a new way of communication that is interactive and creates a new space for the younger generation to search for self, God and anything else they may want according to their interest and tastes. It is a fast, hypertext-based, audience-centred, mainly secret and cheap means of communication. On the internet, many are engaged in attempting to build and break their relationship and search for meanings of God and of life. On the internet, the virtual self searches for a virtual God where one may discover or destroy one's own faith. This changing paradigm of communication challenges the way in which communication is understood in traditional terms by theologians. This demands us to re-vision the question of God itself as an interactive communicator with people. The relevant questions are: does God himself change according to the changes in the world? Or is what changes our interpretation of God in the light of these changes to the world as we experience it, our theology? To this end, Frances Plude's interactive method will be analyzed from a theological perspective.

The internet provides a huge range of means to search for meanings of God and of life according to one's own expectation and personal interest. This shifts the quest from a theo-centric to a human-centric approach to theological paradigms. Thomas Thangaraj [1999:1–7] in his book, *The Common Task: A Theology of Christian Mission,* demands a paradigm shift in doing mission in which we need to emphasize the '*missio-humanitatis*',, the mission of humankind rather than the '*missio-Dei*', the mission of God. This provides a platform for re-visioning the image of God as a participatory, interactive and dynamic person. This chapter will discuss how the understanding of God is being influenced by the way the culture of communication has emerged through the internet.

Community media have emerged as counter media to the mainstream media in the developing countries but not many have taken their religious roles seriously. They enable people to organize themselves and to express their concerns among themselves and with others. This has brought radical social changes using folk, alternative and technological media. Community media are readily available, accessible and affordable by the people. Among many communities this has brought radical changes in terms of social, economic and political enlightenment and awareness to the people at the margins. From simple chalkboards to news media, these media are making a marked impact on people's religious faith. People have increasingly become critical of the religious institutions and their leaders through such media. Our question is to search for the theological response to such media practices and to assess their impact on those who use them.

The mass media play the role of informer, educator and entertainer whereas community media interact with communities in their search for religious meanings or to engage the communities themselves in such searches. Theologically we are invited to develop a concept of God who is also communitarian in nature. Maintaining communitarian values does not mean losing the freedom of individuals, rather finding a negotiated space for individual freedom and creativity and maintaining the positive role of certain agreed values within a particular community. Such a theological framework would also enable future theologians to discover God in their respective ways. This chapter will also deal with Habermas' quest for rediscovering

11

the public space in relation to theology and media. This leads to a discussion about the understanding of community within theological circles. Religious communities understand community in terms of their own religious members. By serving through the community media to others, there is a challenge to theology to persuade people to include others too, in their service towards a fuller humanity.

It is people who 'make' theology and who take much from the media. People are engaged in diverse ways to search for meaning through the various media. If this is the case, the way different media provide new hermeneutics for contextual interpretation of the Bible needs elaborating. This book thus highlights the importance of recognizing the media and their culture in doing theology. It also struggles with the question of how theological thinking can become relevant and effective in the public arena and make an impact on the media and their practices.

This book seeks to enable the reader to recognize the importance of imagination, entertainment, representation of 'other', human-centred approaches and communitarian concepts as used in the media and their role in doing theology in today's context. This would enable theologians and media practitioners to rediscover and re-imagine their roles in public and interpret the meanings of God and of life along with the audience.

1 Hollywood – Is Jesus still the Superstar?

Section A: Imagining Jesus in movies

Introduction

When the movie *The Passion of Christ* was showed in Bangalore theatres I was standing in a queue in one of the theatres. It was to my surprise the queue was full of Muslims from the suburban areas of Bangalore. It was a grand success English Movie according to the local newspapers as audience found it as entertaining as well as worthy of watching in the theatre. I read similar success stories of the films even in some Muslim countries in South East of Asia and in other parts of the world.

I had a discussion with an educated Muslim about the film. For him this film has brought together the modern visual display and the gospel story together. The attraction to see the film was due to the criticism that the film has received from Christians and also from media critics. He told me that this film has brought passion explicitly and so brought sympathies from my heart towards Jesus. He added further how technological imagination and display can bring the story closer to his heart. Finally he compared the suffering of Jesus with Palestinians. These were extraordinary intellectual reflection of the film. But he pointed out important issues within the film which will be discussed in the chapter.

In this chapter the following questions are discussed: Can Imagination play a role in retelling faith stories? Can the stories be told a bit differently in media using contemporary visuals and sound systems? What is the role of imagination in theology and hermeneutics? How did biblical communities re-imagine God in different contexts? In order to engage with these questions I use two films as examples and also use some Biblical references in the second section of this chapter. They became popular in the first part of 21st century, at least

John Joshva Raja

in South Asia and all over the world, and were viewed in cinemas by people from all religions.

Mel Gibson's *The Passion of the* Christ (2004) was viewed by audiences around the world. It was critiqued for its visual presentation of Jesus' passion and also for compelling sound-effects and visuals. Thus, the depiction of the suffering of Jesus became an entertaining film for the public, perhaps a reflection of the skill of Mel Gibson and also of the producer of the film. Though the film followed closely the passion stories found in the gospels, but exaggeration of the passion of Jesus using imagination, aesthetic elements and popular images were used in such a way that people were willing to pay to see this film.

Unfortunately, a negative attitude has existed among many Christians about the role of imagination[2] and aesthetic[3], elements in understanding and interpreting God in public. Also, there are references in the Bible that are utilized to attempt to prohibit imagination in any form in the public Christian communication [McIntyre, 1987:5]. Misuse of imagination, it is feared, can lead to 'iconophobia' (fear of icons and also of images) among the many protestant Christians [McIntyre, 1987:8]. Imagination, however, is an important element of hermeneutics. It is the thought to which experience of events and people are described without direct contact or experience. McIntyre [1987:150–162] describes imagination as sensitivity to and perceptiveness of features in the world and in persons which the ordinary observer passes unnoticed.

Imagination is selective from the mass of the material with which the mind is confronted. Imagination is also selective of significant features in any situation or piece of history or of literature and therefore requires a high level of creative and constructive thought. In this chapter, I understand imagination as a thought or an idea that enables people to develop or re-tell or re-imagine a story using contemporary images and cultural tools. It is a dialogic thought between visual images and imageless nouns and concepts. The contemporary film producers in Hollywood use such imaginative thought patterns to retell many old stories.

The *Passion of the Christ*

Whether we accept or reject it, the Christian message is made available to the public in a more imaginative way through films such as *The Passion of the Christ*. This enables a film to play the role of a theologian, disturbing the mindsets and enabling the public to enquire about the meaning of the passion of Christ. The film was produced in Italy with Jewish traditional settings. A few violent graphic sections of this film received R-rating in US[4]. The film was criticized for being anti-Semitic; however, it was also seen by many Evangelical Christians as an opportunity to reach the world. Gary North in his book, *The War on Mel Gibson: The Media versus Passion [2004: 11-40]* referring to various Jewish sources and scholars strongly argues that this film uses stereotypical portrayal of first century Jews. He goes further to argue that Gibson refuses to accept the liberal agenda of caring and sensitive to others including Jewish communities rather sensationalising people against Christ-Killers.

In this sense this film is also anti-Christian in its values *[North 2004:36]. By making profit as one of the primary motives of producing The Passion of the Christ, Gibson was able to convert sensationalising the passion of Jesus into a success in the Hollywood Market.* In spite of all the criticisms, the film ran successfully enabling the producers to make huge profits at the box office. For Beal and Linafelt [2006:3–5] *The Passion of the Christ* is not merely a media phenomenon but a religious and biblical phenomenon. The film provides contemporary visual hermeneutics for New Testament stories although depicting filmatic violence and also anti-Jewish dimensions.

The story depicted in *The Passion of the Christ* provides a broader dialogue between media, popular culture and theology. The graphics, editing skill, technological production, contemporary image use, extreme violence and popular cinematographic settings are all used to enable the audience to imagine and feel the suffering of Jesus both before and during the crucifixion. Using visual artistic elements and the use of Aramaic language, the producer provides a hermeneutics for the story to the mass audience who may not be Christian, but are regular film viewers of Hollywood films. There is a negotiation between the popular imagining process that is done in Hollywood and the mass religious stories that are found in the Gospel. Gibson was successful in maintaining an assumed target audience, that of Christians, while bringing in a new non-Christian audience, willing to pay and view this film in the format of Hollywood filmic imagination.

The Da Vinci Code

While looking at *The Passion of the Christ* and the role of imagination in the portrayal of hermeneutics in public, the challenge for theologians is to look at Gibson's way of recognizing and displaying the old story with new imaginative meanings. However, it is acknowledged *The Passion of the Christ* is within the regular framework of imagination of biblical stories, yet when we discuss *The Da Vinci Code* (2006), based on a best-selling novel by Dan Brown, as a film; many other issues arise about the role of imagination in doing hermeneutics in public. In both films, many theologians were engaged in defending the true stories or in exposing them in one way or another. Many theologians perhaps, did not realize that these films behave like theologians in public, engaging in the search for God and for life, albeit in their own ways. Using imaginary stories with a historical background, the novel writers and film producers make their product very attractive and entertaining and thus, as a result, reap huge profits.

Hollywood is a film industry where people invest money in order to realize immense gains. Any marketable story that is likely to bring back money to the producers in Hollywood is being bought and converted into film; controversial themes are often used by this industry to boost the sale of films. The question at issue is: when a historical figure is converted into a mythical figure will there not be a tendency to change his or her character altogether through an imaginary narrative?

Such construction of stories is part of human nature. Even the oral tradition created Jesus into a more imaginary figure with embellishments of other-worldly characteristics. Adding some imaginary characters and contemporary images to the story in order to make the story alive to the Hollywood audience is not such a great issue, even if it happens to deviate a little from the original story. However, when the characters are imagined in a deviational way, such as depicting Jesus getting married to Mary, as yet not established historically, then the question arises how theology needs to take into account such deviational imagination. The immediate reaction is to reject the story altogether, pointing out the weakness in the historical background of *The Da Vinci Code,* for example.

The question of, can deviational imaginations also contribute to the thinking of theology, is the most difficult one to answer. It can be argued that even the deviational imagination is a way for the media to engage in the search for meanings of God and of life. This is because theologians have often failed to recognize some of the subversive texts and secondary meanings in the main stream texts, and have often found themselves comfortable with the accepted meanings, and have negated or rejected different or deviational meanings. The 'other' meanings are often sidelined in the mainstream readings of the text that are revealed through such a popular reading of the text.

Subversive meanings

If the imagination of an author such as Dan Brown can bring out such subversive meanings that are not even embedded in the main text rather in the deviational text, then the film becomes interesting not only to view but to overcome the curiosity of knowing the 'other imagined' meanings that are added to the text. In the book *Exploring the Da Vinci Code*, Strobel and Poole [2006] argue that this novel and the movie have certainly raised the questions about the role of women in Christianity, which is often neglected in the main stream historical narratives. It could be that people were already searching for meanings of the texts from women's perspectives and for the role of women in preserving and sharing the faith to the people. In such contexts of the search for alternative meanings, Dan Brown engages along with others in their search for contextually relevant meanings in a radical way. The questions such as whether Constantine or Jesus started Christianity were being asked from different quarters. Such questions are also raised both in the film and in the novel.

From the Hollywood perspective, it also means popularizing Roman Catholicism and the power of the Roman Catholic Church among their audience. The word 'imagination' refers to imaging the imageless either through a dream or through a thought or through an image. The phrase 'deviational imagination' refers to the imagination that is not confined within the historical or moral rules. Theologians have to take this 'deviational imagination' seriously in order to expose those meanings of the text that were never heard of before, even if they are disturbing to the faith. Many theologians, even the liberals, have tended to defend the narratives within the New Testament arguing against the total change of the character of Jesus and of his marriage, which is historically unacceptable to them. 'Deviational imagination' is an alternative imagination. It does not need to prove itself because it works within the imagined world. It only disturbs the mind of people to the extent of challenging regular stereotypical images, even if they are positive.

Such imaginative narratives still make Jesus a superstar in the Hollywood movies. While most of the churches in the West have lost their access to the public sphere and appear unconcerned about it, Hollywood film producers bring to the public Jesus, the controversial person, and create him as a hero worthy of discussion publicly, even today. In this way it is such movies that make people talk about Jesus Christ and to show interest in reading about him, whether in a positive or negative way. Thus, imagination plays an important role in the popular religious films and provides a hermeneutic tool for engaging in the public search for meanings of God and of life. This can be viewed by theologians as a learning process for interpreting the word of God in the contemporary context, to the public.

Drama of gods

In Hinduism, even such imagination of the negative side of the gods is seen as their *leela* (play/drama of gods[5]). In Hindu Puranas (myths), gods are described as those who interfere in the lives of the human beings, this interference at times is playful to test a person's loyalty to gods and at other times the gods play a negative role in order to make sure that human beings find the need of God in their lives. In essence, gods play negative roles in order to make sure that human beings return to them after their adharma (unrighteous act). In many Hindu stories, gods play the opposite roles such as Ashuras – villains tempting people to do wrong thing in order to test the worshippers and see whether they can sustain such temptations.

However, if the person is strong, the gods accept their defeats in tests and grant them their wishes. Similarly the 'deviational imagination' is a compelling way to highlight the weakness and failure of the mainstream readings of the text. It can be construed as the failure of theologians to read the secondary, sidelined and subversive meanings of the text that has led to such an outcry of the public towards this phenomenon. Thus the film makers engage in such unusual search for meanings and 'play' with their plots to highlight such meanings and initiate dialogue with the public about such meanings, through their narratives. This God-talk in the public sphere is no longer facilitated by the church or by theologians but by novel writers or by film makers.

The Da Vinci Code also refers to some Gnostic texts, where such assumptions and deviations had already been made. The question remains whether this should be seen as an exploration of an alternative way of looking at history and texts. Interestingly, Christianity is presented as a religion constructed by the fourth-century Roman emperor Constantine in contrast to the radical movement within Judaism begun by Jesus. Strobel and Poole [2006:104] painstakingly try to defend the claims within the New Testament, that Jesus was the Son of God and that these claims were not constructed by Constantine.

For this study, the main interest is not whether the gospel stories describe something that actually happened or were written at a later stage as an attempt to preserve a particular interpretation of the memory of Jesus. This study focuses on how far the 'deviational imagination' is helpful in recognizing the voices within the historical stories that were not heard before. Imagination can play a role, not only in deconstructing but also in *re*-constructing a text, so that its relevance can be widened to the emerging contexts. While accepting the main reading of the gospels and its defence as reasonably based on a minimum of historical facts, such deviational readings are needed because of the danger of the main reading being fixed and used by a few for their own advantage. Within the imagined world of faith, the dominant readings and meanings tend to get fixed and thus can become destructive at times. Counter or deviational imagination becomes essential to test the dominant readings and, at times, to shake the dominant discourse, and thus to make sure that other meanings are also explored that were earlier often neglected. The 'deviational imagination' is useful to help us to explore new or alternative meanings of the text but not to replace it.

Theologians need to take seriously the role of such imagination in the making and shaping of Christian faith. Having looked at 'deviational imagination' as a counter act to the dominant readings of the text, the cultural context of the audience should also be taken into account in imagining the alternatives. For a Christian from India, such an imagined alternative is an offence to the basic thrust of Christian faith, unless the story proves to be true. In the western media, it is part of their regular practice of critically evaluating anything that is religious and traditional. This is also part of the western media culture of selling and popularizing anything that is controversial as well as anti-religious. Information about any religion is often negative and tinged with suspicion and flippancy.

This is where the Eastern perspective of faith may differ to some extent in approaching a religious faith or tradition. Granted, there is no monolithic culture specifically separating West and East, there are possible perspectives that many share in common in the East and also in the West. When such a differently imagined story is presented to the public, the Eastern mind raises the question of their authenticity and their relevance, not merely their entertainment value and their counter imagined world matter but also their usefulness and the truth within them are important for the East. If it is not so, such narratives should not be made available to the public.

Da Vinci Code: Responses

In India this Supreme Court refused to ban the Da Vinci Code film saying no predominantly Christian countries have banned this film[6]. The Catholic Secular Forum (CSF) released a press note about the film saying, "The Da Vinci Code is offensive as it hit certain basic foundations of the religion."[7] In Hong Kong, the Catholic archdiocese, "has not called for the movie to be banned, nor asked its members to stay away from it. Instead, each priest is free to do or say what he wants within his parish"[8].

According to Al-Jazeera (a television channel) among the predominantly Islamic countries this film was viewed by a large number of audiences[9]. One of the top Vatican official urged people to boycott the film[10]. The Catholic scholars who head the research in *Opes Dei* (a particular order within the Catholic Church - its meaning is work of God) engaged with Sony Corporation to clarify matters regarding *Opes Dei* but with little success. At least it shows interest on the part of the Catholic Church to engage creatively and critically with the media industries.

David Walsh of the socialist writer comments the film as a 'counter cultural' myth[11]. There are number of critical responses point to the fact that the film and the book on Da Vinci Code claim itself to be a novel[12]. But both in the East and also in the West the ban on the film slowly were lifted and people flocked to see the film. There are many who wanted to the film to be displayed in public thinking that many would be interested to know more about the facts in Christianity and so this could be a good starting point. But there are a few who think that this film can shake the foundation of people's faith in the historical person Jesus through its fictional narrative. There are a few

John Joshva Raja

who wanted people to ignore or dismiss the film as less-factual and so need to educate their congregation about the film and the story rather than try to ban the film. The reactions to the film fall into many categories but highlight the complex nature of the audience and their background.

The Passion of Christ:
This film was generally created a mixed reaction among the audience in Asia. In Pakistan this film received much space in the mass media. James Lal, a Director of the Teachers' teams-Pakistan, felt the film showed too much violence and was a bit exaggerated. He told the news agency there, "Some scenes are not from the Bible, like the crow snatching the eye of the thief near Jesus on the cross, and Judas hanging himself on a tree. We don't read such things in the Bible[13]". According to an Iranian audience a reporter claims,, "Islam prohibits the visible depiction of holy figures, and says that Jesus was neither crucified nor the Son of God, Analysts say, however, that Jewish anger over the film has encouraged many Islamic countries to break their strict censorship rules and allow 'The Passion' to be viewed"[14]. Among many Hindus this film was received with an appreciation.

Anjan Srivastava, a Hindu censor for the Central Board of Film Certification noted, "Undoubtedly, it is a visually violent film. However, its universal message of non-violence, forgiveness, tolerance, harmony and peace warrants that it be seen by all people, including children"[15]. The release of the film during the time of Easter provided an additional popularity for the film (2004). The use of Aramaic in the film created an enthusiasm both in East and West[16]. The critics of this film in the West demonstrated disappointment, that the film pictures suffering, without giving hope for catharsis, to the enlightenment, purification. They charged Gibson with the superfluous forcing of passions, with the gloom of the atmosphere[17].

In the United States the film was critiqued for its exaggerated violence and its display of anti-Semitic sentiments[18]. Some of the Vatican representatives argued, "The film neither exaggerates nor downplays the role of Jewish authorities and legal proceedings in the condemnation of Jesus. But precisely because it presents a comprehensive account of what might be called the 'calculus of blame' in the passion and death of Christ, the film would be more likely to quell anti-Semitism in its audiences than to excite it"[19]. For this film too the reaction is mixed and varied according to the context and religious affiliation of the audience and scholars.

While engaging with the two films theologians, film critics and the audience tend to be appreciative or critics of their content, theology, history and impact on people. Not many of them have engaged in a creative way highlighting how the producers used their imagination to recreate the Biblical stories for the public, film industry and also for people around the world. The main question that is the role of imagination and aesthetical elements in interpreting the gospel to the mass audience has to be asked in order to recognise the significance of the films that tend to retell the religious stories. While recognising these stories' variation from the original stories it is essential to raise the question how far one can deviate from the original story. It raises an important hermeneutic and historical question in terms of using imagination not only to recreate the old story but also deviate from it. This gives raise to the tension between freedom of expression in the public and the sensitivity to people's faith in particular Biblical narratives.

Hollywood's presentations

In this section the role of imagination in the search and description of one's faith is being discussed in relation to the film industry and in relation to theology. Hollywood film producers found Jesus as their hero and imagined a new story for him and thus sold their products to the public. Their films reflect and engage with the audience in their search for meanings of Life and of God in different ways. Rather than asking the question in what ways theologians respond to these films and the issues that are raised by these films, this section tries to highlight the importance of recognizing the imagination in doing hermeneutics for the public and thus engage with the public in their search for meanings.

Even the attempt to deviate from the story through imagination enables an audience to see the possibility of other meanings though they are controversial and unacceptable. It is also argued that we need to negotiate between creating an imaginary narrative in the public and respecting people's faith and religious traditions. Recently, 'deviational imagination' without negotiation has created a lot of suspicion, loss of identity and misunderstanding and hatred between different religious communities.

Imagination, media and theology

This calls for a new way for theologians to engage with the media and with the audience and also new directions for the media that deals with theological issues. The media's attitude towards religion is often sceptical though, the media use the technique of imagination as the Bible story tellers have done, long ago. B. B. Scott [1994] in his book *Hollywood Dreams and Biblical Stories* argues that even the recent imaginary stories borrow concepts and values from the biblical stories. His book provides a dialogue between films and the Bible. He argues that films tend to address contemporary issues of conflicts, isolation and displacement through imaginary stories and myths and therefore they present reality in a way that entertains and satisfies the audience who are thus content. [Scott, 1994:5–7]. Scott begins this hermeneutic dialogue between film and Bible by highlighting the themes and theologies that are used and interpreted by popular films [1994:13]. However, the attitude of the theologians towards media often remains negative because of media-phobia and the ethical concerns that arise from the media's impact generally on the lives of the people.

Wesley Carr [1990:83] argues that imagination is not just desirable but indispensable for the survival of people. Imagination plays an important role in shaping our faith in God and also our attitude towards the media. If the common ways of sharing, challenging and engaging through a creative and constructive imagination are accepted by both media practitioners and theologians, new areas would open up for further discovery of another world or of a new age. People are always engaged in groups or masses or as individuals in search for new meanings that are relevant to the ever-changing contexts. Both media and theological institutions can engage in people's search for meanings of life and of God using such elements of imagination that are available in the public.

Even using 'deviational imagination' public attention can be sought and challenged in certain ways. Nevertheless, there is a need to consider the respect for the majority and the minority cultural groups as well. This takes us beyond Paul Soukup's [1991] categories of attitude, ethical issues, advocacy and use of the media to venture into the common space created by imagination between theology and media[20]. Such common space provides not only a space for imagining alternative worlds while trying to maintain some continuum but also a space to hear those meanings and voices that were never heard before, constructively and creatively. Imagination in media and theology can enable both institutions to participate with people in their struggle for relevant meanings. This takes us to the next quest which is how the media sells a message using the popular entertainment code. People are accustomed to entertaining themselves by using religious content of the media.

Hence, imagination can be a point of contact between theology and film studies. Imaginary stories ought to be used for doing hermeneutics in the public domain. When popular cultural visual or aural texts interpret religious stories, they tend to entertain as well as bring the story alive to the context of the audience. Theologians need to recognize the active role of popular religious films and develop theological discussions on the role of imagination in their hermeneutics. The 'deviational imagination' can enable the readers to deconstruct the text while the theologians have to take it further, thus enabling the readers to reconstruct the text by critically reading the popular text along with the traditional text.

Whilst recognizing the role of 'deviational imagination' in bringing out those voices that were never heard, we also need to recognise and respect the religious faith and dignity of other cultural groups. This should lead to negotiation between diverse points of view rather than a conflict of cultures. In a way, only imagination can help us to find a way to allow different meta-narratives to co-exist and to nourish each other and to correct each other. It is a challenge for theologians to imagine alternative worlds where such realities can be achieved.

It is impossible to imagine an alternative world without imagining God differently. In order to hear different voices we also look at the narratives that describe God and describe within the narrative the different aspects of God. This would enable us to re-imagine God as one who listens to the opposites and take their views seriously while God too struggles in communicating his views to the human audience. A few narratives in the Bible would enable us to imagine God differently and thus highlight those meanings and voices that were not often heard or written.

God and imagination

Imagination plays an important role in every religious faith. It means in faith often one has to imagine God through available anthropomorphic images such as father, shepherd or king. The creation story presents God as one who creates the earth and sees it as good. According to the creation story the earth comes out of God's own imagination as part of the creation and its beauty as art and follows an appreciation to the art of God's hands[21]. These stories are not merely imaginary stories rather they tell us about the creator God and his artistic design behind the creation using imagination. Without imagination, the Old Testament and New Testament communities would not have described God through the narratives or stories. It is through imagination that these stories were handed over from generation to generation with some additions and reductions and thus interpreted to listeners using immediately available images and concepts. Garett Green affirms this by arguing that the Christian community carries out the hermeneutic task of retelling story as faithful imagination [1998:126].

In this way, the story was preserved, interpreted and made relevant to every context and cultural group that promoted faith and traditions in a creative and constructive manner. Such a hermeneutic role of imagination needs to be emphasised again and again in order to make the religious texts relevant and effective in the emerging contexts. In a context where there is no experience of God directly as in the Old Testament or New Testament period, people can only imagine God. Imagination is inevitable to preach and to communicate religion to others. Theological language has to remain metaphoric and cannot be explained in a scientific narrative [Avis 1999:51].

Paul Ricoeur talked about the role that imagination plays in reading and interpreting the Bible. For Ricoeur, *imagination* consists of (1) "a rule-governed form of invention" (it is this reference to rules that limits the otherwise free-for-all scope of imagination), and (2) "the power of re-describing reality" [1995: 144-5]. Using Imagination "We must allow ourselves to somehow be moved by the text, to change the way we view our lives—or, as Ricoeur puts it, "in drawing on the semiotics of texts . . . the notion of intertextuality . . . dynamizes the text, makes meaning move, and gives rise to extensions and transgressions . . . insofar as it makes the text work" [1995:148]. Only one option that is available for theologians and pastors to retell the Bible stories to today's audience is to use imagination as a hermeneutic tool.

Through imagination one may rediscover and re-describe the Biblical realities for the audience today. Some questions that can be asked at this stage are: Did Biblical communities use imagination as a hermeneutic tool to retell the stories? When they retold the stories, how far were they close to their original stories? Did they use deviation from the original story as a method to retell it to their own context? These questions demand us to look into the Bible whether the variations between the same stories were part and parcel of the hermeneutic practices of the Biblical communities both Old and New Testaments. This may be true even post-canonical writers such as

27

Iraeneus when they tried to imagine Christ within the Old Testament Texts [Boersma 2005: 23-25].

Bauch in his book on Storytelling: Imagination and Faith, highlights the paradoxes of stories in which the tension lies between Spirituality and Earthiness; Freedom and Obedience; Security and Uncertainty; Absolute and Personal and Triumph and suffering. In these paradoxes imagination plays a major role in retelling the story in relation to the readers' context. In the negotiation between the context of the audience and the context of the original communities, the medieval writers tried to use allegory as a method to interpret and to some extent deviate from the original intention and purpose of the story and thus contextualised into their audiences' versions [Gasque 2005: 57-70].

Even the four gospels are good examples of expansion, addition; editing and deviation of stories shared orally by the New Testament communities and then handed over them to the next generations. In this sense there are number of examples within the Biblical communities that show deviation from the original narrative to retell the story with new meanings and new insights to the new emerging communities. This was seen as part of revelation itself and as part of rediscovering one's faith through the participation in the Eucharistic celebrations [Ricoeur 1995[22]] Though this does not deny the possible authentic experience of God of the Biblical communities, they described their experiences through available imageries and metaphors with the help of imagination. They held the contradictory ideas of God together through such metaphors. For examples in many instances they identified God as a universal creator and saviour while God was seen as the God of Israel and God of Abraham.

A particular God Yahweh had chosen a particular people - Israel. Such paradoxes are kept together through the stories. In the following sections I will give a detailed example of how the writers at times deviated from their original intentions of a strong monotheistic description of God by recognising the communities within Godhood. This is a radical deviation as there can be no other God than one God

– Yahweh and Elohim but there are selective examples where God is seen as community where decisions are made through discussions, negotiations and arguments. This supports my argument that deviational imagination is part of hermeneutic practices of Biblical Communities. When the films have used them in their display and retelling of the Biblical stories, we need to recognise and possible consider using them in interpreting the gospel stories today to the new emerging communities and their contexts.

Section B. Bible and Imagination: Selected examples

Imagining God through Biblical narratives

The Old Testament and New Testament communities attempted to explain God within their limited understanding of the narratives and religious experiences. They maintained the narratives orally, though later these narratives were preserved through writings. Kaufman [1981:21f] argued that these communities constructed the concept of God through their narratives. During the oral transmission those who preserved tradition used creativity, imagination and aesthetic elements to hand it to next generation.

When these oral texts were written down, the writer began to search for original stories. Because they could not find one absolute story, they had to put together different stories in writing. The written texts began to search for original narratives and thus began to eliminate all other narratives. These narratives describe God in different ways. They are also interpreted by the different media to relate to people's context example – a film on Jesus. As I argued in the previous section, the visual media, particularly films, interpret the story of Jesus either through the accepted narratives or through imaginative narratives that are not confined to the accepted narratives.

Through oral or written narratives the communities were asked to imagine a God who is often authoritative, authentic and unilateral in decision making. God is often seen as making decisions on his own. They interpreted 'God' in the way they wanted to accumulate power through such an idea of God, and thereby neglected voices from the margins as they did not want to hear those meanings from the periphery of every community. They were not minded to listen to the other and opposite voices and so imagined God in a way that was comfortable for them. Nevertheless, there are images of God in which God is seen as a community or a parliament where decisions are made through discussions, engagement and even listening to the opposite voices.

The Old Testament stories present God not only as one who is authoritative, powerful and unilaterally deciding God but also as one who holds dialogue with opposite voices and even discusses with Satan in arriving at decisions. Such presentation of God deviates from the accepted descriptions of God in the Old Testament. This supports the argument that Biblical communities not only used imagination to interpret their faith experience and stories but also through their imagination they changed the nature of the stories and deviated from their traditional beliefs in order to relate their stories to their contemporary contexts. As the films have thrown challenges theology, I will highlight using examples from the biblical narratives, how God is listening to the opposite and how Jesus is engaging with his opponents. This leads to a theological challenge to interpret the 'Self' in dialogue[23] with opposing 'self's' within, as it inherits the image of God. The following sections will make a study on the image of God, Jesus and Self from this dialogical perspective.

Dialogue within God

Interpretation is an art of spiritual imagination [Boersma, 2005:32-33]. When one allows imagination to be shaped by spirit, a creative narrative evolves. In this section, I will argue that within the Godhead, opposite voices are heard and attended to at times. I too interpret the biblical text using a few contemporary imageries; God is a God of dialogue, a God who communicates. He is a communitarian and Trinitarian God and in him[24] there is a community of God. The Book of Genesis (Chapter 1) informs us that God spoke in first person plural noun (Let us create human being in our image) and the Hebrew word 'Elohim' (Eloah – singular noun) refers to gods rather than God[25] and this can also be called a "Community of God in complete Unity and Oneness".

This can also be interpreted in terms of Trinitarian understanding of God from the Christian perspective. .This is similar to Moltmann's concept of 'Mutual indwelling' (perichoresis) of God which binds three persons in the community of God[26] It also provides the picture of God as one who communicates within himself and this communication involves both listening and speaking. God has to be understood as a community of God in oneness. There is also a dialogue within this community of God at particular times. God holds a dialogue with Satan in the book of Job (Chapter 1), in other words God is presented as one who allows Satan to appear in a "Parliament of God" everyday.

Within the parliament of God, Satanic voices are equally heard and are listened to by God. This does not mean that Satan is part of God as Jung [1969] would like us to imagine. Even with the opposite parties, God contacts, listens, communicates and establishes relationship. He communicates with the other which clearly proves that God establishes perfect communication even with the opponent by listening and speaking with him (1 Kings 22). God also lets part of his community play the role of the opponent in the life of the human beings. The underlying unity of God does not refer to the uniformity of perspectives and ideas. The oneness does not refer to sameness of personalities within the community of God. The Trinitarian concepts explain to us the way different personalities exist within the oneness of God (Dynamic Monotheism).

Jung and 'opposites within God'

Such a concept of God holding dialogue with the opposite and playing the role of the opposite is slightly different from Jungian concept of 'opposites within God'. For Jung, God is the archetypal image of the collective unconscious. Jung argues that Christianity is dualistic and if it claims to be monotheistic then the opposites must be contained in God. In God, insight goes together with obtuseness, and 'loving-kindness along with cruelty'. The coexistence of these opposites means God is unconscious or just feebly conscious. Both good and evil exist in God so He is a 'totality of inner opposites', and God 'does not care a rap for any moral opinion and does not recognize any form of ethics as binding' [Jung, 1969:11,358–369]. Jung argued that the Old Testament reflects the primitive human beings' concept of God as they conceived God as one who was unconscious and morally primitive. Jung points out that the paradoxical nature of God has an effect on humanity; it splits us into opposites and delivers us over to a seemingly insoluble conflict.

Psychologically, what happens is that in such situations of conflict the unconscious in any number of ways (dreams, fairy tales, myths, etc.) throws out signs of the union of opposites as symbolized by a variety of means, for example the child-hero, squaring the circle and so on. To Jung [1969] this motif appears again in the dreams of modern humans and it always has to do with the bringing together of darkness with light. This union of opposites is a problem that the revelation set out, that alchemists have tried to resolve for seven centuries and that confronts modern people. For Jung, [1969] God is the archetype and a construction of the 'collective unconscious' of people. For me, the religious narrative is a construction of human beings to promote an idea of God.

The concept of God is also possibly constructed by human beings; however, the experience of God cannot be a psychological construction of the collective unconscious. Perhaps, the derivation from the experience to the concept and the narrative is possibly a psychological construction. Psychological explanation is among diverse perspectives that tend to analyse the experience, concept and the narrative of religious people. It is difficult to come to the conclusion that God himself is the construction of the collective unconscious. If the experience has to be studied it has to be done more scientifically or objectively which is also difficult to do with religious experiences. The narratives have to be considered as a construction, being developed by faith communities from their experience of God in whatever ways they felt and communicated their experience through whatever words, means and methods that were available to them, though they have their own limitations. Within what is narrated and experienced, God is seen as one who holds dialogue within himself.

God and many voices

Within God there are multiple voices and perspectives underlying oneness but which hold dialogue amongst them and this shows the nature of God in the Bible as one who is a dynamic and interactive God. The prophets show us that God is one who accepts all as his people so this means that not only the Israelites are the chosen race, rather others are called and led by God just like Israelites. In Isaiah 19, God calls Egypt his people, Assyrians as his handwork and Israelites as his chosen race. In this sense, God is shown as a universal God who leads every culture and people according to his ways and teachings, thus God is engaged in different communities in revealing himself. With specific purposes he might have revealed diverse perspectives to people of God. No religion and no culture are perfect in describing God and so they can only serve people to relate themselves with God and with one's neighbour. They have often failed in their basic objectives; rather they have misled people against God and against their own neighbour.

God is seen as one who establishes contacts, communicates, renews relationship and develops understanding with himself, with others, even with his opponents and with those whom he may not agree with. This is because within the Godhead there are multiple perspectives that are in constant dialogue, this is what I call God's dialogue, and it needs to be recognized and extended to human relationships as well. There are many other examples in the Old Testament that portray God as one who listens, communicates and understand the others. It is interesting to note that the change in God is to be seen as inbuilt nature itself rather than as one who changes from righteousness to unrighteousness; this is because God is a dynamic God and not

John Joshva Raja

a static God. God tends to recognize different perspectives, that he may understand human beings better. God breaks his rules (Sabbath observance), transcends the laws of nature (clock set backwards) and changes himself at times in order to re-establish a relationship with human beings.

God can be seen as a jealous God who does not want his creation to worship any other than himself while he has to be recognized by all and is working through other people to bring the Israelites, the chosen people, back to him. So God is also working among and through other people besides the chosen people of God. In this way, the Bible projects God as both exclusive as well as inclusive of different people and their faith. God is also seen as one who is engaged not only with Israelites but also with others in their search for meanings of God and of life. In every culture and community, God has been working in some ways that have been developed into a religious narrative and structure. Whether every religion (its institution and narrative) leads one back to God is not possible for anyone to conclude or affirm.

Dialogue and the Word

In terms of establishing contact, relationship and understanding with human beings, God breaks his own natural law, religion, reason and science and thus became the son of a woman who did not follow the natural rules to beget a baby. The expected messiah is therefore dwelling among people in an unexpected and unacceptable format, people did not understand that the Word can only become flesh and dwell in the form of a simple human being called Jesus. The protestant equation of Word with word is a major disaster in theological thinking. The Word can never be equated to oral or written or visual word. The words can only interpret the Word event and cannot objectify Word into a narrative. The Word can only be experienced by people in the form of flesh. The spoken or written word can only provide multiple descriptions of Word that should lead to its experience.

When the experience of the Word is narrated in human words this leads to a diversity of narratives and therefore no single narrative can claim to be absolute and perfect. The purpose of the narrative is to lead us to experience the Word which is ultimately with God and is God and we accept limitations in human communication. The Word can only become (because it cannot be merely spoken or written or visualized) and can communicate through the incarnation and the life of Jesus Christ, Jesus is the embodiment of the Word. Because human communication is constrained by its limitation, even the narrative about Jesus has to be shared through four Gospels that are different at times in narrating the events.

Dialogue within Jesus

Jesus can also be seen as a role model in dialogic communication. He established contact, relationship and understanding with others including those who were identified as sinners by the community. Jesus engaged in discussion with his contemporaries – such as Pharisees and Sadducees who were often opposed to some of Jesus' radical views. He created a public sphere by holding dialogue with them and challenging them within their own narratives. He was also critical about their interpretations and their authority. Nevertheless, he was not undermining the narratives of faith that they shared with him; Jesus shared many perspectives with his disciples as well as with his listeners. Very often Jesus had dialogue within himself from different perspectives and he shared this dialogue with God whom he called 'My Father' and also with his disciples. He was struggling to decide on taking up the cup of suffering and prayed to his Father to remove it if possible, therefore showing a dialogue within him that he extends to God.

When Jesus had dialogue with those who were questioning his teachings, he was listening, recognizing and trying to establish understanding with them. Though his expectations to convince the other groups failed he did not give up either. He was in anguish at the cross even asking the father 'Why have you forsaken me?' But his mission was to hold contact, dialogue, relationship and understanding with all people with whom he was interacting. This is the greatest model for us to hold dialogue with others, even those who are opposed to our perspectives and views. Jesus did not change his vision and teaching of the Kingdom of God rather he was trying to enable the opponents to see the problems within their interpretations and approaches. Through dialogue he continued to interact with people from every section of society regardless of their refusal to accept him and his teachings.

This sets us an Christological model for our dialogue. Jesus tells people that there is no other name besides my name on earth. He also asks his disciples to proclaim the Gospel to the entire world. He says, 'I am the Way, the Truth, and the Life' (John 14.6). In many ways, he is presented as an exclusive person. At the same time, there are instances where he accommodates others as they are. He accepts the Samaritan woman (John 4.21–24) and tells her that God will be worshipped everywhere. He also tells the Gentile man who was healed from among the graves to go back to his people and proclaim what (his) God has done to him. He wants his disciples to accept him and him only, but when it comes to other religions he seems to hold a dialogic and listening style. For Jesus, the religious narratives are secondary to people and their lives, so when he says, 'The Sabbath is made for human beings rather than human beings for the Sabbath' Mark 2:27), he recognizes people's faith in God and appreciates it.

At one point he was convinced by the Gentile woman's faith (Mark 7.25f/ Matthew 15.21) in coming to him to heal her daughter. He recognized and emphasized the importance of people's lives, their faith, the need to share resources among themselves and their relationship with each other. Jesus is presented in the Gospels as inclusive as well as exclusive. He might have been exclusive when he says go to the Israelites only, but was certainly inclusive when he says to the Samaritan woman that God will be worshipped everywhere. Jesus can also be seen as one who heals the deaf and dumb people and as one who dines with tax collectors and sinners. Thereby, he affirms the life of these people and makes them whole. His mission is to guide people to recognize themselves, realize along with others and thus become divine beings in this world.

For Jesus this means to enable the people to become full human beings. If a person cannot speak and hear, Jesus makes him a fuller human being by enabling him to speak and listen. If there are not many chances for tax collectors and sinners to listen due to the rejection of the main stream society, then Jesus goes there to listen and speak to them. Jesus also listens to his opponents and contemporary leaders who want to eliminate him and then attempts to interact with them by engaging in their search for meanings. By listening, Jesus communicates and for communicating Jesus listens. Because Jesus communicates within himself from different perspectives as an extension of his communication with God he was able to hold dialogue with anyone with different perspectives. He also creates an atmosphere to have dialogue with the other and thus attempts to lead humanity towards becoming a divine community.

Conclusion

This chapter discussed the issue of the role of imagination in interpreting God to people. Popular films often tend to enact the role of theologian to the public by interpreting the stories of Jesus, conversely this shows people engage with the media in their search for meanings of God and of Life. Theologians need to study the role of imagination in doing hermeneutics seriously. Using examples of two films, *The Passion of the Christ* and *The Da Vinci Code,* I also argued that 'deviational imagination' can enable the public to see the subversive meanings that may not be otherwise available. Such subversive meanings often strengthen the main argument by widening and interpreting it to different contexts and to different cultural groups. Such engagement with the films has shown that we need to see God from different perspectives even if they are contradictory, deviational and purely imaginative narrative.

As I discussed in the second section, within biblical narratives God can be seen as one who engages with the other and also with those who hold different views. Such opposite views and voices can be heard within the community of God. I have used two films as examples to show how imagination can play a major role in interpreting religious stories through the mass media. When the films also deviate from the story plots by using contemporary visual images and plots, they try to relate Biblical stories to the contemporary contexts and their issues. They use deviational imagination as part of hermeneutic tool to highlight those voices which were not recognised. Using the Biblical examples I argued that even the Biblical communities have used such deviational imagination to retell and interpret their past stories to different audience in order to relate to the emerging contexts and issues.

Even God is seen as one who holds dialogue within heavenly community an as one who listens to opposite voices. This highlights that there is no uniform description of God within the Biblical narratives which reveals the diversity of interpreting and even diverse ways of retelling the stories. It also means to use deviational versions and imagination to interpret stories and thus make them relevant to their respective contexts. God is not merely a God who commands people to follow his commandment but also who listens to his own people and even to opposite voices including Satan. This sets the direction for this book in terms of dialogue and engagement with the other, which will be explored in the following chapters.

2   Tele-Preachers – Marketing God in the Public

Section A - Tele-evangelists and commercial gospels

Introduction

An Indian Engineer in Birmingham uses Skype to pray with his parents in India along with his sister in United States. Other family members are in London and in Gulf who often join with them. As a Christian minister from their place they invite me to join with this family prayer on his children's birthdays. I offer a prayer of blessings for them. His wife works as a nurse in the hospital and they relate to others through their engagement in the church. It is also interesting to notice that besides me they also listen to Tamil Christian channels where their own favourite tele-preachers speak. For this family more than worshipping in the local church their prayers with the family keeps them united and spiritual in many ways.

While I recognise them as faithful Christians I also notice that the whole family watches Tamil serials and films regularly via other Tamil Channels. They describe this as being in touch with the culture in India. My experience with this family shows that they tend to keep cultural entertainment and Christian faith as two distinct but essential for their living in UK. Much part of their lives depends on one or the other media both for the growth of their faith and also for their entertainment and so on. It is interesting to note that the media enable them to relate to their parents and relatives from around the world while they faithfully maintain their Christian tradition. This provides a lot of challenges for the churches, theologians and leaders locally and globally.

First challenge is that there is a wide range of choices in terms of Christian faith and teachings from the wide range of media that people can choose and follow. Secondly the theology of entertainment is widely used by the tele-evangelists in communicating their faith.

John Joshva Raja

They are successful in converting it into an income. Thirdly prosperity gospel makes an impact on the people's faith.

At times without proper awareness and education about tele-technology some of the tele-evangelists dramatic healings and proof for their prayer fortunes before the camera, the audience often assume that these are real. The primary questions in this chapter are: How can theologians engage with the popular tele-evangelism? What is the role of entertainment in communicating the gospel? How do the churches educate their member to understand and use media creatively and critically through media literacy? What are the theological issues with religious claims and counterclaims in the media?

Religion has become part of people's entertainment in a media-dominated world. By entertaining the public with their demonstration of miracles before the camera, the tele-gurus become popular and persuade large numbers of the audience to become their followers. Although, the term 'tele-evangelist' is more widely used in North America, in this chapter, I prefer the term 'tele-gurus' to represent the wide range of religious gurus, evangelists, mullahs and other religious leaders who try to use the television as a means to attract an audience, convert many of them, sell their theologies to them and buy their time in the channels.

One cannot deny the fact that some of them perform healing either by using miraculous power or by using natural medicine or some other techniques. They make sure that their popularity is converted into donation and gifts for their programmes or their institutions[27]. Many of them follow strict fundamental concepts of their religions and claim that they have a special authority from their God. They assure their followers of an entry t heaven and thus grant them prosperity in their lives here through some methods such as prayer or rituals. They follow certain media values in popularizing and selling their packaged faith like any other goods in the media market.

When some television channels have used religion as a product sold by a few popular religious personalities, the response from theological circles was often critical and negative. In this chapter, the tele-gurus' different methods and presentations are highlighted and critically looked at from different perspectives. This subject has been studied and has been written about by many scholars since the 1980s. Neil Postman's book *Amusing Ourselves to Death* [1985] is the best example, where he deals with how the visual images have come here to entertain people and thus convert the messages into merely an entertaining medium.

The medium of entertainment has often been seen from a negative perspective among theologians and religious scholars [e.g. Neil Postman, 1985 and William Fore, 1987]. While recognizing the importance of the critical engagement of theologians and media scholars with these television gurus (include television evangelists and also other religious television gurus,) it is essential to study how entertainment has become part and parcel of the search for religious meanings in the public. A theology of entertainment is the need of the hour and preachers must learn to listen to the popular preachers who use such media skills of entertainment to promote their faith, to raise funds and to interpret faith in public. The tele-gurus use contemporary images and cultural codes, particularly visuals, in order to attract the audience.

The visuals are used in an interpretative way that demonstrates to the audience their faith and thus persuade them to accept the 'tele-gurus' doctrines and faith statements. Tele-gurus create audio-visual display of their own programmes carefully so that the mediated message is communicated clearly to the audience and create an enthusiasm and persuade them to join their followers. Thus they provide a public interpretation of their faiths using visuals and sound technology. Thus their programmes provide a visual hermeneutics [interpretation provided through visual images] by using visual imagery to interpret and relate the tele-gospel to the context of their tele-audience.

Their visual imagery is often both contemporary and popular. In this chapter, a critical study of the popular use of religion in the media will be attempted. It will also highlight the role entertainment plays in the popular media and public hermeneutics of faith, doctrines and texts. This chapter has two sections, the first section deals with the critical study of the tele-gurus and their methods of communication by highlighting the fundamentalist nature of their claims and their subscription to the uncritical values of the media practices. The second section highlights different theological responses to the issues raised by the tele-gurus from a Christian perspective. I also raise questions about the way in which entertainment can play a role in theological discourse as it does in the case of tele-evangelism.

I. Tele-gurus and the media market

Theologies have been in the public and private sphere for a considerable time. The word 'theologies' is used because of diverse theological engagement with the media and their impact on the multicultural and multi-religious communities. Religious institutions which were once influential in promoting values and worldviews for their students and their public have been replaced by the media in a new form and genre [Gregor Goethals, 1990]. In this, there is a breakdown of barriers between secular and religious spheres. Also, both media and theologies depend much on the language (oral, written, audio and video) of different means of communication. Many questions arise in the interaction between media and theologies of different religions, these questions become complex where media range from print to convergent media.

The word media refers to radio, television, print media, telephone and all other technological means that people utilize today. I will confine myself here, to the mass media (TV, newspapers, radio and so on). The word 'theologies' include a wide range of theological and doctrinal statements that are faith expressions of the tele-gurus from Hindu, Muslim, Jain, Christian and other backgrounds. I limit the word theologies to the mass and popular theologies that are mediated through the mass media and accepted by the masses. This raises a number of questions: how are various theologies of popular religious gurus mediated through the mass media? How do people use such mediated theologies in their faith, value, social and political formation? How do media interpret religions using entertainment as a form? How do the media and theology interact through entertainment?

Christian Television ←→ Popular Theologies	
Culture ←→ Religious contexts	

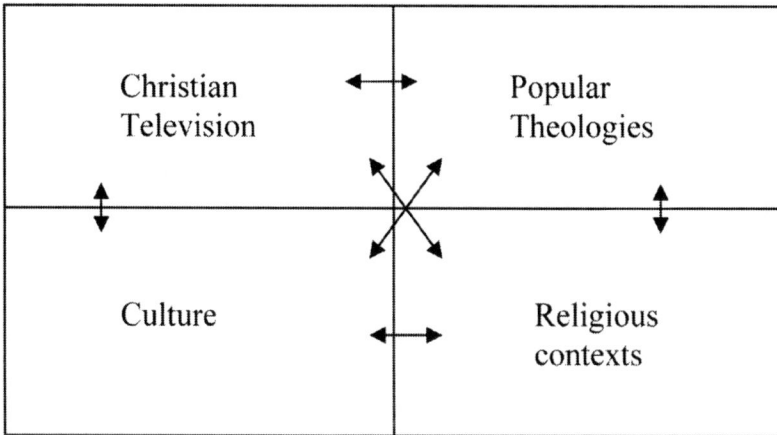

From the above diagram it can be argued that the media are dependent on other social processes and institutions. Television makes an impact on theology, culture and society while reflecting the changes and realities within other processes. These elements can be both interdependent and independent of each other. Thus they influence and are being influenced by the other social processes in a particular context at a particular historical time. In the interaction between television and theology a few issues are discussed in this chapter, by focussing on mediated neo-religious popular cults, whom I call tele-gurus (e.g. astrologists, numerologists, tele-evangelists) and the way television uses entertainment as a means of communicating Christian content.

A few of the above stated issues will be discussed in the following sections. Many scholars have discussed these groups and their theologies in a systematic way [Stewart Hoover, 1988; William Fore, 1987; Quentin J Schultze 2003; Peter Horsfield, 1984]. Their studies focus mainly on the Christian tele-evangelists within the context of the United States. They look critically at the way the tele-evangelists emerge and operate within the culture of popular Christian movements in America. Though their thoughts have influenced this chapter, this study focuses on similarities and differences between different religious tele-gurus who are popular in Asia and elsewhere.

Mediated theologies

Jacques Derrida [2001] argues that both popular theologies and television are mediations bridging the interior and exterior. In line with the above argument, de Vries points out that there is a negotiation between the private and public sphere in the relationship between faith expressions and television. There is a privatization of religion with public consequences, for example the Islamic revolution in Iran [de Vries, 2001:17]. Religion and media play mediation roles in society and thus theologies themselves undergo mediatisation in the process [Derrida, 2001]. Mass-mediated theologies are a new evolution of the interaction between television and neo-religious movements. Technological display of popular theologies has become a reality, an everyday affair in publicly displaying and popularizing one's own faith. Television content is reflecting the already popular theologies through their public-ness.

The religious communities are using television for various purposes, such as to promote their religious faith, values and ideologies. Television industries often use tele-gurus to reach out to the particular audience and thus earn money through their popular theological contents. In India, one can watch 24-hour religious channels, such as God Channel and Trinity Broadcasting Corporations (American channels) as well as two Hindu, one Islamic and one Jain channel. Besides these channels out of 78t channels that are available through the cable networks in the urban and rural areas in India, not less than ten would have an hour morning religious programme besides these regular religious channels.

Beyond this, a particular kind of audience views these popular programmes regularly and has been supporting these through their donations. The reasons behind the sudden popularity of a particular tele-guru cannot be completely explained, for example some of them perform miracles in front of the camera which surprises many and some of their miracle performance poses a direct assault on science and rational thinking. The media present these miracle stories in such a way that people regularly switch on their channels, and thus they can sell their advertisements.

The sudden popularity of a few religious sects in the public sphere encourages the media to broadcast such programmes that perpetuate the popularity of such cults to the public. In this interaction with the media, some tele-gurus were successful in selling their popular theologies to the public, whereas others have not survived. Some of the American tele-evangelists combine scripture, race and politics in their sermons in the Trinity Broadcasting Network (TBN) which is broadcasting throughout the world [Melling, 1999].

Ananda Mithra [1994] in his book, *Television and Popular Culture in India: A Study of Mahabharat,* claims that it is the Ramayana and Mahabharatha serials that popularized the Hindu religious consciousness. There is a possibility that the media may also construct or create a popular cult or media guru. It can also be argued that media reflect the ongoing popularity of a few cults and gurus of different religions as some people would like to worship a kind of god who would enable them to fulfil their wishes and thus are willing to pay those who would do this. They are after 'Ishta Devas' who would enable the worshipper to succeed in everything that they wanted and needed.

Thus neo-religious movements have become popular among people through television publicity such as Amirthanmaye Amma (in India), Benny Hinn, Pat Robertson, Sri Sri Sri Ravi Sankar, and Zakir Ali and so on. Media have created a number of media gurus who have not only become popular but also fit themselves with neo-liberal values and this means selling their 'gods' along with other goods, in this world of competition ,their success or failure depends on how long they could sell 'gods' and also how wide their market is. Television tends to use all such content that is saleable, including their theological content. In such a context, the religious experience is being explained in emotional and mystical terms rather than faith, community-based and rational experiences, and thus the media sell their theologies through the promise of prosperity.

Those who use such beliefs and spirituality seem to use

psychological and physical demonstrations as proof and those who follow them are keen on taking all that is given to them seriously. The popularization of the charismatic movements in all religions by the global media has become a reality today. On the one hand miracle performers, exclusive evangelicals, and some charismatic leaders use the global television networks because of their popularity and the support that they receive from the masses. On the other hand Nameologists (luck with changes in names), numerologists (fortune tellers with numbers), Signaterologists (predicting with signatures) and astrologists, special powered *pujaris* (priests), gurus and *ammas* have become popular religious gurus and leaders emerging through the global media.

Many of them follow the style, presentation and content of the Christian television evangelists. These religious people and groups have popularized their beliefs and ideologies through various evidence and proofs and people tend to follow their teachings and try to become 'religious'. It is interesting to recognize the fact that many church goers have found viewing such religious material enables them to increase their 'spiritual activities' and also their participation in their church programmes [Christopher, 2007].

Mediatised theologies

Religious fundamentalism is a major problem all over the world, particularly in India. In India, people are increasingly becoming aware of their religious and cultural identities. Any public fundamental claims are seen as a threat in a pluralistic society to religious coexistence and any religious group that makes exclusive claims of their faith may indeed question the basic thrust of Indian society. In such a context, the tele-gurus need to be studied critically so that the churches might become aware of the problems created by them. Through these programmes the tele-gurus popularize their religious beliefs and doctrines by emphasizing the sensational aspect of religious faith, working like commercials and thus commercializing religious beliefs and, it could be argued, have therefore technologized religious faith.

They make various claims about religious authenticity, beliefs and practices and highlight contradictions, this is part of the theological content which is popularly sold in the media market.

Popular theologies

These tele-gurus are popular among villagers, the poor masses and the lower middle class people who struggle with their daily or monthly income. This does not negate the fact that urban and upper middle class people are equally attracted by these programmes. Interestingly, tele-gurus have often supported the rightwing politicians whether it is in the United States of America or in India, thus they make their programmes popular with their irrational statement in favour of a particular war or in favour of the majority people in their country. Some of the charismatic programmes were popular even before they came on television, yet they have now established themselves as popular images through television and thus have widened their fold.

Popularization means success in terms of large audiences, however, not all these programmes are universally popular as some are successful in drawing large audiences whilst others are successful in converting their audience. In order to become popular, these programmes use formats that are similar to advertising and utilize other crusades, such as anti-nuclear campaigns. Many of them follow the US tele-evangelists in their methods of communication and so follow the trap of individualism, popular superstitions, self-help philosophies, prosperous view of life, miracle-centred faith and folk religion.

Cheap grace

This popularization of the religious content takes people away from their traditions and displays faith in the images of popular culture as the preachers offer what we wish to hear. Their genre conforms to other popular programmes, with only a slight difference as in order to achieve popularity these programmes use entertainment elements that attempt to capture the attention of the listeners or viewers. They offer special prayers according to people's needs and give publicity for their 24 hours prayer phone lines.

They promise that through their prayers many of people's problems would be solved and so people are demanded to support their ministry. They claimed to have healing and foretelling power which they have received from God. Thus they try to get as much donation as possible for their ministry by selling God's grace to the people. Such kind of programmes is popular among the rural and urban masses. Having moved away from their traditional village or from a community life the people from urban areas look for new sets of values and beliefs that provide popular meanings to popular problems for their new context. For example, mediated religion challenges science through miracles and psychological strange phenomena.

The media are interested in these strange events, of course miracles are real public events for them as they engage in the popular search for meanings of life and of God in their own style and methods. Many of these popular tele-gurus provide such popular meanings through television among the wide market of meanings. It is not only attractive for those who are urbanised but also for those in the village who are poor and who struggle for everyday life. These tele-evangelists seem to provide immediate solutions to daily problems through prayers and miracles.

Christian tele-gurus are forerunners in this regard of promoting a popular gospel to the public, something, the German theologian Dietrich Bonhoeffer describes as "cheap grace" [William Fore, 1987]. Their main aim is to make their doctrines popular and as saleable goods in the media market and they also use their popularity to influence the public with their political views. At times their remarks and views can be very influential in the political process, particularly during elections. Robert Bosten [1996] in his book on *The Most Dangerous Man in America* writes about the way Pat Robertson combines politics, race and religious ideas and thus distorts the Gospel itself in the public domain. Such activities can be found among Hindu tele-gurus as well [Gupta, 2004]. In a way the tele-evangelists are not only popular with their cheap grace but also influence the political thinking of their audience using religion, and television as means and methods of their communication.

Sensational theologies

Tele-gurus' religious beliefs are sensational because of their promise of an extraordinary and fortunate life. The content is focused around miracles, sensational happenings (such as falling down), emotional activities (ecstatic dances), and strange theological concepts (no medicine or baptisms) and the performance of miracles on television and examples of those strange events realized through tele-visual means. One of the popular Indian charismatic television preachers D.G.S. Dhinakaran and his programmes (such as the "Ilam Pankalar Thittam" which means to pay and be part of Young people clubs for better future) are very similar to the 800 club of Pat Robertson and his programmes in the United States of American where the proof of miracles are often displayed in order to gain support for their programmes.

These health-and-wealth oriented religious gurus are successful on television as no questioning or critical thinking is relevant to their programme and the purpose of the programme is merely to authenticate what these charismatic gurus want people to believe. Their faith is linked more too strange events, superstition, irrational phenomena than to the historical continuity of Christian faith, false hopes are provided and no arguments are encouraged. Faith is therefore developed on self-authenticating mystical experiences rather than on reason, evidence, scripture and tradition.

In Indian culture, among Bakthi movements there is a practice of gathering before the temple early in the morning. The community gathers in the street, sings Bhajans and goes to the temple to worship and sometimes to hear expositions before they go to work. This practice is often followed in many Christian churches too. This is reflected in radio and television programmes because whenever people go to any daily work, they wish to hear God's words and

49

promises for the day in a similar manner to Bhakthi traditions. Every morning, the audience listens to the radio or watches the television so that the whole day might be a blessed day for them where they are promised good marks in an exam for example or perhaps a successful day and therefore, these programmes flourish.

This perceived success is only possible, according to some tele-evangelists, through miracles and through strange events. However, by sensationalizing religion, they misuse the freedom of expression that is enjoyed by the public in India and elsewhere. Because of the freedom of the media, many channels are connected to houses either through a set top box or through cable. A policy of self-regulation is practised by the media in general, but some Christian channels misuse this freedom at times to broadcast these programmes to the Indian public, even if they degrade some Indian leaders and so on[28]. Some of the tele-gurus ask people to touch the television in order to receive a miracle, which is often guaranteed and thus the audiences are sensationalized into the notion of receiving these blessings.

Commercial theologies

Religious beliefs are commercialized using the practice of asking people to contribute money by means of telephone and email. Whilst the established religious institutions do not have the method of visa card payment as a means of donation, some of these tele-gurus encourage their audience to pay through their Pay-Pal system, VISA or Master cards. Their magazines ask for sponsorship of one or two television programmes, in this their televised faith works well with the commercial set up of the cable networks. They justify the way in which such social, cultural and media institutions operate by being a part of them, therefore they too become 'clever entrepreneurs' who, it can be argued, take advantage of the physical and psychological weaknesses of audiences.

There is such competition among tele-gurus and rival ministries that they actively report their successes and the progress of ministry and mission among people. Religious proselytization is similar to methods used in advertising. They are also concerned about copyrights of their products and programmes. Their purpose is to get the money for their programme through popularity and by sensationalism. Thus they adopt their way of presenting the gospel to reflect the demands of television popularity. They make the gospel into a package and sell it through the media. They are not opposed to individual beliefs but to institutions, including churches.

In South Asia (particularly in India), the cable television networks found an audience market for Christian programmes as well as other religious programmes. These tele-gurus make use of such times that are available to them at a reasonable price. To broadcast in Tamil on one of the television channels one has to pay around ten thousand rupees. It is interesting to see that every morning the cable channels offer some religious or good word to their audience and so the demand has created a market for such programmes. Tele-gurus are making use of such demands and markets and turning the preaching of the gospel into a profit-making business. Being on television boosts their popularity, as well as increasing awareness for their public meetings.

By offering 'prosperity theologies' they make people's life seem easy whereas, it can be argued, they are in fact encouraging an escape mechanism from the realities of life. They shape the worldview of the audience giving an individual's achievement or salvation priority regardless of their relationship with others. Life in a society is linked with the extra-ordinary experiences that one has. Television plays a major role in bringing the evangelist visually to people and whenever they get some success in their lives they think it is because of the tele-gurus.

There is less emphasis on the struggles and ability of the individual, so many are encouraged to believe that even without working hard things could be achieved easily through some miracles. This is visually proved with the witness of those who have succeeded in their lives through such miraculous experiences. But since gospel values are negated by these life values it is a challenge not only to the churches but also to the basis of the gospel itself. The whole programme and organization revolves around a single individual guru or preacher or leader who happens to speak or preach well or perform some miracles. Occasionally, there are scandals which make the popular, charismatic leader very unpopular and this often leads to a crisis of faith in leadership among the viewers.

Fundamentalist theologies

Some of the television and radio preachers promote a kind of fundamentalist theology in the public sphere. A few of them claim that they are following the fundamentals of Christian faith and often interpret the Bible literally. The word, 'fundamentalism' refers to all religious movements that seek to return to 'fundamentals of their faith' [Hippler and Lueg, 1995]. It is also 'the affirmation of religious authority as holistic and absolute, admitting neither criticism nor reduction' [Lawrence, 1989].

Their teaching is not a problem as long as they do not offend other Christian and non-Christian teachings. Some of them fall into the following category of fundamentalism. While they use entertainment as a form of communicating the gospel to the public they determine and state their doctrines in fixed narratives and create new communities of their own believers using various technologies and media. The following are some of the characteristics of their faith and doctrines.

- Their theologies often have fixed narratives of faith. Thereby their doctrines fix God within these narratives and thus play God for their own ends. They promote a belief in absolutism and inerrancy of their revelation. These sects are often very selective of their tradition. They defend it at all costs. They feel threatened by erosion of religious values.
- Their theologies are often highly dualistic. They create a myth of the other. Their members are chosen and are in the light whereas the outsiders are under darkness and so the other is an evil. The other is the enemy of God and can be seen as a threat to their faith, culture and so on. They often propagate

negative information of the other and thus promote ignorance about the 'other'.

■   Their theologies tend to view the outsiders 'as Infidels', 'Pagans', 'Heathens', 'Jihads'' or 'Western' though they follow another religion and thus see the other as a monolithic group (Homogenous). They create a fear of others among their members. They create a stereotypical theological image of the other which indirectly portrays them as enemies of the people of God.

■   They create a myth of the Golden Age or ideal world that is peopled only with their members. Often their idea of the Kingdom remains exclusive such as – Ram Raj; Umma; Kingdom of God/New Creation and thus they often support or join with right wing politicians to establish it.

These characteristics of fundamentalism are present in mass mediated broadcasting. At times they offend the other religious groups by publicly excluding them or categorizing them into negative imageries. They entertain the audience through their claims of miracles and their fortune telling. Many of them promise that if the audience buys their religious icons or contributes to their ministry then God's blessings will certainly be bestowed upon them. Having critically evaluated some of their characteristics this section will highlight their ways of approaching the public and thus lead to a dialogue between theology and media.

Section B - A theological reflection on Fundamentalist theologies

Tele-gurus have raised old questions of exclusive and universal claims of religious truth by their public demonstrations of miracles, fortune telling, and predictions or name-calling practices in which the preacher calls the individual by his or her name from among the crowd without knowing them beforehand. They not only make their claims exclusive but also critique other inclusive theological approaches. They have posed a challenge to these pluralistic and inclusive approaches. Among theologians these approaches are already discussed and written about. Tele-gurus public remarks on these approaches raise serious questions for theological thinkers particularly about inclusive and pluralistic theological approaches. In the following sections, I will highlight three main approaches and critically engage with each approach and then develop a new possible direction.

No other name?

This section will begin with a discussion about exclusivist views that are often used and displayed in the public by tele-gurus. Many Christians share such an exclusive faith in Christ. 'No other salvation is possible except through Jesus Christ' is the kind of statement the exclusivist would point to, supported by verses such as 'There is salvation in no one else, for there is no other name under heaven given among men by which we much be saved.' (Acts 4.12) and also Jesus' sayings such as 'I am the way, the truth and the life; no one comes to the Father, but by m.' (John 14.6). Christianity is identified with this truth and so claims were made to establish such truth.

First of all we need to accept the fact that there are a number of verses in the Bible that clearly point to an exclusive faith in Christ and a need to spread this faith to all in the world. The universal relevance of the Gospel cannot be denied by any Christian. There is uniqueness of the message and revelation of Christ. It is difficult to see this uniqueness which makes the Christian faith an exclusive one. The gospel is often seen by many Christians as an exclusive one within the framework of Christian faith, doctrines and biblical narratives.

The twentieth-century Dutch theologian Hendrik Kraemer objected to the surface-level similarities between religions. According to Kraemer [1938], every Christian should proclaim the truth about God and humankind which is revealed only in Christ. But Christians should strive for the presentation of the Christian truth in terms of modes of expression that make its challenge intelligible and related to the peculiar quality of reality in which they (non-Christians) live

[1938:303].

Any revelation can only be effectively discerned in the light of the special revelation of Jesus Christ[29] [Kraemer 1956:232]. Such claims were also made by tele-evangelists who made an impact on the popular faiths. It is interesting to note the fact that similar claims were made by television gurus from other religions too. Recently gurus such as Zakir Naik, one of the famous Islamic television preachers, challenge through his comparative study of different religious texts and make an exclusive claim of Islamic faith[30]. Other tele-gurus follow the same method and format to make claims similar to Christian claims.

Critique of exclusivist approaches

One needs to recognize the other passages or verses in the Bible where Jesus is seen to have other kinds of approaches towards other faiths. The claims of superiority of the revelation of Christ over other religions cannot be substantiated as Jesus himself was a Jewish religious person and he did not begin a separate religion as such. Even though Jesus lived in actual time and space, many things were reported from a faithful early Christian community which had undergone a post-Easter transformation. Many scholars have highlighted the problems with exclusive claims of Christian faith. Gavin D'Costa argues that people cannot neglect the dynamic nature of religion as well as the creative interaction between beliefs and practice which result in the development and changes within religious traditions because of this emphasis on the totalitarian nature of religion [1986:61].

The demand by Jesus to proclaim the Gospel to all did not mean to spread Christianity or to proselytize people into another doctrine or ideology or faith, rather it means to invite people to the Kingdom of God and to practice its values. The exclusive claims are often made to defend institutional Christianity or to protect the power structure of the church or to hold on to the deadly denominational doctrines which often divide people rather than unite.

The claims of the uniqueness of the revelation of Christ are also made within the framework of Christian gospels. In simple words, the uniqueness of Christ is that the logos became flesh and dwelled among us. The gospel narrative contains both the words of Jesus and also the words about Jesus (Christ-event). The Christ-event was unique and complete revelation; nevertheless it could not be communicated through a single absolute gospel. Rather four gospels were kept together in order to explain and interpret the event of the Word becoming flesh. The early Christians who kept the four gospels together recognized the difficulty of explaining the Christ-event from one perspective or within one Gospel and so left each writer to explain the event in his own way and thus left them together.

Though the experience of the event was unique and truest when the event was interpreted and communicated through narratives, the early Christians accepted them as they are rather than absolutizing the language of the gospel itself into an exclusive format. Rather they continued to interact with the creativity of the narratives and thus provided new meanings for new issues that arose in the context of the first or second century. Many of the early Christians were Jewish and Greek and thus brought their respective religious experiences into their religious practices.

Narrative idols

For me, there is no problem with the uniqueness and universal relevance of the gospel. The gospel must be proclaimed to all because it is expected of every Christian. At the same time, there is no need to claim superiority over any other faiths or doctrines because the gospel that one preaches is shaped and packaged within one's own doctrines, ideologies and also within one's own conviction. The gospel's main content is the announcement of God's love to the world to all, in particular, through Jesus Christ and a demand for all to love God and neighbour. The uniqueness of the gospel is that Jesus went to the extent of giving his life for the sake of bringing people to God and to understand their neighbours. In this light, God's revelation continued even after the death and resurrection of Jesus Christ.

God's revelation cannot be contained within the Gospels that are written down because of its dynamic continuing activity in and through the Holy Spirit. Limiting God's revelation within the narrative of the gospels means we are idolising the narrative and thus placing it above God and replacing God with the narrative of God. God's revelation is continuously active and will be active in diverse ways. One cannot limit it to mere narratives of the Bible even although they guide us into an experience of the revelation again. Exclusive claims have only succeeded in making the Gospel a static and dead narrative, which amounts to idolizing it.

The uniqueness of the Christian gospel can be expressed only in the emptying of oneself and thus becoming the gospel itself. The churches often find it easy to proclaim the ideal gospel without practising it and thus distance the content away from its praxis. Thus the major purpose of the gospel is to bring people to God and also to their neighbours. If this is the case then the uniqueness of the Gospel is that it is ready to crucify the uniqueness itself for the sake of building communities and for the sake of bringing people to God. If any claims of the uniqueness of the gospel become a stumbling block for other religious people then we should stop making such claims, rather our service, mercy and love towards others should help them to understand the gospel and thus bring them back to God and to their neighbours.

There is a uniqueness that we can embody in ourselves rather than claim it and so we become silent in claiming it in a mature state. Christians are called to proclaim the Gospel to all which means we need to communicate not only through our words but also through our being (life) the Good News. When language fails us (creating confusion in the claims of uniqueness), our being becomes a means of communication (life in silence). In John 1:14 the word became flesh and dwelt among us. It refers to Jesus' incarnating event in which God's word (logos) took the form of the human body in order to reveal the glory of God. Jesus demands his followers to bear witness to his message and to become one with the gospel message.

Becoming one with his message means to serve others (diakonia); to show God's love (agape) and to show solidarity with the people who struggle to come out of their poverty and oppression. In this way Christians can embody the message and thus become the gospel itself. It is in this becoming of the gospel that Christians can witness the gospel. Even when we proclaim the gospel, we do not need to claim absoluteness and superiority of the gospel over the other religious narratives.

Hidden Christ?

Tele-evangelists and other charismatic Christian leaders often criticize other approaches that encourage people to take a positive attitude and have relationship with people from differing faiths. One such approach is an inclusive approach. This approach holds together two convictions: that God's grace is operating in all religions of the world that are searching for salvation, and secondly it is the uniqueness of the manifestation of God's grace in Christ which makes a universal claim as the final way of salvation [Alan Race, 1983]. Representatives of this approach believe that all non-Christian religious truth belongs to and points ultimately to Christ.

Bible verses such as Acts 10.35 ('Truly I perceive that God shows no partiality, but in every nation anyone who fears him and does what is right is acceptable to him.'); 14.16f and 17.22–31 are often quoted by those who support this approach. It is interesting to note that most of the Hindu tele-gurus do not mind quoting Christian texts to highlight the importance of their points and are often inclusive in their approach. Some of them may think that Jesus was one of the well known gurus of the world who attained a true realized stage in his life[31].

Justin Martyr (100-165 CE wrote, 'It is our belief that those [men] who strive to do the good which is enjoined on us have a share in God... Christ is the divine Word in whom the whole human race share and those who live according to the light of their knowledge are Christians, even if they are considered as being godless' [I Apology 46.1–4]. This summarizes an approach which was later identified as 'anonymous Christianity' by Karl Rahner. Karl Rahner points out the two principles that have to be kept together which are: the necessity of Christian faith and the universal salvific will of God's love[32] [Karl Rahner, 1961-84, Vol 6:391]. One of the Indian tele-evangelists Sadhu Chellappa preaches in Tamil and also English by comparing Christianity and Hinduism, and often tends to prove that Hindu texts are pointing to Jesus Christ. Such inclusive, exceptional preachers can also be found appearing on television. An interesting comparative study between tele-evangelists and tele-gurus has been carried out by a Bible study group online[33]. It is essential to analyse such inclusive theological approaches critically.

Critique of inclusive approach

There is no question about God's grace being active in other religions. Emphasizing the Christ-event as the only way for salvation and Christianity as an absolute religion, points to fulfilment theories. In these theories, the emphasis is on God as being active in all religion nevertheless the respective religious narratives point to Jesus as their fulfilment or will lead to him or finality has to be recognized in Christianity. There is no question that Christ is the centre of any Christian faith. No one can neglect the activities of God's grace to Christian faith. When it comes to the interaction with other religions we may recognize God's presence in a few religions. We need to move beyond our theo-centric as well as Christi-centric approaches because in our interaction with other religious faiths, we need to see God's grace active within all religions and Christ as part of this grace, being active even without any need of being recognized as Christ in other religions.

The Christ, the Logos, was there from the beginning and so identifying Christ merely with the historical Jesus is limiting the motives of Incarnation itself. Christ as God's fuller form of revelation was active, not only before Abraham, and also after the Pentecostal movement, but also outside Christian faith proclaiming good news to different people in different contexts. I am not talking about 'the hidden Christ' but a Christ who is present but not willing to identify himself as Christ in other religions, rather enlightening and confirming with the interaction with Christianity while revealing himself to Christianity from being within other religions. While accepting Christ as the centre of our faith, we do not need to impose him to be the centre of other faiths or even in our dialogue with others. Christ cannot be exclusively claimed by Christians alone. By this I mean, Christ as being active from the beginning of the world, not only in Jewish religion but also in other religions, reforming, reviving, challenging and incarnating in them.

Anonymous Christianity

As we believe in the finality of Christ as being the complete revelation of God, other religious people expect their avatar or prophet to be the final one from God. As I mentioned above, Christ is being active outside Christianity too without being identified as Christ and without wanting to be identified as Christ either. In this way, any revival or reform in any religion that brings people closer to God and to their neighbour can be seen as an act of God's grace and shows the presence of Christ as Logos. It is not an anonymous Christianity or hidden Christ; rather it demands of us the recognition of the other religious people as they are. It also demands us to engage with other religious communities in their search for meanings of life and of God as Jesus himself engaged in his hearers' search.

While we hold on to our Christ- centred faith we do not need to convince others to accept Christ as the centre of their faith too (except those who are willing to accept this line). Others may be willing to hold on to Krishna or Ram as their Saviour and Lord. We need to recognize their experience and their insights through which we may understand Christ more than before and may stand corrected. We are also called to share our experience of Christ with them, through which their faith too might be enriched and nourished. We may join in the same search for meanings of life and of God or we may disagree but still we can live together and find a common platform to serve God and serve our neighbour.

Many names

A few tele-gurus tend to prove their point and demonstrate a miracle in front of a camera as they know the power of the camera and also of the language they use. They often tend to criticize those who tolerate other religious faiths. Rarely one can see them talking about other religions in a positive way, except ancient Judaism. They tend to claim that pluralism questions the basic faith in the uniqueness of Christ. But among the theological circle, tolerance and pluralistic values are seen as part of Christian ethos. Tolerance needs to be seen as a Christian moral imperative and as a Christian theological necessity. Hocking argues that the relation between religions must increasingly take the form of a common search for truth [Hocking, 1932:47]. In tolerant pluralism, knowledge of God is partial in all faiths, including the Christian, and Christianity is the anticipation of the essence of all religions and so contains potentially all that any religion has [Hocking, 1940:249].

John Hick terms his pluralistic scheme as the Copernican Revolution and thus he argues that as the sun replaced the earth at the centre of the planetary universe so too God ought to replace Christ and Christianity at the centre of the religious universe [Hick, 1980:52]. At the level of experience the religions portray a genuine, though different, encounter with the divine, and the differences between religious beliefs and practices reflect the cultural forms and circumstances which embody the experiences[34] [On Hick, comments by Alan Race 1983:83]. The God whom our minds can comprehend is a human image, inadequate and incomplete, of what is ultimately indefinable. Difference in doctrine and theological statements reflect difference in the historical and cultural factors bound up in religious belief. The absoluteness of the experience is the basis for the absoluteness of the language [Hick, in Race, 1983:89].

A genuine dialogue and a mutual mission of sharing experiences and insights, mutual enrichment and co-operation should determine the attitude of Christians towards other religions. Such theological concepts are not acceptable to these tele-gurus. Tele-gurus also make

John Joshva Raja

sure the public is aware of the negative implications of pluralism. It is difficult for theologians, not only to promote pluralism, but also to accept the concept and practice of dialogue among grassroots Christian's. Even theologians do not take the audience seriously in order to begin an interaction with their faith and thus engage them in a dialogue with the other in a conflict situation.

Critique of pluralism

I accept that God is active in different religions. At times, however, God is not active in all religions at all times. At times religion and the name of God are used to persecute or kill other people which are not God's grace but the religion of evil. Any religion that leads people to kill or persecute other religious or faith communities is an evil religion. God's grace is not present in such people's mind. At the same time, one cannot generalize the activities of a few people to be a representation of the whole religion, which is happening all over the world today.

Our God is God for all which means the one who created a Hindu also created me and so his or her God is also my God. God reveals himself in all religions continuously that they may come to him and establish good relationship with their neighbours because everyone is God's creature, and everyone experiences God in his own way. If I am born into a Christian family, I feel Christ is the Truth and the Way, whereas if I am born into a Hindu family I would have seen Krishna or any other gods as the reality.

Out of each one's experience of God religions, culture and practices are established, tested and interpreted over the years and generations. But the question is, to what extent the religious narratives can lead us back to God and to our neighbours, whether it is Christianity or Hinduism or Islam, whether I feel that I am taken closer to God and to neighbour regardless of caste, colour and class. At times, religious narratives do take us towards a destructive culture rather than to a creative way of life in which God is also present. My contention is that not all the religions nor their narratives take us to God nor is

God present in any religion or in any community that destroys other communities or kills other people.

Narrative and experience
The second point that I would like to argue against pluralism is that the experience of God is real, whereas the narrative that describes such an experience is real to the extent of explaining such an experience. In so far as those who have not experienced the same, it is only a narrative, unless demonstrated in a laboratory or experienced in a similar manner. I will not term the narrative as myth but narrative does not explain the whole experience rather it attempts to describe it within the constraints of available language and symbols.

The narrative, with its limitations, cannot claim to be absolute or universal because similar experiences can cause different stories and experiences of the same incident and can also create a variety of narratives and thus is liable to diverse interpretations. In this sense, the different denominations interpret the narratives in different ways and so no one can claim their church or denomination as the true church or denomination. This is also true of different religious claims. These narratives are written in order to preserve the stories of God's revelation and intervention and to tell them to the new generations and thus bring them to God and also establish better relationship with neighbours. At an immature level, the narratives were used to eliminate other communities but in a mature state the narratives are used to create new relationships between all living beings.

Narratives of God often unite and at times divide people. Each individual determines the way he or she uses the narratives for his or her own growth or destruction. Each community uses these narratives the way they want, at times exclusively and in a destructive manner and at times in a creative and constructive manner. Communities and individuals receive the narratives which contain both constructive and destructive narratives. According to their interests, they highlight those elements that they want and thus determine the way they want to use religious narratives. At the same time individuals and communities are also engaged in a search for meanings of God and of life that would continue to help them to interact with God and also with their neighbours within and outside their communities. Religious narratives enable people to experience God's revelation continuously and to add more narratives or also reinterpret existing narratives.

For this one religious narrative does not become the basic criterion to evaluate other religious narratives. Rather everyone is engaged in the search for new meanings of the mystery of God's grace and revelation and also of life. In this process one religious friend may help the other without compromising one's own conviction and beliefs. While engaging along with others we may learn together from each other and find out that our faith is enriched by the other and vice versa.

Taking the audience seriously in doing theology
It means to begin with faith statements such as, 'Christ is the way'. Such faith statements do not need to be changed while encouraging Christians to engage in search for meanings along with other religious friends. In this way, dialogue can be very helpful and even Christians at the grassroots level can be convinced of such dialogical efforts. At times pluralism itself becomes an exclusivist view point. Because those who hold this view argue that unless one agrees that God is active in all religions and demands to give up the claims of uniqueness of Christ, one cannot have a dialogue. Even though I criticize the claims of uniqueness in the previous sections, it is the reality of Christian faith at the church members' level which one has to take into account. This is where I am blending two concepts – 'existential pluralism' which arises out of the demand for existential realities.

In a multi-religious context, the communities were pluralistic and were accommodative of other religions. Nevertheless, recently different religious communities are increasingly becoming conscious of their identities and trying to return to the fundamentals of their religions. Some of them feel threatened by other religious communities and thus try to form alliances among themselves in order to protect their faiths, cultures and religions. This can be explained using an example from the Indian context. A few Hindus and a few Muslims are engaged in violent activities against each other in the name of religion. Recently, there was a clash between these two communities in a place called Godhra, one of the north western states of India, where many people were killed in the name of religion. This incident was not an isolated one. This has led to a misunderstanding and suspicion between different religious communities in Gujarat, particularly between Muslims and Hindus. Such a misunderstanding is spreading all over India between these two communities. In many parts they could not live together as village communities anymore and so the majority ask the minority to leave the village or the place where they stay or to otherwise adopt the majority's culture.

Engaging with the 'Other' –theologising in public

Many of the tele-gurus are not interested in promoting awareness of the Other. In many multicultural contexts the confrontation between different communities is an everyday reality. They often ignore such conflicting realities or defend their own religious groups in the conflicts. In a reality where an interaction between fighting communities would reduce the terror and the deaths, one has to see establishing peace as part of Christ's mission. In such interaction no one needs to compromise one's own faith for the sake of dialogue. This is being identified as an existential pluralism, which means the existential demand for a dialogue towards removing ignorance and misunderstanding of one by the other has to be taken seriously.

Otherwise many people's lives are lost in the name of religion and the misunderstanding could lead to major confrontations and conflicts between different religious communities. Such a dialogue forces us to take part without losing our convictions and our faith experiences. Christians can believe that Christ is the way, the truth and the life as it is part of their lived experience. They can also proclaim the gospel to all inviting them to enter into the kingdom. But at the same time, they do not need to offend others by saying that their experiences, traditions and narratives are wrong or inferior to Christian claims, as Christians have not experienced such traditions and experiences.

Hindus can hold on to their experiences as true experiences without contrasting or without imposing their way of life on others. This seems somewhat 'contradictory' or 'a chaotic proposal' but let me try to clarify this. We do not need to accept other religious faiths and narratives in their fuller form nor need to adopt their traditions and experience to hold dialogue with them. We do not need to misunderstand them or misquote them as pagans or heathens. We do not need to misunderstand other religions such as Islam and label them terrorist religions. We cannot understand their faith, their doctrines and their experiences fully. As outsiders we cannot understand other religions at all. However, what we can do is try to remove our ignorance about them. If our ignorance about other religions costs people's lives then why not try to remove such ignorance and thus allow others their right to live in this world? It is not only our ignorance that has to be removed but also others' too needs to be corrected.

For this we need to engage in interaction with other religions and also encourage other religions to interact among themselves. This is what I call 'existential pluralism', where we try to live together as a community of communities, where religion will not divide us rather it will help us to relate ourselves with the other. There is an existential demand for us to live alongside the other with a better understanding and this demands us to accept the others as they are, while encouraging them to accept us as we are. While engaging in the interaction, not only the misunderstanding or ignorance about the other would be reduced, but the participants will realize that others too are engaged in a similar religious search for meanings of life and of God. If the participants in the interaction decide to travel together further in the search for meanings then they may correct, nourish and enrich each other's faith and thus enable each one to come closer to God and also closer to a better relationship with their neighbour.

Theologians and tele-gurus

From the interaction between the theologies of tele-gurus and the media there is a demand for theologians to develop alternative paradigms of theology. Such alternative paradigms would take the audience seriously in their theological thinking. While enabling people to see the realities around them, their simple faith should also be given first and foremost importance in hermeneutics. In this way, without compromising their faith, people need to be guided to see the reality around them. This is where theologians can also provide a public discourse and challenge these tele-gurus. These tele-gurus do not show any concern for the contextual realities except in raising some funds for charities. They tend to assure people of prosperity and thereby distract them from looking at their realities and their problems.

If theologians do not take the audience's faith seriously (in their claims of uniqueness and so in their proclamation to all), it is very difficult to find a point of contact and so to share a sphere with them. A few tele-gurus would certainly mislead the mass audience by misrepresenting and misinterpreting them. By providing what the audience wanted and how they wanted it, the tele-gurus have succeeded in capturing, maintaining and manipulating the public for their causes. It is essential to start with an acceptance of the audience's faith and their expectations in order to engage with them in their search for meanings of life and of God.

Section C Facing Challenges of Telegurus

Telegurus provide two kinds of challenges to the theologians and churches in general. First they work closely with the media marketing principles and so they promote a kind of emotional and prosperity gospel. They attract the public and convert them into their income. Their presentation of other religions and other denominations in their programme are often negative and thus publicise a false fear or give wrong assurances for the sick and the poor through their prayers and other activities. They tend to manipulate the audience and promote a false understanding of their own religion and others' too. They tend to create tension among multicultural and multi-faith communities by using and displaying stereotypical imageries. This provides a challenge to the theologians regarding the use of media by the Telegurus – particularly by the tele-evangelists. Theologians need to take media literacy programme seriously so that they can promote awareness, education and learning of the people about their own and other religions through critical thinking and reflections rather than simply through media.

The second challenge is to explore the possibilities of using entertainment, emotion and feeling in religious communication. Particularly the use of such characteristics of the media, the Telegurus have succeeded in reaching out to the public and persuading them to their followers. A systematic study of theology and entertainment needs to be taken in order to promote within the churches and among other religious agencies to develop their communication effectively among the people. This would enable those who are engaged in promoting ecumenical relationship, theological awareness and contextual issues would not only succeed in reaching out but also enable the public to support and engage in such activities as well. The following two sections will highlight the importance of using media literacy – particularly using Paulo Freire's learning methods and also using aesthetic elements in religious communication.

A need for media literacy and theological literacy

Having highlighted the issues of tele-gurus and their theologies, it is essential for theological formation to include media literacy programmes as part of their training. People use media without having the ability to read the texts and meanings embedded within the texts. Many of the audience often do not understand how a miracle is created using a camera, to look like a miracle. The viewers often remain as illiterate and do not recognize the fact that the media construct realities with particular perspectives and ideologies.

Within such constructed realities the tele-gurus operate creating their own faith-centred realities. In such a context, a media literacy programme should be carried out enabling people to read the visual, aural and convergent texts creatively and critically [Raja, 2004]. Not only media literacy but also a theological literacy has to be promoted among the public so that issues related to theologies of prosperity and entertainment are freely discussed by people. Thus the public will become aware of those issues and be able to read these popular texts of tele-gurus critically.

Media literacy as liberative praxis

It is essential to explain the media literacy in the context of theological education so that its importance can be recognized. Media Literacy, in a very simple way, can be looked at in three ways. Media Literacy is a critical awareness of what the mass media is all about. The structure, ideology and techniques of the media are studied and reflected upon. This awareness leads to an action which culminates in the making of alternative media programmes with a simple methodology, but which delivers a powerful message. Media literacy [Manuel and Boyd, 1992] [35] is the ability to sift through and analyse the messages that inform, entertain and are sold to us every day.

It is the ability to bring critical thinking skills to bear on all media — from music videos and web environments to product placement in films and virtual displays. It is about asking pertinent questions about what is there, and noticing what is not there. And it is the instinct to question what lies behind media productions: the motives, the money, the values and the ownership and to be aware of how these factors influence content.

Media literacy also involves the process in which a community of people creatively and critically participate (production, distribution, and exhibition) in using traditional and technological media in the liberation and development of oneself and one's community. It leads to what can be called 'democratization of communication'. Media literacy [William Bowen, 1996][36] seeks to empower citizens to transform their

John Joshva Raja

passive relationship to media into an active, critical engagement —
capable of challenging the traditions and structures of a privatized,
commercial media culture, and finding new avenues of citizen speech
and discourse. Media literacy aims to encourage an awareness of
how the media are influenced by commercial considerations, and
how these affect content, technique and distribution. Most media
production is a business, and must therefore make a profit. Questions
of ownership and control are central; a relatively small number of
individuals control what we watch, read and hear in the media.

Media educators follow eight key concepts and principles. These
concepts provide an effective foundation for examining mass media
and popular culture. The first principle for media literacy assumes
that all media are construction[37]. The second principle of the media
literacy is that the media construct reality[38]. The third principle is that
audiences negotiate meaning in the media[39]. The fourth principles
are that media have commercial implications. Media Literacy aims
to encourage an awareness of how the media are influenced by
commercial considerations, and how these affect content, technique
and distribution. Most media production is a business, and must
therefore make a profit.

Questions of ownership and control are central: a relatively small
number of individuals control what we watch, read and hear in the
media. The fifth one is that media contain ideological and value
messages. All media products are advertising, in some sense, in that
they proclaim values and ways of life. Explicitly or implicitly, the
mainstream media convey ideological messages about such issues as
the nature of the good life, the virtue of consumerism, the role of
women, the acceptance of authority, and unquestioning patriotism.

The sixth principle is that media have social and political
implications. The media have great influence on politics and on
forming social change. Television can greatly influence the election
of a national leader on the basis of image. The media involve us in
concerns such as civil rights issues, famines in Africa, and the AIDS
epidemic. They give us an intimate sense of national issues and global

70

concerns, so that we become citizens of Marshall McLuhan's "Global Village." The seventh principle is that the form and content are closely related in the media.

As Marshall McLuhan noted, each medium has its own grammar and codifies reality in its own particular way. Different media will report the same event, but create different impressions and messages. Media are extensions of human beings and shape the message and meanings (McLuhan). The eighth principle is that each medium has a unique aesthetic form Just as we notice the pleasing rhythms of certain pieces of poetry or prose, so we ought to be able to enjoy the pleasing forms and effects of the different media. The media are here to stay to entertain us, to turn information into an infotainment and also education into an edutainment. At times they provide aesthetic elements that are good and are essential for our leisure.

If we follow these principles in the tele-evangelists and Telegurus, we will start understanding the fact that their content in the television are merely constructions. The miracles and other happenings are not just happening but are also constructed for the audience. It is constructed to promote and popularise their programmes and then persuade the audience to pay for it. They construct a reality which satisfies the audience. Their religion is constructed according to what the audiences wanted and according to the demands of the media industry. Even though the audiences construct diverse meanings in their engagement with the media, the success leads to survival of the best persuasive programmes in the television. These gospel messages have commercial implications.

Thus they carry an ideology and values system which would be in favour of the mass media industries and businesses. In order to get audiences to their programmes they have to use some of the methods and techniques of the entertainment industry and thus survive the highly competitive public space. In this sense tele-evangelists or tele-gurus have created a new religion of making money by proclaiming successes/prosperity, good luck promises and assurances with guaranteed solutions. Unless the audience become aware of these

71

issues, they can easily be sensationalised into particular issues and thus show the other as a potential threat and as enemy imageries. Media literacy needs to be taken very seriously by the churches and thus enable them to engage with people in critically studying the content and practices of the mass media.

We see people's faith being challenged or misled by neo-tele-evangelists who appear on the cable screens and who speak on radio programmes. They spread the gospel of success and fortune. For everyone, life must be a success which can be achieved by believing in what the evangelist says and also by donating to him or her. These evangelists assure people of a successful, painless and easy life. Many of them emphasize healing miracles and an easy solution to the many problems of life. They work, like advertisers, for money. Their practices are in conformity with other media practices which work through persuasion methods. They are taken into a 'False Consciousness', a term invented by the twentieth-century political philosopher Antonio Gramsci [1973], where disparities between rich and poor and values of life are not taken seriously. Success and fulfilling one's desires through faith have become prime factors of their theology.

This enables people to accept voluntarily such realities and remain passive about them. It maintains and justifies the 'culture of silence' theologically. This brings about challenges to theologians to liberate people from such false consciousness that is promoted by these television evangelists. Such false consciousness can be challenged theologically only when our understanding of communication moves from old model in which the movement is from sender to receiver to participatory model. Paulo Freire has suggested a shift in the understanding of education methods which may be used for engaging and challenging mass mediated communication in today's context. Freire's model of education provides a challenge in our ways of communicating to people within the churches and also the ways that a few tele-evangelists try to popularise their versions of the gospel. Only by critically engaging with the media's religious content the Christian audience can become media literate and thus able to differentiate between commercial and gospel proclamations.

Section D – Conscientization as part of Media literacy

Paulo Freire

The Brazilian educator Paulo Freire has influenced many scholars from Asia, Africa and South America in his emphasis on the participatory aspects of communication. His primary aim is to develop a dialogical method in education. Even though he has developed his method primarily for education, the principles behind such a method can help in developing media literacy at grassroots. I identify three principles that he highlights the education methods in his book, *Pedagogy of the Oppressed* [Freire 1972]. They are: Banking Education; Liberating Education and Action and Reflection; His three approaches enable those who wish to promote media literacy to develop theoretical framework for their awareness and education programme about media. Using his liberative and action-reflection method may enable educators to eliminate or reduce the false consciousness and thus liberate people from uncritical use to a critical and appropriate reading of the media.

A. Banking Versus Liberating

Freire uses the imagery of a teacher-student relationship in order to identify the problem of banking education and to point out the importance of liberating education. In the banking method, education becomes an act of depositing, in which the students are the depositories and the teacher is the depositor [Freire 1972:47]. In this sense communication is a transfer of knowledge from the communicator (teacher) to the audience (student). Freire is critical of this method of communication. For him it is to minimise or annul the audience's creative power and turn them into containers to be filled by the communicator. The banking communication is similar to that of the instrumental approach in which the communicator is a sender and the audience is a passive receiver.

Against this banking method Freire proposes a liberating or problem-posing method which bases itself on creativity and stimulates true reflection [1972:56]. This view considers people as beings who are authentic only when engaged in inquiry and creative transformation. Liberating communication consists in acts of cognition and not in transfer of information. Freire's writings reflect his own South American context in which oppressors used certain existing forms to socialise and to oppress a large mass of people.

In the liberating method of education, the teacher of the students and the students of the teacher cease to exist and a new term emerges: teacher-students with student-teachers. The students are now co-investigators along with their teachers [Freire 1972:56]. Methods of communication should not be based on the banking model. They should view the communicator and the audience as equal participants in the communication process. The gap between the communicator and the audience disappears as they both engage in this process with the freedom to share their views and with critical thinking. In the media literacy programmes we need to use this technique of critical thinking and freedom to share to enable people to become aware of some of the issues from the media.

B. Action and Reflection

Communicators share with their audiences in such a way that the cognizable object mediates their capacity for understanding. The reality cannot be transformed without posing the audience's false consciousness of reality as a problem. Thus the interaction between the communicator and the audience should lead to the transformation of reality around them. This transformation needs to enhance the process of humanisation of the audience [Freire 1972:106]. Pradip Thomas notes: In Freire's pedagogy, action and reflection are not separate activities but an organic whole and it is this dialectical interplay of action and reflection that constitutes the process of conscientizacao (concentization) [1994:50].

Only when the action follows reflection then is the communication true communication. So reflection is only real when it sends the communicator and the audience back to the given situation in which they act and live. The communicator and the audience become aware of these issues by participating in the communication process [Freire 1973: 36].

C. 'Freire and Communication'

In Freire's views of education, the communicator and the audience are equal participants in the investigation of knowledge. Their participation in the communication process would lead to the disappearance of distinctions between them [Thomas 1994:51]. The act of critical thinking is the primary element of participatory communication. The task of the communicator is to enable the audience to become aware of their critical faculties and to relate them to the tasks of political struggle and development. Freire's concept is relevant to my study because it attempts to view communication as a process among various other social processes. The social, cultural and political contexts in which communication occurs are given importance.

Because in his Latin America powerful oppressors violently subjugated many people, Freire wanted communication to reflect and address such issues. For him changes in material world alone would not bring about changes in social structures. The dominant mythological concepts that serve the oppressors should be challenged and replaced through critical thinking by alternative principles arising from the people themselves. The task of the communicator is to participate in their audiences' process of communication in such a way that the audiences become aware of these issues.

While recognising the importance of Freire's work, my study suggests that communication does not merely arise from the needs in society. It attempts to address the social and cultural issues while enabling the audience themselves to find a solution. The primary task of Christian communication is not merely to humanise the audience (to liberate from the oppression) but also to bring people closer to God. The aim of the communicator's participation is not only to liberate the audiences from their oppressors but to guide them to establish faith in God. This implies a continued interaction through which the Christian communicator would present the meanings of God along with other social meanings. This interaction may bring awareness among the audience and enable them to interpret or to reinterpret their religious faith. Without enriching faith in God, humanisation may become meaningless. This will be explained in the interactive aspect of communication.

Section E - A need for a theology of entertainment

Entertainment is the essence of every culture and religion. Without entertainment there is no worship and there is no religion. Entertainment refers to the way people celebrate their lives through participation in events or activities and also enjoy their presence using cultural or religious expressions, forms and means that provide pleasure to them. Any act that provides amusement and attracts the attention of the audience can be also identified as an entertaining act. People go to worship not only to relate themselves with God and others but also to entertain themselves. Because the word 'entertainment' is used so negatively people might be shocked to see it used positively here.

Christian worship is an event in which participants celebrate their lives together with others in the presence of God. It means to enjoy their presence together as community and celebrate their lives in worship. Some of the elements of entertainment are well discussed by Clive Marsh [2004] in his book *Cinema and Sentiment: Film's Challenge to Theology*. The tele-gurus recognize these elements of the media and use them to their advantage. They provide entertainment as well as promote religious faith. The way they struggle to get the attention of the audience to convey and persuade them to accept their popular theologies, clearly show their priorities of communication.

From the tele-guru's perspective the audiences' attention is as important as their content. So they use the techniques of the media, miraculous demonstrations, contemporary icons and the popular story telling methods to maintain the attention of the audience. This is a challenge for theological thinking where the audiences' attention has not been given consideration at all. The audiences are often seen as empty bottles that have to be filled with theology that flows from universities and seminaries.

Tele-gurus are blamed for creating and selling Ishta Devas (gods who fulfil desires) to the audience. They create in the mind of the audience an eagerness to pray to God for a proof or a demonstration. Such appeals lead to a demand from God that whatever the audience desire should be fulfilled, and their desires can be achieved through prayers and rituals. Thus the tele-gurus end up providing a god who fulfils the desires of the audience. While critically pointing out the problem of such effects of tele-gurus one cannot deny the fact that entertainment is the basis of religious experience and thus 'audience-attention' must be viewed as a concept that requires as much importance as the content in the process of communication.

McLuhan's [1994] famous statement, 'the medium shapes the message' provides us with another dimension of entertainment which is often used by tele-gurus to communicate to the public. Morris [1990:181] argued in a similar way saying that genuine religion may enter the system at the camera but it is entertainment that emerges at the other from the domestic television set. Media often tend to interpret the messages in their own way. Tele-gurus work with a team of skilled professionals to popularise their theologies to the public. They have recognized the effect of the media in interpreting them and their faith in the media market. It is such mediated interpretations that enable them to raise financial support and thus buy space in the media. Entertainment is part of media technology, mediated content and presentation to the public. The outcome of the media in the public is entertainment that can distort the texts and meanings originally intended. However, tele-gurus have successfully exploited such technology and methods.

Traditionally people find it hard to accept entertainment in a positive manner, though they enjoy being part of it. It is the division of the sacred and secular worlds that has led people to have this view of isolating entertainment from religious activities. But for tele-gurus entertainment is a God-given means to promote their gospel while they themselves are often critical about some elements of it. The fundamental aspect of entertainment refers to free time and free space that people give for themselves and others. It refers to a leisure time where one can enjoy oneself in relationship with God and with others.

In his book *Free Time Towards a Theology of Leisure*; Neville highlights the importance of entertainment, leisure and pleasure. Neville strongly argues that the elements of leisure and entertainment had been developed by theologians such as Augustine, Thomas Aquinas and others [2004]. The fundamental implication of leisure seems to be freedom [Neville, 2004:7]. If there is no entertainment the creativity and joy of the religions would disappear and thus religions themselves would fade away.

Another study on the theology of entertainment is done by Wilson [1999] in his book *Worldly Amusements: Restoring the Lordship of Christ to Our Entertainment Choices*; Wilson argues in favour of being present in the world of entertainment. Interestingly, this book collects references from various sources including Bible references to justify the use of entertainment by the churches. The theology of beauty and entertainment has been discussed a lot among theologians using the word 'Aesthetics'. Theological aesthetics is concerned with questions about God and issues in theology in the light of and perceived through sense knowledge (sensation, feeling, imagination), through beauty, and the arts[40].

Balthasar [1994] wrote seven volumes of theological aesthetics by restructuring theology around aspects of aesthetics such as form and beauty. After analysing popular culture, Lynch [2005:189] proposes to develop a theological aesthetics of popular culture. He demands theologians to come up with an aesthetic language to make sense to the popular language and also to develop aesthetic criteria for evaluating popular culture. The tele-gurus emphasise the beauty of God that enable them to use the new technology, its genre and its form easily and communicate to the public in the way they wanted. It is essential to take aesthetic elements in doing theology very seriously. If so many of the theologians may have to communicate their concepts through poems, arts, dances and drama, rather than through arguments.

Theologically, when God saw everything good he decreed the seventh day as a day of leisure. Thus even seeing good and beauty in everything is part of entertainment. Jesus entertained the crowd telling them parables and stories while trying to communicate the meanings of life and of God. Jesus was placing his own meanings among other meanings through entertainment narratives such as stories and parables [Raja, 2000]. He often did not exclude or condemn other meanings rather placed his meanings as an inescapable entertaining and imaginative reality for the audience. The audience found themselves creating their own 'self's' and judging themselves in and through such articulated and imagined world of parables.

Even the Old and New Testament communities entertained themselves telling and retelling their traditional stories about their forefathers and relating them to their context. In an emerging and ever-changing context (some identify this as a post-modern context) any meaning has to be placed among a wide range of meanings in a more attractive way. While entertainment possibly diverts the attention of the audience from the real issues and possibly distorts the original meanings of the text it still is the only means of reaching out to the people with alternative concepts for theological thinking. Theologians need to be present in the public in order to challenge the dominant thinking and meanings. This is possibly the best means to engage in the public sphere, that is, to use entertainment as a means to interact with the audience. I would like to discuss how the use of aesthetic elements in the media provides a challenge to look at the way Christian communities and their leaders communicate among themselves and to others. This raises questions about the use of aesthetics in Jesus' use of the parables as well. I will discuss in the following sections about the use of aesthetics in hermeneutics of the Gospel to the contemporary context.

Kierkegaard and Aesthetics

In his book *Training in Christianity,* Kierkegaard [(1850) 1941A] argues that by his very nature Jesus did not directly communicate himself to the world, even to those closest to him. Jesus' message, Kierkegaard notes, was indirect and his followers were asked to believe in it. Indirect communication is defined as the opposite of direct communication that can be produced by the art of reduplicating communication24 [1941A:132]. This means there is no objective way of communicating Christ[41]25.

In Kierkegaard's concept of indirect communication, Christ did not communicate directly to his followers through his teachings. Those who believe in Christ could recognise the 'sign of contradiction' in him. For Kierkegaard [1941A:124] Christ is a sign, 'a sign of contradiction'. A sign of contradiction is a sign which contains in itself a contradiction. To be a sign of contradiction is to be another thing which stands in opposition to what one immediately is [1941A:124-5]. Christ is a sign of contradiction[42] because on the one hand he 83 says he is one with the Father and on the other he is an ordinary human being like others and thus contradicts himself. The sign of contradiction that Christ offered was offensive, and so, too, the indirect communication of a Christian will also offend [Arbaugh and Arbaugh1968:274].

Kierkegaard was critical of the Christendom28 that has transformed the whole of Christianity into direct communication [1941A:97]. For Kierkegaard, until now, people taught Christianity as knowledge that has triumphed over actuality and reduplication [Pattison 1992:74-6]. By making it a dogmatic and apologetic confession, the act of communicating faith becomes merely an imparting of knowledge and information about God, and about Christ, which for Kierkegaard, is a misunderstanding of Christianity.

A. Aesthetic as Hermeneutic starter

This aspect of indirect communication is explained with the help of the mid-wife imagery. Kierkegaard borrows the midwifery image (*maieutic)* from Plato and uses it in his *Fragments.* The imagery appears in the dialogues of Plato where Socrates says,

I am so far like the midwife that I cannot give birth to wisdom... all who are favoured by heaven make progress at a rate seems surprising to others as well as to themselves, although it is clear that they have never learned from me. The many admirable truths they bring to birth have been discovered by themselves from within [Hamilton and Cairns 1963:853-5].

The midwife's role is to help a woman in the process of delivering her child; it is the woman who delivers the child by herself with the help of the midwife. For Kierkegaard the communicator's role, like a midwife, is to help the learners (audiences) to become free and to stand by themselves in the process of believing and entering into the God-relationship [(1847) 1995:276-78]. The communicator remains anonymous in the process. Arbaugh and Arbaugh [1968:274] point out that for Kierkegaard the teacher, like a midwife, should deal with the learner where the learner is, in whatever state he or she may be, and seek to progress from that point towards the eternal. Both are concerned with seeking eternal truth.

The purpose of indirect communication is not to bring the learner into a relationship with the teacher but rather into relationship with God. In an essentially aesthetic age[43] if the teacher is to start where the learner is the teacher must start with the aesthetic – even though the aesthetic is incapable of expressing religious truth [Pattison 1992:72]. 87 Kierkegaard defines aesthetic as a pleasure, which is more than an art, and as personal interest which is more than sheer pleasure. With an aesthetic attitude one is caught up in various attractive experiences of the moment, in a state of immediacy which does not reach beyond itself [Arbaugh and Arbaugh 1968:64].

John Joshva Raja

B. Aesthetic Hermeneutics and Choices

Kierkegaard is also concerned with moral life that for him is learnt by practising the art of such living, together with observing this art as demonstrated by noble examples. In *Either/Or* he uses another metaphor of a judge who views the aesthetical, the ethical and the religious as three great allies [1959(2):150]. The ethical will not annihilate the aesthetical but transfigure it. In this way Kierkegaard combines indirect communication, Christology, aesthetic and ethical aspects together in the teacher (communicator) and learner (audience) relationship. In combining these aspects of communication, he sets out the goal and the role of the Christian communicator.

The goal of Christian communication should be to bring the audience not into an intellectual acceptance but to a personal acceptance of spiritual and ethical principles through aesthetic characteristics. Kierkegaard notes, "The ethical must be communicated as an art, simply because everyone knows it. The object of communication is consequently not knowledge but a realisation" [1967 (4): 272]. The learner needs to be prodded into self awareness in relation to these principles by means of irony, pathos, and dialectic. Such communication addresses an individual, a constituent of the audience, to help him/her to see inwardly and then to choose these principles in the light of his/her God-relationship[44]. It is to enable the individual to seek for himself/herself these principles in communication.

Arbaugh and Arbaugh argue that in Kierkegaard's understanding this ethical communication develops a response, but does not seek to inform [1968:272-3]. They interpret Kierkegaard's ethical communication as to coax the ethical out of the individual because it already exists inside him or her. They also point out that in ethical and religious communication the teacher is himself a learner who benefits from the response of his pupil [1968:272-4]. This characteristic of ethical communication, as explained, recognises those religious and social meanings as already present in the audience, waiting to be shared and interpreted through the communication process.

It has been noted that a wide range of competing meanings is available to the audience through various social processes. In these circumstances the best way to communicate the ethical meanings is to present them among a wide range of social values that are available to the audience. It is vital to relate those ethical principles to religious beliefs through the aesthetic aspect of communication. This would enable audiences to read themselves and might make them more aware of the God-relationship.

Parables and Hermeneutical Aesthetics

A. The Use of the Aesthetic Elements in the parables

Jesus enabled his hearers to participate in the hermeneutic process by introducing aesthetic characteristics to the parables. He attracted their attention through his use of aesthetic elements – such as familiar characters, forms and genres in the parables. The hearers were already aware of some of these characters and forms. The later Jewish interpreters used a similar technique [Stern 1991:8f]. While interpreting their beliefs, he entertained them by adopting these aesthetic elements. As people had already experienced these with other interpreters, they could readily engage with Jesus in this process. The aesthetic aspect of the parables enabled Jesus to capture the attention of the audience and to interpret their religious beliefs.

This study argues that Jesus used parables not simply to impart certain information (message or meanings) to his hearers but also to enable them to interpret their beliefs and establish their relationship with God. He used the characters, genre and aesthetic elements that were familiar to his hearers. Some examples of the aesthetic elements in Jesus' parables are embellishment, shock, turns and twists, contrast, numbers, open-ended stories and unexpected endings33. The aesthetic elements in the parables enable the audience to participate in the interaction by appreciating and enjoying the beauty of the images and stories. From a communication perspective, genres are "cultural media (conventions) which function on levels of linguistic competency beyond the scope of the sentence within every linguistic community" [Petersen 1974:137].

John Joshva Raja

Wilder describes Jesus as a teacher and as an artist. For him Jesus brought together his eschatological sayings with his humanistic concept achieving an aesthetic balance [1982:79-80]. For Wilder the parables represent a unique fusion of theological and moral mystery combining ordinariness, naturalness and secularity. In Wilder's understanding, the hearer not only learns about the reality but also participates in it. He searches to establish a relationship between the one who spoke the parables and the text. He is right in pointing out that the relationship between eschatological imagery and layman's language is established by the aesthetic balance.

My study recognises the fact that Jesus' parables are not merely motivating stories even though they have the characteristic of compelling imagination, of spell, of mythical shock and transformation. It should be noted that the parables not only reflected the everyday reality of his hearers but also interpreted their belief and related it to their context. Jesus' parables mediated everyday reality in order to enable the hearers to read themselves in them.

Via [1974] identifies a parable as a story46 and not as a discourse. For him, parables are aesthetic objects, carefully organised and self-contained. He wants the parables to be interpreted without relating them to their historical context [1967:95-101]. Even though parables propose certain values in their structure, they do not present them as universal moral or existential values. One can easily fine the use of the aesthetic elements in the parables. Jesus captured and maintained the attention of his hearers by sharing aesthetic elements in the parables. These elements of the parables encourage the audience to participate along with the communicator in the hermeneutic process. They provide attractive and entertaining aspects in order to capture and maintain attention.

A sensational story like the parable of the Wicked Tenants (Mt 21:33-46; Mk 12:1-12; Lk 20:9-19) not only maintained the attention of the audience -particularly chief priests and the Pharisees – Mt 21:45) but also enabled them to identify themselves with the character of the tenants. Using sensational images and aesthetic forms, parables display and challenge the audience's faith. They lead the audience to act out the roles in their imagination. By sharing the audience's characters, settings and forms, the parables display their taste and interests and help them to become active participants in the construction of meanings.

Using Familiar Characters

First Jesus interacted with his hearers using familiar characters (such as a priest or king) and familiar narrative forms as well as using contemporary events or incidents. By displaying the characters, situations and forms which can capture and maintain the attention of the audience, Jesus enabled them to engage in the hermeneutic process along with him (Lk 15:8-10 - lost coin; Mt 20:1-16 - servant wages). It is essential to recognise the fact that Jesus and his hearers were aware of the characters used in the parables and their meanings. For example, Jesus drew symbols and characters from nature and from human society such as mustard seed (Mk 4:31), leaven (Mt 13:33), lost coin (Lk 15:8) and denarius (Mt 20:2) and political characters such as king (Mt 22:2-14). Scott [1989:374- 375] points out that not only did the audience know these characters but also meanings similar to them were available from later texts such as in those in the Mishnah (M Kil 3.2).

Young [1989:207] points out the relationship between the image of the mustard seed and its proverbial smallness which Jesus exploited in his parable. Young records the similarity between the imagery of the mustard seed in the parable and the tree in Daniel (4:11). He also notices that the Halakhic issues related to the planting of mustard seed in the garden and in the field and are not related to the imagery in the parable [1989:206-7].

It can be argued that Jesus used these popular images and forms in order to interact with his hearers. Jesus chose to use these characters or events even though they did not perfectly interpret his audience's beliefs. The characters and their roles in the parables carried cultural, social and religious meanings. These meanings might have provided a means of capturing the attention of the hearers and could have enabled them to play different roles within the parable. When the religious beliefs were interpreted through this parable the hearers could interact with the story and construct their own meanings in the light of the understanding of the kingdom.

ii. Using Contemporary Forms

Secondly Jesus shared his hearers' forms of communication and used them in order to encourage his hearers to participate in discursive form of communication. Borsch [1988:1] notes that the parables were designed to lure the hearers to become participants and invite them to play several roles. He highlights the characteristics of the parabolic stories that enabled hearers to realise the extraordinary in the context of the ordinary. He notes: By looking and listening beneath the surfaces of human life one discovers that ordinary decisions and actions are often fraught with all manner of unexpected consequence... The brevity of the story ...leaves space for allusion and imagination to interact and be at play [1988:15].

It is essential to widen Borsch's argument by placing parables in the ongoing process of communication in which Jesus and his hearers engaged. Their interaction occurred within a particular cultural and historical framework. The purpose of using aesthetic elements was not merely to entertain the audience but to interact with their belief and worldview.

Jesus' parables helped the audience to imagine and play the roles in the story and thus interpreted their beliefs. Jesus took part in his hearers' communication by attracting them to the story and by allowing them to create their own social and religious meanings. By identifying different forms in Jesus' parables, Stein [1978:7-33] argues that in a storytelling culture, they sought to describe the arrival of the kingdom of God through stories. It is argued that Jesus engaged in his hearers' search for meanings by using their images and stories and by reconstructing them into his own parables. In the parable of the Great Supper[45] Jesus described a feast or a banquet. The characters such as servants, feast, and high street beggars are used to construct an imaginary situation in which the genre and story form place the characters in a different dramatic action.

Parables were less used in some of the contemporary Jewish texts[46]. It is very difficult to trace any story form of parables among those writings except in later rabbinical writings. The editorial work for more than two centuries on the original tradition makes it difficult to compare them with the parables of Jesus. This study mentions a few references that could support the argument that Jesus' audiences might be familiar with the parabolic way of communication[47]. Some of these references point out the possible use of some forms of parables by the Jewish contemporaries of Jesus. Young's work depends greatly on the later rabbinic documents which can be dated from third century Christian Era[48]. They also suggest that the parables did not take a story form during the time of Jesus. Many of them used the aesthetic elements in the parables in various forms.

This study agrees with Stern [1991:43] that the ideas and assumptions from two and a half centuries after Jesus cannot be imported into his parables, even though the rabbinical preservations of the oral tradition (such as Hillel's) might point to the presence of parables during the first century Christian Era. McArthur and Johnston [1990:107] argue that if the attributions to R. Johanan b. Zakkai (90 C.E.) are correct, then parabolic communication was already known among the rabbis at the time of Jesus. It is argued that

Jesus' hearers might have been aware of this hermeneutic process in which aesthetic elements were used to interpret religious beliefs. In Jesus' parables, religious and cultural beliefs were mixed with aesthetic characteristics in such a way that they helped the hearers to participate and construct the meanings of their beliefs along with Jesus.

iii. Using Familiar Scenes

Thirdly, the process of merging an audience's beliefs and the aesthetic aspects happened within the framework of their context.

In the parables, Jesus displayed a familiar event in their life[49] or a familiar scene[50] and presented it as a story in order to interact with the audience's beliefs and worldview. These characteristics were part of the hermeneutic process that one can identify from the Old Testament and later rabbinical parables. In the book of Job there is a story similar to that of the sower in which plants grow differently in different places and this is used to differentiate the people of God from those who forget God (Job 8:9-19). In this narrative one of Job's friends tried to interpret the relationship of people with God and used a familiar event in their lives. In Isaiah 27, the prophet communicated with his audience by using their images (vineyard), by interpreting their beliefs (reconciling with God), and by addressing their social issues (bringing back Israelites) in a similar way to the parable of the sower.

Jesus interacted with his audience's religious beliefs and worldview as in the case of Haggadah. As in Haggadic method of interpretation, Jesus used these aesthetic elements such as characters, narrative forms and familiar scenes in order to capture and maintain the attention of his hearers. Strack [1965:7] defines Haggadah (aggadah) as all scriptural interpretation which is non-Halakhic in character.

After an extensive study on the Haggadic exegesis, Fishbane [1985:408] concludes that within the framework of their new historical and life setting the new (Jewish) teachers using Haggadic method revised and interpreted non-halakhic materials. Their (Jewish teachers) interpretations displayed new literary milieux and literary modes as well. This clearly shows that Jewish teachers were also engaged with their audience in this interactive process; a form which Jesus adopted. In the parable of the Good Samaritan, the story form, the characters and the genre were constructed in such a way that they not only attracted the attention of the hearers but also interacted with their beliefs and worldview.

IV. Haggadic, Aesthetic and the Parable of the Good Samaritan[51]

The aesthetic characteristics of the parable have similarities with other stories used by Old Testament and other contemporary texts. Fishbane [1985:285] argues that the vast majority of cases of Haggadic exegesis in the Hebrew Bible involve implicit or virtual citations. He also notices that this exegesis existed within the Old Testament [1985:291]. He points out that the Old Testament prophets have these procedures of Haggadic exegesis in their narratives [1985:429]. My study agrees with Fishbane that Haggadic exegesis was a familiar method of interpretation at the time of prophets. Jesus' contemporaries might have developed this form and used it in different ways.

In the Haggadic interpretation the form of the folk tales was blended with the interpretation of the text with a freedom of structure [Schwartz 1983:85]. In the light of this argument, it can be argued that the parable of the Good Samaritan could be a Haggadic exegesis of the narrative in 2 Chronicles (28:5-15). Spencer [1984:314] has identified this link between the parable of the Good Samaritan and the passage in 2 Chronicles. By comparing the parable of the Good Samaritan and the narrative in 2 Chronicles (28:14f), this study argues that similar characters and meanings might have existed among some sections of Jewish society at the time of Jesus.

The form and the words used in both these narratives (the parable of the Good Samaritan and thereby in Chronicles) support an assumption that the parable could have been an outcome of Haggadic interpretation. This method of interpretation and the genre of Jesus' parables could be traced to Hillel and Shammai, teachers in the early first century. There are examples in the later rabbinical parables that have similar narrative forms and genre to the gospel parables.

Among them, Haggadic exegesis combined different narrative forms and genre by using aesthetic elements. It is difficult to compare rabbinical texts with that of Jesus' parables because most of them came from a later stage or underwent editorial changes. It can be argued that Jesus' hearers might have been familiar with Haggadic technique of interpretation. Jesus might have been aware of different forms and means as he engaged himself in parabolic communication with the people. In order to capture and maintain his audience's attention, he moulded characters, forms and genre into a genuine parable by using aesthetic aspects of communication.

'Aesthetic Elements and the Parable of Good Samaritan'

The meanings of the characters arise from the contemporary experience of Jesus' hearers and are brought together in the parable by the aesthetic elements. The meanings that are developed in the parable of the Good Samaritan coincide with that of the dialogue. The aesthetic elements enable the hearers to develop the wider meaning of the word 'neighbour' within the context of their beliefs in the law and in eternal life[52]. This aesthetic aspect in the parable of the Good Samaritan was enhanced by the use of certain devices. Other details about the Samaritan's beast and his possessions have added colour to the narrative. The connection between the dialogue and the parable also contributes to this aesthetic aspect of the narrative.

By not disclosing the identity of the traveller the story implicitly points out to the hearers that it could be one of them. The character of the suffering man, and the way in which a priest and a Levite neglect this man leaves the hearers in an aesthetic state where they either feel sympathy for him or identify themselves with him. The suffering (half-dead) traveller remains on the road until the Samaritan comes and the other two religious persons pass by. The priest and the Levite who are expected by the law to show mercy to the neighbour do not offer help to him.

The climax - the arrival of the Samaritan near the suffering man - links the plot to the aesthetic aspect of communication. Crossan [1974A] and Funk [1974B&C] make clear this aspect of communication - the unexpected happenings and climaxes - in the story and the progress with which it reaches its end. Crossan [1974A:75] notices the first climax in the balanced reactions of priest, Levite and the Samaritan in Luke 10: 31-33. He states: The linguistic balance places the rift between priest and Levite on the one hand and the Samaritan on the other. The second and final climax is the rhetorical question of 10:36. In the literary sequence the robbers recede (into the) background, clerics follow them into stylistic oblivion, and in 10:36 the hearer (s) has one person left to face, and to face by his own necessary decision: the Samaritan judged as good [Crossan 1975:75].

The aesthetic characteristics of the parable of the Good Samaritan were constructed by displaying the characters through the story setting. Some New Testament commentators have pointed out these elements without referring to them as aesthetic elements. Fitzmyer [1985:883] identifies the storytelling devices in the episode: the threesome in the dramatis personae; the Palestinian details; the answer of the Jewish lawyer, which studiously avoids using the Samaritan's name, and a certain improbability.

Nolland [1993:591-92] notes that the parable itself began with the introduction of a man on a journey, clearly the chief figure of the parable, who continued to be on stage. He described the traveller's condition as one who is reduced, in an isolated place, to a desperate need. He dramatised the arrival of the Samaritan in the story by stating: In what seems to be a lucky break, the arrival of a situation of high-grade potential helper raises hopes, soon dashed, for the man's rescue. This scene is then replayed, with a not quite so likely potential helper, who again brings no joy. Next on the scene is a classic villain figure, a Samaritan, who nonetheless has compassion on the sufferer. The story climaxes with the mention of the Samaritan's compassion [1993:591-92].

This dramatic interpretation clearly highlights the interest with which Jesus entered into his hearers' imaginative world. Nolland [1993:585] also describes the state of the hearers by noting, "the hearer is brought down gently from this high point of tension with a somewhat extended account of how the Samaritan attended to the injured man's immediate needs and took responsibility for his restoration to health". These are some of the aesthetic elements used in the parable of the Good Samaritan. The negligence of the priest and of the Levite might have increased the sympathetic attitude of the hearers towards the traveller. This was followed by an element of shock in the story that challenged the stereotypical thinking of the audience. The lawyer and the hearers might not have expected the Samaritan to help this man.

Funk [1966:204] points out that the first sentences of the story were in accordance with everydayness but the shock came with the introduction of the Samaritan. He notes that the logic of everydayness was broken upon the logic of the parable. Funk [1974C:74] identifies the meaning of the parable as the way auditors take up roles in the story and play out the drama. As a drama into which the hearers are drawn, the parable suggests that in the kingdom mercy is always a surprise. For Funk [1966:206], the parable is a story, a parabolic metaphor that opens before the hearers a new vision of reality which shatters the everyday view. If the audience's participation in the construction of meanings through the parable is considered, then the numerous ways of interaction between Jesus and his audience need to be noted.

Some of the Jesus' hearers might have understood the parable as a metaphor whereas some might have understood it as a straightforward teaching or a simple story with certain meanings. That is why it is argued that the story cannot be identified simply as a metaphor. It has already been pointed out that the internal dynamism of the story and the historical situation of Jesus' day agreed [Crossan 1974A:75]. Crossan and Funk demonstrate the elements of communication in the formal structure of the parable that enabled Jesus and his hearers to interact. But the meanings of the word 'neighbour' arise out of this interaction (at this particular historical and cultural context) not merely from the structure of the parable.

If the hearers do not pay attention to the parable, then Jesus' involvement cannot achieve its purpose. It was not only the content that was communicated by Jesus to his hearers but also their involvement in this narration which enabled them to construct meanings. They constructed the meanings of the word 'neighbour' out of the role of the Samaritan in the story, out of their beliefs and out of their context. Jones points out that the function of this aesthetic element was to obtain the interest and approval of the hearer until the tables are turned on him [1964:118]. In order to achieve this, Jesus had to use those elements that could capture and maintain the attention of his hearers - the aesthetic elements that they shared in common.

The parable of the Good Samaritan developed a situation in which the suffering traveller was in need of someone's assistance to pick up his life again. Funk [1974C] argues that an unexpected turn in the parable of the Good Samaritan caused the audience to look through the commonplace to a new view of reality. Nevertheless Funk points out that: The parable does not, therefore, involve a transfer of information or ideas about an established world from one person to another. This means that both narrator and auditor risk the parable; they both participate in the narrative and venture its outcome [Funk 1974C:77]. This argument clearly supports the view of my study that Jesus and his hearers were involved in their ongoing process through the parable without knowing the outcome. Their engagement in the parabolic communication was made possible by the aesthetic characteristics of the parables which were popular and contemporary to the audience.

It has already been pointed out that Jesus presented characters and aesthetic elements that were known to his audience. By analysing the use of characters, plots and aesthetic elements in the parable of the Good Samaritan and in the Jewish texts, this section has argued that at the time of Jesus the Jewish public shared some of these characteristics of parabolic communication. These characteristics of communication (characters, plots (genre) and aesthetic elements) were familiar to Jesus' audience.

Even though no story similar to that of the parable of the Good Samaritan can be traced at the time of Jesus, these elements of communication can be traced in some of the stories of the Old Testament and of other Jewish texts. This shows that at the time of Jesus, Jewish people may have enjoyed sharing the aesthetic characteristics by retelling the parables and historical narratives among themselves in various forms. In order to interact with his hearers Jesus took part in a process in which many of them were interested. This clearly shows that the use of these characteristics in the parable of the Good

Samaritan enhanced the interaction between Jesus and his hearers and their participation in the ongoing process of communication.

Aesthetic Elements and Hermeneutics

It was noted that Jesus used aesthetic elements in his parables. By inviting the hearers to enter into the story, to feel and to play the roles, Jesus enabled them to become aware of the meanings. By describing the condition of the traveller after the attack from robbers as a half-dead man Jesus raised sympathy among his hearers. By identifying the third passer-by as a Samaritan he astounded his audience. These are some examples of the aesthetic elements in the parable of the Good Samaritan. By using them Jesus could not only capture his hearers' attention but he also enabled them to read the wider meanings of the word 'neighbour'. Such a display of aesthetic elements was not unknown to Jesus' audience as was shown in the previous chapters. It is vital for the Christian communicator to recognise the role of aesthetic elements in interpreting the religious beliefs of their audiences.

Without attracting the attention of the audience, there is no possibility of interaction. Jesus used the aesthetic elements in the parable because he wanted his hearers to participate in the construction of meanings. He had to begin from the place where his hearers were. Kierkegaard argues that as the audience (learner) was in an aesthetic age, it was essential for the communicator (teacher) to begin from this point even though the aesthetic is incapable of expressing religious truth [Pattison 1992:72]. Christian communicators have to identify the tastes and interests of the audience and use the aesthetic elements and popular forms in order to interact with them. They cannot use all available aesthetic elements, but those which can interpret the gospel without offending any section of the audience.

As technological developments extend people's tastes and interests, communicative forms must change accordingly. Christian communicators need to be sensitive and shift their use of means, and thus their method of interaction, according to the need created. Some modern theologians have emphasised the use of aesthetic elements in

Christian communication. Balthasar [1982] points out that the reality of Christianity should be constructed from starting points in human culture: the beautiful (aesthetics), the good (dramatics) and the true. In his fourth volume on theological aesthetics, Balthasar defines *aisthesis* as a beholding of the glory that reveals itself [1991:9]. It is an act of beholding the living God that presupposes a transporting of the creature beyond itself and its natural cognitive faculties.

In his third volume, *The glory of the Lord: a theological aesthetics,* he points out that Biblical revelation took root in the concrete historical terrain of human thought, feelings and imagination, always using all these forms for its own expression [Balthasar 1986]. Thus all myths, philosophies and poetic expressions are innately capable of housing within themselves an intimation of divine glory [Balthasar 1991:11]. Theologically and practically there is a need for the use of the aesthetic elements in Christian communication. By using technology, communicative forms and aesthetic elements Christian communicators not only attract the attention of the audience but also enable them to participate in the ongoing process with reinterpreted beliefs and a challenged worldview. Hunt [1993:17] argues that one way of interacting with the audience is by reclaiming the poetic, and so a new narrative/symbolic form of communication should be introduced. Christian communicators should take note of this new emphasis on the poetic and aesthetic aspect of their work.

These aesthetic aspects of communication include the visual images, characters, popular narratives, folk genres, emotional plots, suspense and thrills and other elements that enable the audience to participate in the imaginary world created by the communicator. Babin [1991:182-84] argues that narrative/symbolic communication should have priority in audiovisual or electronic media because it represents the best way of arousing people's interiority. He notes that the language of emotion and symbols is the language of the highest form of communication used by sages and mystics [Babin 1991:8].

While taking aesthetic elements into consideration, the primary purpose of interacting with the audience in order to share the gospel must not be lost. In a context where new media have taken aesthetic aspects of communication seriously the Biblical interpreters need to develop this hermeneutic role of aesthetics in recognising, using and interpreting the texts to today's audience in order to capture their attention, to engage them in playing the roles and to enable them to participate through their feelings and appreciation while constructing meanings for themselves.

Conclusion

As I have highlighted in this chapter, we need to go beyond the regular questions of use and impact of the media. The real issue here is how the media culture develops belief systems and worldviews in such a way that a few popular theologies have become part and parcel of the public sphere in a more personalized and packaged form. On the one hand this chapter is critical of the tele-gurus, their methods and approaches and on the other it is suggested that their use of entertainment as a method of hermeneutics needs to be studied and discussed among theologians. Theologians also need to create a critical awareness about the media – particularly about tele-evangelists and Christian fundamentalism in the media. This may lead us to empower the audience particularly the Christian audience to become media literate.

At the same time there is also a demand for theologians to be present in the public exploring the use of entertainment and imagination as a means of doing hermeneutics through the media. By looking at the way people use these media for their faith, social and political formation, deconstruction and unlearning can also be developed through media and theological literacy programmes for lay people. This would enable many of the audience to be media literate and competent in using the media content discriminately and effectively.

Theologians have to address these issues at the grassroots and thereby critically engage with the tele-evangelist and their methods of promoting different theologies. Theologians have to also take into account the role of entertainment in doing hermeneutics to the public. This would enable the theologians to use these elements of entertainment effectively in their mode of communication and thereby meet the expectation of the contemporary audience. Tele-gurus use entertainment as a method to communicate their gospels to the mass audience. They have set a number of challenges including a series of questions about inclusive and pluralistic theological views and emphasised an exclusive view of God in the public. This raises a number of issues with religious narratives constructed by them about the 'other' which will be discussed in the next chapter.

3   Media and Myths – Weapons of Mass 'Distraction'

Section A- Mythical media

The media's attitude towards religion

When I held a conference in Kathmandu Nepal (2004) on "Representation of Religious Minorities in the Mass media" as a regional secretary of World Association for Christian Communication, we had representatives and scholars from different countries in South Asia. We also had representatives from Nepal who were claiming that there was no problem for Muslims in their country as they live peacefully with majority Hindus. In the same year an online video displayed 12 Nepali hostages being murdered in front of camera, many mosques were brought down to ground in Nepal[53].

At times selective reporting and popularising some of the sensitive religious stories and interpreting them as religious conflicts make the stories myths and result in large scale violence against some religious communities. In this chapter I will discuss how these myths are propagated and how they provide challenges to our inter-religious engagement and theologies of religion. The primary questions in this section are: Why do the media promote myths about religions? Why do they represent religions often in a negative way? How can theologians demythologise the religion and thus reduce the ignorance of one particular religious community about the other? How can we engage with media to promote interfaith relationship among the members of different religions?

Media reporters are interested in anything strange, even in religion, including miracles and strange behaviours of leaders and so on. Often the media tend to expose the failures of religious institutions and expose scandals. Such news items or reports fit well into their regular practice of exposing the social institutions' non-accountability and irresponsibility. This also reflects part of the sceptic attitude of the media practitioners towards religious institutions and authorities. Further, they report any strange events such as a picture of Jesus or Mary in the Bread or Milk-drinking Vinayaka idol. Anything miraculous or sensational is reported as it fits into the popularization of strange things in the media. Some media tend to ridicule some aspects of religion as blind belief and at times enter into a confrontationist position with religions.

Media bring religion into their every content whether it is soap or film or drama or speech. In Indian films, soaps and other entertainment programmes too often bring gods and goddesses as part of their stories and narratives. These demi-gods and goddesses are seen as those who help the hero and heroines to overcome the evil factors (Superman/ Sakthiman-Hindi version). Media technology creates mystery into a lively act. Media shape religions and their presentations. Media make religion very expressive in nature. They are also interested in the implicit religion of the public and so their own media people. They present religion as an advertisement.

Media practitioners tend to select religious news for their sensational effects, scandal and conflicts and abnormal happenings. Many of their reports or presentations betray their ignorance about the practices and rituals of religions. Very often the media's reports show scepticism of the institutionalized religion and criticism of simple religious beliefs. The recent controversy over cartoons depicting the prophet Mohammed show that the rational mind set of the media journalists and practitioners will continue to evaluate religion with a strong critical approach. Thus making a mockery of religious practises and people has become a part and parcel of media practice. They enter into the clash of media and so of cultures very easily and quickly.

Mediatised realities

Through mass mediated texts, we come to know about places we have never seen and people we have never met and peoples' culture, religion and new contexts. In this sense the mass media can enable us to develop a better understanding between individuals, communities and nations. At the same time, the mass media can become a source of misunderstanding and ignorance and so create division and hostility between people, communities and nations. The media often construct reality for us. Most of our perceptions about other people, our attitude towards them and world views are being shaped and influenced by such a media driven reality.

The relationship between mass mediated text, people and religion is a very complex issue. Using an understanding of hype reality, Baudrillard [1994] argues that the original reality is replaced by the copy. Simulated and mediated reality is taken as the original and real. In a similar manner some religious communities are presented with stereotypical images by the print media and replace their real nature with negative and threatening images. Thus the media have created an articulate ignorance in the public about those minority religious communities. There is a concern in our context that certain religious people are not portrayed properly in the mass media, particularly in representing minority communities.

By doing so, certain stereotypical images and concepts about religious minorities might have been propagated by the mass media. Due to the demand from the media market, the media often turn a reality into a myth and a myth, into a reality. Mass media often becomes a distraction of reality misrepresenting the context and the people. They become a mass distraction in the context of war, associated with powerful and rich countries and individuals. They too side with majority communities and so tend to misrepresent the minority communities. This is particularly true with the print media. They are also directly or indirectly used by particular political or communal groups.

Thus they tend to become 'weapons of mass distractions'. These weapons of mass distraction are more dangerous than Weapons of Mass Destruction (WMD). This leads to a large scale reproduction of stereotypical images and thus creates a huge gap between the national and international communities. In this chapter, I try to demonstrate with two cases how the media can manipulate and distract people and thus tend to misrepresent reality. Market pressure, and the need to make a profit, drives the media to be first in reporting a news item or story, in order to attract larger audiences and so increase their share of the market.

Myths and media

In this process the media begin by popularizing a few myths which are soon backed by a few social players such as politicians or industrialists or advertising corporations. This section will use two cases, one in the Indian context and the other in the international context to highlight how the myths are constructed, distributed and justified by a few social institutions including the media. These myths are created by the media with the help of political groups or religious communities as a way of explaining recent tensions or conflicts between communities. The reports and stories about fundamentalism are identified as myths because most of them are the construction of the media to justify a few groups; to promote an ideology or to label certain communities or groups.

The act of popularising the myths of fundamentalism might contribute towards the ignorance of one religious community about another which may in turn fuel confrontation and lead to communal clashes. One of the reasons for the spread of violence in Gujarat after the Godhra incident was the use of provocative news and rumours by the regional newspapers and magazines [Bunsa, 2002]. Analysing the speeches and words used by certain politicians, and seeing the emphasis given by the media, I would say that this 'mythical language' contributed towards the conflict between Muslims and Hindus in this state. In the aftermath, all of us know what happened to the minority Muslim community there. Though not all newspapers and magazines use such provocative and biased news some of them certainly used them to popularize their magazines.

A myth[54] is a widely held story or belief – a misrepresentation of truth or an exaggerated or idealized conception of a person or institution or community (The New Shorter Oxford Dictionary). The myths of fundamentalism[55] refer to those mediated stories or reports or narratives that contain details about fundamentalists or communal forces that belong to a particular sect or group within a particular religion. These groups may not represent the wider religious community but are popularized by the media as representatives of that community.

The selected stories and statements about these groups are publicised, reiterated and proved through different stages of media reports and news items. Thus they turn a report or narrative into a myth by over-emphasising a particular ideology or highlighting the negative image of particular groups. Such groups become identified with the majority of members of a particular religion and thus the label and stigma, affects the whole community. This is where the myths of fundamentalism in the media become a source of public ignorance about the other religions.

Mediated myths of fundamentalism

Sometimes the myths of fundamentalism may be partially true and represent biased views about a particular religious community. They do not represent the majority in the religious communities that are often against such fundamentalism. These myths are created, circulated and popularised by a few politicians, by a few rich people and by a few who hold power in order to maintain the tension between different religious communities. While constructing stories about fundamentalism, myths are constructed about minority and majority religions, thus creating ignorance about one's own religion as well about the other religious groups. What happens in the media is that the fundamentalists are shown as those who try to protect their own religion at any cost.

The fundamentalist groups of the majority religious communities are seen as defenders of the nation and are the representatives of the majority of the community. The fundamentalists are seen as neo-nationalists, or even cultural defenders who are protecting people against a liberal culture that is seen as a threat to traditional societies.

Though the fundamentalists are small in number, and do not represent the majority, the media portrays them as the voice of the majority by providing more space for their sensational words in the media. It is a myth of fundamentalism constructed by the media, politicians and other dominant power seeking groups.

Myth and ignorance

The media alone cannot be blamed for this myth; intellectuals who contribute to the wider thinking also rationalize this myth. This is particularly evident in Huntington's thesis on *The Clash of Civilizations* [Huntington, 1996:217]. Though Huntington recognizes the plurality within civilizations, his explanation of the conflicts seems to represent a misunderstanding of Islam and other cultures. For Said, Huntington reduced 'civilizations' to what they are not: shut down, sealed-off entities that have been purged of myriad currents and counter currents. Civilizations animate human history and help[56] different communities and nations to contain wars of religion and imperial conquest but also to be one of exchange, cross-fertilization and sharing [Said, 2001:2]. For Said it is the clash of ignorance – which means ignorance about the other.

It is not clear whether being unfamiliar with 'the other' causes a natural ignorance, or whether being exposed to the tiny negative side of 'the other' causes an articulated ignorance[57]. Thus myths in the media are rationalized and are marketed as reality which creates ignorance and fear in the minds of the people. The myth not only creates ignorance and misunderstanding but also contributes towards a confrontation and conflicts between the religious communities. Ignorance is often built into the narratives and is then articulated and used by certain political groups. It becomes difficult for other people to challenge this ignorance because it has reached an accepted and rationalized status.

2. Analyzing the myths –case 1

At the outset, I would like to highlight a few ways in which the media constructs such myths of fundamentalism in their texts. Then I will analyse the way such a mythical construction is being used by some politicians as a means of persuading the public in their favour. First the media often publishes reports about the activities and statements of many fundamentalist groups. Whenever a controversial statement is made by them it is often reported and any rally with arms is often recorded with photographs. The media often highlight their reports with a particular colour – for Muslims it is usually green and for Hindus it is saffron. These fundamentalist groups are more popular than any other groups within the same religion. Thus media popularizes the fundamentalist aspect of every religion.

Some characteristics of the myths can be found from the media reports about fundamentalist groups. In the market-driven news media, an event is reported only when it is negative or abnormal or unexpected[58]. Religious activities are often reported when they have negative or unexpected characteristics[59]. The news media should be seen as one of the sources of images, perceptions and representations. Let me begin with a few popularized statements that were given 'front page' coverage in the media. I have two types of study to justify my argument. I take Islam as one case study but will also include reports on Christians. First, I have selected two English magazines and analysed samples for two to three years and then selected the news reporting of the Godhra incidents by Gujarat Newspapers in 2002.

From my analysis of the English magazines I came to a number of conclusions which are supported by the table in the Appendices:

(a) There is a sharp increase in reporting about religion in general and Muslims in particular

(b) Muslims are seen as a monolithic community and thus Muslims in India are identified with Muslims across the world and the same language is used to describe them. Muslims are fundamentalists; they practice polygamy; they (Indian Muslims) sympathize more with Pakistanis than Indians and thus with terrorists (thus anti-Indians); they do not follow family planning and so have many children; they are of Arabian origin and they eat beef (the cow being considered a holy animal in Hinduism). Islam is often shown as a religion of terror, sword, the enemy and aliens[60].

(c) Muslims are portrayed as fundamentalists, uncivilized, anti-Indian and religious fanatics. Majority of the Muslims are seen as fundamentalists, sympathizers of terrorists, vigorously promoting their religion, supported by the Pakistan ISI (intelligence agency[61]) if they are in the majority they would force minorities to become Muslims, trained in Madrassas to attack others.

The media often refer to the September-11th incident and the attack on the Indian Parliament House as being an attack on Islamic terrorism, while Godhra was a proof of Islamic fundamentalism[62]. Kashmir Muslims are shown as if they are trying to 'Islamicize' the state.

The word 'fundamentalists' is applied to all Muslims because they want 'to return' to their original faith[63]. Such myths are substantiated by political and religious leaders' statement and small incidents[64]. These are myths constructed in the media about the religious minorities in India. The following will be specific cases where explicit misrepresentation and manipulative statements of the minorities are publicly displayed by media and vested groups.

Media Statements

Mr Modi, the Chief Minister of Gujarat (one of the Western states of India) who belongs to the Bharathya Janatha Party (BJP), a political wing of the Rastrya Swyamsevak Sangh (RSS), a Hindu fundamentalist outfit, said that the Muslims' slogan was *,"hum paanch, hamaare pachhis" (we are five and we will be twenty five)[65]*. This was said in the context of the Indian government promoting a family–planning scheme among Hindus to have only two children .This myth was then created about Muslims that a Muslim will marry four women and have twenty five children and thus have more Muslim votes against the Hindu votes.

This was disproved by the statistics of the government that showed a decline in the percentage of Muslim in the population growth and also for 1000 Muslim women there are 1068 Muslim men. This statement was made so popular by the media that the Prime Minister who was in the United States of America had to react to it. He also made remarks about Christians and other people and the media took them to the public. Whether it is his attacks on the "fair-skinned, Italy *ki beti*" Sonia Gandhi (wife of the former Prime Minister of India and Leader of Opposition Parties) or the "Christian Lyngdoh" (the Chief Election Commissioner in India), or his remarks aimed at Muslims, senior BJP leaders are finding it difficult to defend him beyond a point. Modi's latest salvo has been directed against Pakistan President Pervez Musharraf, and BJP leaders are at their wits' end to justify this particular one.

At one of his public meetings, Modi called upon the "five crore (five millions) people of Gujarat" to chop off the hands of "Miyan Musharraf" for raising a "dirty, accusing finger" at the State. Incidentally, posters and advertisements, asking the people to choose between him and Musharraf, have sprung up in the State, apparently released at the behest of Modi, coinciding with Modi's diatribe. These statements are given front page coverage in many of the regional newspapers in Gujarat and elsewhere in India[66].

The second statement was made by the RSS (one of the Hindutva outfits – Rashtra Swayamsevak Sangh) which is that, 'The Minorities (Religious) need the Majority's Goodwill'. Strongly defending the stand, RSS Chief K.S. Sudarshan told reporters here after a meeting with top Christian leaders that "many people" supported his organisation on the issue. For him, 'It is not a sentiment but a statement of fact that minorities have to earn the majority's goodwill to live in any country.

Can the minorities in Britain or France go against the majority Christian community?' he asked. Sudarshan contended that minorities, instead of 'cultivating enmity' should blend with 'majority samskrithi' (culture). 'The three per cent Hindus in Kashmir were hounded out on the basis of their religion. There were attacks on pilgrims in Amarnath. Naturally these are piling up in the Hindu psyche. The government cannot provide protection to each and every individual' he maintained (*Times News Network*, March 23, 2002).

Myths and Media – an incident at Godhra

In February 2002, a train carrying Hindu Kar Sevaks who were returning from their worship and service at Ram Temple in Ayothya (a disputed area both for Muslims and Hindus) stopped at the railway station of Godhra. The train Sabarmati Express, coming from Faizabad and proceeding towards Ahmedabad caught fire a few minutes after it left the Godhra railway station on February 27, 2002, killing an estimated 58 people. It is claimed that a small dispute between a station shop Muslim vendor and Hindu Sevaks spread the rumour in nearby Muslim villages that a Muslim girl was taken into one of the compartments of the train. The villagers stopped the train and burnt one bogie of the train with people inside. This incident was a precursor to a spate of widespread communal violence in the state which lasted nearly three months[67]. The role of the media in reporting this event played a major role in intensifying communal violence after this incident[68].

Post-Godhra Statements

The Post Godhra reporting in the Gujarathi News papers contained more negative myths about Muslims. The examples are: on 6 March 2002 the headlines screamed HINDUS BEWARE: HAJ PILGRIMS RETURN WITH A DEADLY CONSPIRACY[69]. In reality, hundreds of terrified and anxious Hajj pilgrims returned accompanied with heavy police escort to homes that could have been razed to the ground[70].

The statements do not need any interpretation and show how the politicians and religious leaders make irresponsible statements and how the media often report such statements and kindle the existing myths[71]. Many religious leaders and politicians have made objective statements and engaged in a positive manner but their words are not often reported[72] . Media personnel argue that this is what the public often want to read or hear or see. Such practices have also become part and parcel of their media industry without which they claim that they cannot survive in the market of news making and entertainment.

Mediatised myth

The media use an interesting dualistic approach in presenting the fundamentalist groups. As in the case of a myth, they often pit one group against the other portraying one in the image of the villain. Thus the media seem to take a strong dualistic approach in which at times they are absolutely sure about what are good and bad people in the society. On the one hand they often claim to be 'objective' in their news and reports but on the other they tend to generalise or overstate particular characteristics of religious minorities. This creates or reimposes or reiterates the stereotypical perception of a particular group of people. As I have given examples from India it seems that when a few radical Muslims become violent then the news media reports as if Muslims are violent in that part of the world. These small minority radical Islamic terrorists do not represent majority Muslims in India as India has 133 million Muslims and are not at all violence[73].

The media often tend to generate an interest in the public on the division of religious communities in such a way that the majority religious communities' interest is given more importance than the interest of minority communities. This is particularly true during the conflicts between religious communities or terror acts [Flanders 2002]. Of course to sell the newspapers or journal or any other content of the mass media this is seen as a normal practice. It is often argued as if this is what the audiences wanted to read or listen or see. However the minority does not deserve to be presented with a negative and monolithic representation by highlighting a few terror incidents or events or clashes.

These media also tend to be the first in reporting. While hurrying to report first their regular strict regulations are missed out at times in terms of reporting with some accuracy. Ignoring the good practice of investigative journalism they report on whatever they have heard or received from less dependable sources without verification particularly at the time of war or conflicts. The reasons are: the media reporters want to be the first; economic interests are given more priority than public interest; the reporters' national interests and their own adventures and promotions are given priority in reporting. So reporting negatively about Muslims and Christians has become part of the media practices in India[74]. This has been developed into the editorial, reporting and collecting practices of the media in such a way that alternative ways of reporting becomes very difficult. It means those who wish to report in a different way about the minorities cannot survive in the media industry.

There is a fear that if they write in favour of Muslims, they can be identified as traitors or pseudo-secularists who favour Islamic terrorism. Thus the media can be blamed for siding with the outside terrorists and considered as a threat to the integrity of the nation. In this sense the media's role in the construction of myths of religious fundamentalism contribute towards public ignorance of the other religious communities. Though different religious communities have lived side by side for decades the media have successfully created an atmosphere of suspicion and fear by their popularization of myths, extreme or bigoted statements and articulated ignorance. There is always a need to engage with, and confront the media personnel educating them about the consequences of promoting negative images and ignorance about other communities despite their avowed need to survive commercially as stated above

Myths, media and violence

The incident at Godhra was waiting to happen as was the violent aftermath. This event was not an isolated incident but a culmination of small incidents that occurred earlier. More than events the myths that were circulated among people through the politicians, media and religious institutions against the other religious communities were the causes of such confrontation and conflicts. The myths create ignorance about the other religious communities. Media popularize such myths through their display of colour, photographs, language, rumours, headlines, sources, selection and inaccurate reporting.

These myths often lead people to a 'culture of suspicion'; to a 'culture of confrontation' and thus to a 'culture of violence'. There is a strategically well-planned attempt to create a fear of minorities (such as Islamophobia) in the minds of the majority through such myths. This is done with the help of the articulated ignorance by a few groups with vested interests. Their statements have ready access to the media; myths are popularized by the media and broadcast to the public.

Section B– The Media and the 'Clash of Civilizations'

Conflicts and confrontations are part of everyday life in a few places in India such as Kashmir, the North East, and Gujarat. The primary motives behind these conflicts are communal, caste, racial, social, political, tribal and religious beliefs and narratives. Even the international conflicts have to be explained on the basis of such beliefs and narratives. The conflict between Israel and Palestine can both be interpreted as political as well as religious conflicts. The war on Iraq has to be interpreted from economic as well as political perspectives. Some conflicts existed even before religion was brought in as an effective means to group people together against the other groups. Nevertheless religion is very much used by a few people to enhance these clashes.

In the summer of 1993, *Foreign Affairs* published an article entitled 'The Clash of Civilizations'[75]" by Samuel Huntington. His article generated discussions among many intellectual communities. He wrote:

> It is my hypothesis that the fundamental source of conflict in this world will not be primarily ideological or primarily economic. The great divisions among humankind and the

110

dominating source of conflict will be cultural. …the principal conflicts of global politics will occur between nations and groups of different civilizations. The clash of civilizations will dominate the global politics. The fault lines between civilizations will be the battle lines of the future
[Huntington, 1993:1].

For him, the evolution of conflicts began from the clashes among kings, emperors, nations and then moved to conflict of ideologies (Communism and liberal democracy). After the collapse of the Soviet Union, the main conflict is between civilizations. The countries will group themselves in terms of their culture and civilizations rather than on the basis of their political or economic systems or of their ideological similarities. Huntington argued that the final clash will be between Islam and the West. Thus most of the clashes in the world are studied under the purview of clashes of cultures or civilisations.

He identified seven major civilizations[76] in the world which are Sinic[77], Japanese, Hindu, Islamic and Western, Latin American and African. He argued that the Western civilization ends where Western Christianity ends and where Islam and Orthodoxy begin [Huntington, 1996:159]. Huntington's thesis was widely read and appreciated as a description of what is going on in the world. Among the civilizations, he highlighted the clash between two – Islam and the West. He argued,

The underlying problem for the West is not Islamic fundamentalism. It is Islam, a different civilization whose people is convinced of the superiority of their culture and is obsessed with the inferiority of their power. The problem for Islam is not the CIA or the US Department of Defence. It is the West, a different civilization whose people is convinced of the universality of their culture and believes that their superior, if declining, power imposes on them the obligation to extend that culture throughout the world
[Huntington 1996:217].

Though he recognizes the internal differences in some nations and cultures his division of West and the rest, particularly of West versus Islam has been criticized by many scholars.

Neither the Western nor the Islamic communities have a monolithic culture, as he seems to argue. It is difficult to understand why he speaks of West versus the rest, particularly Islam. While he identifies Islam to be a single cultural identity, why did he not point out the clash as between Christianity and Islam? The main clash should have been between Western Christianity and Islam but he selected the word 'West' rather than 'Christianity'. These are some issues which are not addressed in his thesis.

Chomsky on Huntington

Asghar Ali Engineer noted that the enthusiasm in the West for Huntington's dubious hypothesis shows widespread prejudice against Islam since the period of the crusades [Engineer, 2001:16]. Noam Chomsky [2002:100–1] criticized the thesis by saying, 'Huntington wanted (us) not to think about rich powers and corporations exploiting people, that can't be the conflicts, but, as a clash of civilizations – between West and Islam and Confucianism'. Pointing out the United States' support for the Saudi Arabian government, Chomsky argued that the main reason for this support is that Saudi ensures that the wealth of the region goes to the right people: not people in the slums of Cairo, but people in executive suites in New York. For him there is a clash with those who are adopting the preferential option for the poor no matter who they are [Chomsky, 2002:101].

Though Chomsky's examples of clashes between Catholic churches and US in Central America support his emphasis on economic elements, he generalizes in the same way in relation to Islamic countries[78]. The clash between nations and religious communities is more than at cultural or economic level because the grouping of nations or communities cannot simply be explained using Huntington's or Chomsky's theses. In a few contexts or incidents their theses might be true but that does not mean that their theses apply to all conflicts in all contexts.

Tariq Ali on Huntington -

Taking a different view, Tariq Ali [2001] in his book *'Clash of Fundamentalisms: Crusades, Jihads and Modernity'*, argues that the clash is between American hyper-patriotism which is interwoven with market fundamentalism and radical Islam. For him, Huntington's thesis is reductive nonsense. The fundamental political relationship between 'civilizations' is better characterized by terms like 'inter-related' and 'imbricated' than by the zero-sum notion connoted by 'clash' or 'conflict'.

When different civilizations interact with each other, they do not necessarily end up in clashes and conflicts [Ali, 2001:274]. In some interactions between the Western countries and Muslim countries, there is a closer co-operation and co-ordination between the nations rather than conflicts (such as Pakistan and US in the war against terrorism). Even within so called western countries there is no general agreement on the war on terrorism (German's objections). In this sense, Tariq Ali's argument was right in his emphasis on the inter-relatedness of civilizations. It means the relationship between cultures and nations is more complex than what Huntington classifies as the West and the rest.

Said on Huntington -

While appreciating the argument as compellingly large, bold, even visionary, Edward Said [1997:1] argues in his article, 'The Clash of Ignorance' that Huntington did not have much time to spare for the internal dynamics and plurality of every civilization or even the interpretation of each culture. For Said, a great deal of demagogy and downright ignorance is involved in presuming to speak for a whole religion or civilization. He argued that huge complicated matters like identity and culture are simplified by Huntington like the Popeye and Pluto characters in the Cartoon network programmes 'where both bash each other mercilessly with one always virtuous pugilist getting the upper hand over his adversary'.

According to Said, Huntington reduced 'civilizations' to what they are not; shut down, sealed-off entities that have been purged of myriad currents and counter currents. Civilizations animated human history and helped different communities and nations to contain wars of religion and imperial conquest and also to be one of exchange, cross-fertilization and sharing [Said, 1994:2]. Huntington recognizes the plurality within civilizations. Nevertheless his interpretation of the conflicts as 'the clash of civilizations' represents Islam and 'others' as monolithic culture. There is no such homogenized western culture just as there is no single Islamic culture common to all Muslims. Having lived only in the 'West' and having read about Islam through books, media and conferences, Huntington seems to know more about Islam than those who lived among Muslims.

Ignorance and conflicts

'Ignorance' about other civilizations is the major problem of the world today. Many of us know other people and their cultures mainly through the media, through what we see or hear or read. We are often exposed to negatively tinged news and information about 'other religions or cultures' primarily through the media. Sometime we believe all this. Thus those stereotypical images and meanings in the media shape our perceptions and attitude towards other religions and cultures and resentments begin in the mind regarding the other. They are often misunderstood and often mistaken as an enemy of one's own culture. This is where one needs to systematically study the problem to discover how ignorant people are about 'others' and how much media is responsible for this.

Ignorance and the 'other'

Reviewing Huntington, Tariq Ali argued that it was the clash between American nationalism and Islamic fundamentalisms. However, Chomsky has pointed out the problem with the economic exploitation and its links with clashes. A strong argument is being made by Edward Said who wrote an article on 'Clash of Ignorance'. It is the ignorance of the other that causes the clashes between groups and communities. Ignorance does not mean not knowing the other but knowing in a wrong way or knowing only the negative aspect of the other.

Ignorance is exaggerated not merely by the media but is also misused and articulated well by the power centres (economic, political and religious). This articulated ignorance is widely spread and confirmed with a few select publicised incidents. Many of the politicians, media practitioners and the public know the other communities mainly as terrorists and fundamentalists. The misuse of this ignorance by the politicians aims at polarizing religious communities and thus helps the power centres to maintain the status quo even at the cost of many people's lives.

Even if they (those who hold media or power centres) know about the positive characteristics of the other communities, some of them intentionally or knowingly articulate this ignorance to save their power or political status or wealth. Some of them even publicize this ignorance about the other for protecting their own interests. This is also done in the name of national interests, religious revival and defence of the local culture.

Religious narratives and ignorance

Religious narratives, unfortunately, have often fallen into hands of those who often want to pitch one against the other. The creation, articulation and misuse of ignorance about the other among the religious communities is basically due to the religious narratives while economic, social, political contexts and population expansion contribute to the wider problem. We do need to blame religion for the problem but we should be careful not to isolate religion alone for the conflicts and clashes. Because we are part of religion we need to look at ways to address the issues of conflict. We need to address this problem through religion by interpreting its narratives. Of course, in some contexts religion is the cause of the problem whereas in others religion is not directly responsible for the problem. But we must try to address and solve the problems through religious narratives. There

115

are many ways of looking at the problem and addressing it.

The way religions look at the other and the image of the other is built in the religious narratives including basically accepted texts. Let me use examples from Christianity where the other is often looked at as heathen or pagan which is nowadays challenged, and are no more used by many of the 'others'. Children are also taught by a few Christians that other gods are evil gods. This terminology is unfortunate. Within each religious narrative the way the other is developed is related to the ignorance about the other. Those who have lived or interacted with the other have shown a wider knowledge about them.

Whereas those who were brought up without any knowledge of the other and also with a negative image of the other can easily be influenced by the articulate ignorance of the media. Even the people who live with the other and know about the other are nowadays influenced because of the lies that are also propagated in the name of religion and national identities. If we are looking at removing ignorance we need to look at the way the religious narratives operate in promoting the ignorance about the other. While trying to address this issue by providing a positive image of the other, we need to reinterpret religious narrative in such a way that it would support our own initiatives and others within our own religious communities.

Having highlighted the problem of negative information as ignorance in the above section, it raises a question: how can the 'other', particularly minorities in the Indian context be represented positively in the public or how the ignorance about them can be reduced? For Christians it provides a missiological challenge by emphasising the Christians' involvement in reducing or removing this ignorance of minorities and thus in establishing a better relationship between different communities. Having highlighted this issue at national level I am analysing how the media at global level can create such image of the other, particularly at the time of war. A similar challenge can be identified for theologians regarding the representation of the other through various media at global level. I try to analyse the embedded media's role during the Iraq war and their representation of the 'other'. This representation of the other in the media at local and global levels provides challenge for theologians to challenge present practices of representations in the religious and non-religious narratives.

Section C – Embedded Media

Introduction

Today the role of the international media in reporting of war has become one-sided and biased towards certain religious and cultural groups. It becomes essential for theologians to reiterate the question of truth-telling in the media. For the sake of reporting first and of capturing the market, the audience, and the embedded media have manipulated the public in a number of ways particularly during the recent war on Iraq. This section analyses a few select incidents and reports in the media and presents a case against the embedded reporting. Such analyses are carried out already by a few scholars but this section focuses on the representation of the other in the embedded reporting during the war in Iraq [Schechter, 2003 & Katovsky and Carlson, 2004].

The new practice of 'embedded reporting' during the recent Iraq war by the media has questioned the ethical principles of journalism and thus raised questions about truth telling in the context of mediated myths. These media myths create a negative image of the other through such reporting and thereby this case study too provides a challenge to theologians about the mythical representation of the other in the media. First, I would like to address a few questions: What is embedded reporting? What are the advantages of embedded reporting? What are the disadvantages of embedded reporting? What are the ethical issues involved in this reporting?

Embedded reporting

The British Broadcasting Corporation (BBC) news[79] service identifies 'embedded reporters' as those who were on the ground in

117

Iraq, moving with the coalition forces seeing and reporting the fighting at first hand. They ate and slept alongside soldiers and brought live reports of firelights and artillery onslaughts into our living rooms. The word 'embedded' refers to placing or securing something within a particular entity. The general instruction from Pentagon begins with a note saying:

> Embedded Media operate as part of their assigned unit. An Escort may be assigned at the discretion of the unit commander. The absence of a PA escort is not a reason to preclude media access to operations[80].

It means to fix a media crew with a military unit and report according to their respective broadcasting rooms. The security is in the hands of military unit with which the media crew is being embedded. The BBC had 16 embedded reporters in Iraq during the war.

The Pentagon announced before the war that about 800 journalists from select Western media agencies will be embedded into the US military[81]. According to Navy Chief Petty Officer Diane Perry of the Defence Department, there was a broad range of media representation.

There are a couple of golden rules here. The journalists cannot give specific details of locations or outline the future plans of their unit. Both sides have been getting along amicably, with trust intact. There is no general review process for media products. The Pentagon document says, "If media are inadvertently exposed to sensitive information they should be briefed after exposure on what information they should avoid covering. While seeing sensitive information, reporters must agree to a security review of their coverage, not to censor articles"[82].

This document clearly shows the way the US government has used the media for their purpose. On the one hand media are shown as if they are neutral and democratic while they report the war. On the other hand their reporting should not provide sensitive information to the enemies which means should not be against the armed forces who are protecting them. Thus the embedded media should broadcast only those which the coalition forces want them to communicate.

The US Public Broadcasting Services, Bryan Whitman, deputy assistant secretary of defence for media operations says, 'We want to be able to protect that information that is going to determine the success of an operation.' Reporters were pre-briefed and were often told what is appropriate and inappropriate for the operation. Reasonable people agreed and disagreements were rare"[83]. The embedded media reporters accompanied the armed personnel wherever they went and were protected by them. This has created a risk on the part of the coalition forces while it has helped them in winning the media war against the Iraqi regime.

The 'Other' in embedded reporting

There are many issues that arise from embedded reporting but here I would like to highlight three issues that may be relevant to journalists in our contexts too. In this theme there are three issues that are involved namely: manipulating the truth, misrepresenting of the 'other' and irresponsible journalism. First, the real picture of the war is manipulated whenever and wherever needed and thereby truth became those reports that would favour the coalition forces. If any report was to be objective, it should reasonably justify the occupying forces. If any images were likely to create uproar in the West, it was considered against the truth. The reporters feared being blamed for not being patriotic enough. In a hurry to be the first to report, very often, the principle of truth telling was compromised.

Secondly, there is continuity in reporting the 'other'. The other in this case is a 'Muslim', an Arab or the Iraqi people. The 'September 11th' event changed the way the media presented Muslims and Islam. Though there were attempts to present them in a positive manner, the majority of the media presented them as if the convergence between Islam and terrorism is real. It often reflected an ethno-centric approach which was incorporated into the practice. The communities are often divided into broader groups 'we' versus 'them' and fault-lines are drawn at wider levels between the West and the East and so on.

At times of conflicts and war, the presentation of the 'other' is stretched to its extreme levels where the other is seen as an enemy or linked with terrorists and so on. In the case of embedded reporters, the image of the other is already in the mind of the reporters. They search for those images, events or stories that would fit into their preconceived concepts about the others. Those positive images that would radically change the image of Muslims are of no value for a news item.

Thirdly, the responsibility and accountability of the media practitioner for the wider audience was not taken seriously at times for the sake of being patriotic or for fear of being blamed as allies of terrorists. These three issues are discussed in this paper in a general way. This is not to blame the journalists or frontline reporters nor the editorial groups or even the institution for reporting one-sidedly. At times they have to fit themselves into the expectations of their own public. Yet, within the practice, how far can they be accountable to their own nation and people and be responsible to the international audience without losing certain basic ethical principles of communication?

From truth to un-truth

For theologians, asking ethical questions about telling the truth in public are an everyday affair. A Few media scholars and theologians question the truth claims in the mass media particularly during the time of war. They even question the ethical practices of embedded media and their truth claims. At the time of war those who work strategically for winning would also try to use media in their favour. Two major books have emerged critiquing the embedded media – The WMD Mirage: Iraq's Decade of Deception and America's false premise of War by Craig R Whitney a former reporter of the New York Times and also Embedded: Weapons of Mass Deception – How the Media Failed to cover the War on Iraq by Denny Schechter a former ABC and CNN producer. They have clearly pointed out that tactics of war not only included a lack of telling the truth about the war at times but also manipulation of myths or misinformation into a kind of public news and thus as truth.

Embedded reporting has brought to light these issues of truth telling and thus challenges theologians to recognize the myth-making process of the media and address it. The following definition for truth is given to proceed to the issues in the embedded media reporting:

Truth should correspond to some external set of facts or observations...Truth has become increasingly tied to that which is written down, to that which can be empirically verified, to that which can be perceived by the human senses, and to that which does not vary among people or among cultures – Enlightenment Concept of Truth [Patterson and Wilkins, 1991:22]

Many media analysts have criticised such an enlightenment view of truth and claims of objectivity. Within these constraints, journalists are supposed to maintain accuracy, dignity and diversity to the extent possible in their reports. It is difficult to report objectively.

Any claims to be objective in the news media can also be considered as another myth. Media practitioners need to accept these constraints while they report about other cultural and religious communities, particularly during the time of conflicts or war. In 1942 a commission on Freedom of the press was set up at the request of Henry Luce, publisher of Time and Life magazines, by Robert Hutchins, then president of the University of Chicago, to recruit a commission to inquire into the proper function of the media in modern democracies. A statement was published in 1947 by the Hutchin's Commission[84] that states, 'the right of free public expression does include the right to be in error, but not the right to be deliberately or irresponsibly in error'. [Gunewardena, 1997:4]. If one's safety is in the hands of soldiers, one will be unwilling to criticize them. If life gets difficult for the soldiers on one's side, there will be extra strain on journalists.[85].

121

John Joshva Raja

Reporters were instructed to follow 'guidelines' to avoid coverage damaging to the war effort. With rare exceptions, journalists engaged in self-censorship. Journalists who agreed to go with combat units effectively became hostages of the military, which could control the movements of the journalists and, more importantly control their ability to file the stories. Transparent identification with the military authorities will further tarnish the credibility of the media, especially since millions of people now have access to alternative sources of news information and analysis via the internet. But as the toughest critics would say, The mere fact that journalists are so enmeshed with the military makes it difficult for them to think objectively. If your safety is in the hands of soldiers" the argument goes, "you will be unwilling to criticize them" [Craig Whitney, 2005].

There were a few news stories which were manipulated by the media and military to deceive the public during the war. Schechter [2003] has recorded many of such stories in his book on Embedded: Weapons of Mass Deception. If one had followed the news reporting on 22 March 2003 of the grenade attack in Camp Pennsylvania in Kuwait, one may understand the way in which the reports contradicted their first, second and final reports[86]. At first, the Fox news reporter, Luzader, quoting Associated Press and Reuters said, 'Apparently one or more terrorists infiltrated the perimeter of this camp'.[87]

A few moments later, Sky News Reporter Stuart Ramsay argued over the phone that by now what was only a possibility a moment ago is becoming an alleged fact, which is one or more perpetrators, have become two foreign nationals, "It seems that two Kuwait or Arab nationals entered the headquarters tent in Camp Pennsylvania[88]". Ramsay dressed them saying they wore desert camouflage gear and one wore a helmet. Within a few hours, it turned out to be a lone US soldier who was taken into custody for the attack. The report about this event clearly shows that the embedded reporters were not reporting the correct information about the war to the public. Rather such information has been manipulated to suit their side during war and their version of the events was given priorities by the news media.

Greg Mitchall[89], the editor of *Editor and Publisher* magazine which covers the newspaper industry (March 27, 2003) identified 15 different stories in which the media got it wrong or misreported a sliver of fact into a major event. Saddam might have been killed (March 20); even if he wasn't killed, Iraqi command and control was no doubt decapitated (March 22); Umm Qasr has been taken (March 22-24); most Iraqi soldiers will not fight for Saddam and instead are surrendering in droves (March 22) and so on.

These examples show that there was distortion of reality in the embedded reporting. The problem was the truth claims that were attached to such reporting in which the other is seen not only in continuity with the stereotypical images but also with an image of the enemy in mind.

'Us' versus 'them'

The image of the 'other' in the media to some extent shapes one's attitude and perception of the other. If the other is the next-door neighbour one may have a variety of ways with which to communicate and understand them. But, unfortunately, the 'other' in the media, particularly Muslims in the mainstream Western media is given a monolithic as well as a negative image. Such images to some extent contribute to our perception of Islam and Muslims.

The embedded reporters or editors or journalists report what is already in their minds. Because of the perceptions of the journalists or because of the public reception and acceptance of such images and representations, they highlight only those events or incidents or pictures that will be in conformity with the established perceptions and attitude. Anything that would provide a positive image of the enemy or the other is avoided for fear that one will be identified as a sympathiser of terrorist groups or accused of being unpatriotic.

Bob Steele from the Poynter Institute, an organization founded by Nelson Poynter in 1975 for journalists in the United States of America, cautioned that "While closeness can breed understanding, journalists must remain objective and not write about, "We" or "Our" but about "them'"[90]. There is nothing wrong with having respect in our hearts for the men and women who are fighting this war, or respect for the men and women who are marching in the anti-war protests. The key is to make sure those beliefs do not colour reporting." (News Hour Extra)[91].

It was a systematic elimination of other voices too by the coalition leaders. For them even the other voices that might provide an alternative image of Iraqis in that context should be eliminated in order to justify their action. War does strange things to both military and media. The Bush administration has also been at work on limiting and ideally silencing opposing or challenging viewpoints and factual narratives coming from other sources.

On March 25 the New York Stock Exchange revoked Al-Jazeera's credentials. US Administration has pressured Qatar Amir, Hamad bin Khalifa al Thani to force Al-Jazeera to give more emphasis to their versions of events (Alternet.org[92]). The website of Erich Marquardt, editor of YellowTimes.org was shut down for posting photos of US prisoners of war and dead Iraqi civilians[93]. While there has not yet been widespread censorship, US media outlets in step with the government practised their own form of self-censorship.

Patriotism seems to be running high among journalists covering the war from Iraq in the 'embedded' reporter system. While this offers a decent number of reporters first hand views of the action, critics say the drawbacks are far worse than the benefits. The embedded reporters work is highly regulated by government officials. They are not permitted to interview Iraqis without permission and they cannot interview soldiers off the record, drastically reducing the likelihood that troops will say anything negative about the US effort. 'Embedding is a way to kill the press with kindness' says NYU media studies Professor Mark Crispin Miller, 'You absorb reporters into the advancing military unit and they are psychologically inclined to see themselves as part of the military operation. They even dress like soldiers' (Alternet.Org[94]).

One concern before the war began was that embedded reporters would inevitably become too sympathetic to the troops with whom they were travelling. Some sceptics believed this was a primary motivation on the part of military planners in designing the embedded system in the first place. Feed the media beast enough stories that cast US troops in the best possible light and the job of managing the media is all but taken care of.

Reports from 'Fairness and Accuracy in Reporting' show how truth has been one of the major drawbacks of the media's unquestioning reliance on government sources. The perception is that the Iraqis must have Weapons of Mass Destruction. With this in mind the reports confused the readers. On 20 March NBC, NPR, ABC and other outlets reported as fact the military assertion that the Iraqis had used banned Scud missiles. However, two days later the Joint Chiefs of Staff reported that in fact no Scud missiles had been fired. On 23 March various media trumpeted the government's claim that a chemical weapons factory had been found near the town of Najaf, though a day later that claim was totally debunked.

Responsible Media

The embedded reporting brings us to another question which is responsibility of the media to the audience. If the media reporters and journalists accept that their national interest should get priority because they accompany their army personnel, then why should we all watch their programmes and their reports? It loses its credibility of being an international media and so disregards the international audience who watches their programmes. Other people began to see them being reported as evil or as villains in the so-called self-regulated objective media. If they are not responsible for an international audience which would involve critiquing of their own army at times, then their objective claims and credibility are under serious question.

The priority always is to vindicate the decision to fight. Simon Hoggart, of the *Guardian* newspaper writes in an article titled, 'Anti-war MPs cling to intellectual life rafts', saying, 'Not only is power vindicated, but the few honest voices who dared to stand in the way of violence are exposed as fools – standard media practice after victories'[95]. The objective reporting was the last consideration for many embedded reporters because of their rush to be first to inform the public [Media Education Foundation[96]]. Robert Jensen writer for 'Progressive' said, 'There was no meaningful debate on the main news shows of CBS, ABC, NBC or PBS.

The media did not even provide the straight facts well'. Christ Hedges, a reporter of the *New York Times* says, 'In wartime the press is always part of the problem. When the nation goes to war, the press goes with it… the blather on CNN or Fox or MSNBC is part of a long and sad tradition. The reporters risked giving aid and comfort to the terrorist enemy by being too independent. American networks behaved as though they truly do fear their patriotism will be questioned if they report anything less than a triumphalist tone" [Media Education Foundation[97]]. There was great loyalty shown by the press to the administration because two are one and the same; the wealthy and the elite.

The image of an Iraqi detainee being strip searched by marines, (taken by Cheryl Diaz Meyer, of the Dallas Morning News), who, according to Geiger, was later released, was a haunting and compelling image of the Iraqi opposition, contrasting with the hundreds of photos that were being transmitted by photographers across Iraq, of American soldiers beating a path to Baghdad's door[98].

The Pentagon responded on April 11th by advising the Washington office of the Dallas Morning News that Diaz Meyer would lose her position with the Marines of the Second Tank Battalion, a position she had reported from since the beginning of the war in Iraq. Geiger says it was the one restriction that was "hard to swallow[99]." "We broke the rules," said Geiger. "In our haste to share images as Baghdad fell, we were wrapped up in the bigger picture and we lost sight of our agreement. We should not have published it. We should have been better gatekeepers, given our agreement with the military." Such statements clearly show the way the embedded media reporters and editors failed to maintain even a minimum of decent ethical practice in their communication.

Ultimately the Dallas Morning News (DMN) sent a request to the wire services and the *New York Times* to kill the photo, and DMN editors pulled Diaz Meyer from her embedded position prior to her being terminated, and re-assigned her to Baghdad to pursue other stories independently[100]. Geiger says he has heard the argument from the larger newspapers about the objectivity issue with embedded journalists, but says the price of having someone working unilaterally on the outside, for the Dallas Morning News, who had four embedded positions, was enormous. 'We don't have deep pockets like other larger newspapers,' he said. 'We had an opportunity to tell the story from one perspective and we used other means to tell the other side of the story. It is a finite way of saying that our photographic staff didn't tell the whole story, but our newspaper did.'

There is a clear acknowledgement from different sources that the practice of embedding as well as the pressure from the government and other sources forced the media practitioners to break the regulations and even, at times, their own rules. This led not only to a manipulation of news and reporting but also evolved a new practice where the journalist or editor or reporter thinks only of the way to survive and shine in the world of media.

Learning from embedded reporting

Communication is biased in one way or the other. No-one can be objective in their reporting. Truth can also be interpreted for one's own advantage. The problem is not going to be solved by censorship or control by any government or institutions. It is also clear that self-regulation is no more helpful to maintain decency or accuracy, to an extent, in the media practice. Journalists and reporters should be encouraged to maintain a moral reasoning among them. They must also be encouraged to take up investigative reporting. The embedded reporting is not an easy job to do. We need to appreciate those who were part of such reporting and attempted to be neutral in their reporting. We need to appreciate those editors and other media spin doctors who provided equal amount of space for other reporters besides embedded ones. But such reporting certainly raises serious questions about telling truth in the media.

While hurrying to reach the audience as the first reporter, misinformation was very often provided to the public which could have been avoided. This creates a suspicion in the minds of critics of those journalists and media practitioners though they claim to be objective and neutral in their presentation but in practice are not. They went with bias and reported from such a perspective regarding the other. Establishing credibility is one way of doing business in the media world. By fearing their government and people journalists and reporters began to show their patriotic feelings and support to their armed forces. This raises questions in many audiences' mind whether we need to watch these channels anymore because they have become like any other national television channels across the world.

At the time of conflicts and war there is a need for the media practitioners to play the role of intellectuals who would critique and prophetically raise their voice against their own government. The media critics should use small and alternative media to express their views and enable people to become media literate. I am aware of the fact that journalism and communication courses emphasize ethical and moral principles. There is a need to emphasize, besides skills and technological operations, a personal conviction and commitment to the audience too.

The committed journalism and the practice of media should consider the principles of truth telling, humaneness, justice, freedom and stewardship of free expression [Lambeth, 1992:37]. It is also essential to highlight the importance of 'investigative journalism' where the role of a journalist or a media person is like an intellectual and a social critic. This can make the media industry a major success though many often criticize such attempts. Theologians can also play a role by interacting with the practitioners and helping them to recognize their problems through seminars and training. In a world of chaos the media practitioners can play a constructive role in building communities and nations without losing their business if they are committed to their basic ethical principles.

Section D - Demythologizing the Media

Challenges to Theologies

Mass media provide one of the main sources of information for people about other religious communities. At times, it is very expensive to get access to the media or even to reach out to a mass audience through particular programs. The best way to enable people to demythologize these myths, to remove the ignorance and thus establish a better relationship between different religious communities is to look for other types of communication.

We need to encourage people to deconstruct the media's myths about religious communities by reading the texts critically and also to communicate with other religious communities directly. The first approach is to promote a media literacy programme through which people will be able to read the news with discrimination and critically engage with the public media through verification (with other media) and thus react to any manipulative news items in different ways[101].

It is essential to bring people from different religious communities together in groups and discuss among themselves the ways to coexist. This is interaction or discussion or dialogue at grassroots level. To do this, we need to create the right atmosphere. In order to know the 'other', one religious community needs to listen to other religious individuals and groups. Unless the people at grass root level are prepared to talk with other religious communities it is impossible to bring about an understanding among them.

There is a need for small groups from different religions to engage in dialogue in our own places so that this ignorance about each other can be overcome and be replaced by a new understanding. This is an attempt to establish a culture of dialogue[102] and thus a culture of reconciliation between different religious communities in India.

John Joshva Raja

Such events challenge us to react to the changing reality in altogether different ways, setting us on the mission path of inter-religious dialogue, in order to bring communities together. This is where the dialogue and a need for the theology of dialogue are needed, especially at grassroots level.

Towards a culture of dialogue

The confrontation between Hindus and Muslims in many parts of India is a reality in which other religious communities are also affected. Even Christians are seen as remnants of colonial rule and thus as outsiders. Christians are also blamed for conversions and their institutions and mission workers are often attacked and even killed. In such a context Christians cannot remain silent and should engage in bringing a better understanding between different religious communities. Christians should try to remove any misunderstandings about themselves and also work to reconcile the Hindus and Muslim communities wherever the conflicts and tensions exist. They have to find a way to engage not simply to bring them to Christianity but to show a concern for human lives and for establishing a culture of peace.

Establishing a dialogical understanding between Hindus and Muslims means Christians should engage with the warring communities and enable them to become co-existing human beings while their Christian witness should reveal God's love and care for all. There is already a movement within Hinduism as well as within Islam that is engaged in the search for meanings of reconciliation and peace with other religions. Christians should engage with them in such searches for meanings. This is where it is essential for us to establish a multidimensional dialogic interaction between different religious communities. This interaction will enable people to understand other religious communities and thus find within their religion a way to exist with others.

Previous Models of Interfaith Dialogue

These were the models of communication that were used by a few missionaries or scholars in their approach towards other religions. I am not going to analyse each model rather I just give a pictorial description of the process. The following models are borrowed from C R W David, Avery Dulles, M Pillai, and R Panikkar and also from my first book[103].

1. Coercion Model[104] - The political authorities enforced religion on their subjects. When the Roman empire adopted Christianity as its official religion, the emperors began to force Christian orthodoxy and persecute all other religions including dissident forms of Christianity [Dulles, 2002:2]. Top-Down Model – In this model the missionary is the custodian of Truth looks down at the people and communicates the good news to them. One claims their way is the only way.

2. Triumphalist Model - In this model Christ is seen as the fulfilment, the crown and hidden force operative in Hinduism (R Panikkar's The Unknown Christ of Hinduism). Different religious traditions of mankind are alike the almost infinite number of colours that appear once the divine or simply white light of reality falls on the prism of human experience: it diffracts into innumerable traditions, doctrines and religions[105]. Participants from different religions are engaged in the dialogue but with a mind to search Christ in every religion and their texts.

3. Convergent Model (Avery Dulles) – It is an attempt to bring a synthesis between Christian view point and the Hindu ethos (K C Sen, Mazzomdar and Subba Rao, John Hick). Religions could agree on the basis of theocentrism, recognising their differences about the means of salvation as culturally relative.

4.   Inculturation Model - Taking local cultural roles to proclaim the Gospel and convert them to Christianity (Robert de Nobili). Francis[106] identifies the need for using Dravidian cultural forms of communication in order to interact with people in South India [1983:10]. Though a missionary de Nobili learnt the culture and texts of Hinduism in the South India won over the minds of Brahmins and took up the radical step of being a Sannyasa (sage) and wore Kavi (saffron dress).

5.   Unitary Model – It is an attempt to understand the one reality to which everything belongs to and thus all religions moving towards such a reality. (Ramakrishna Parahamsa). Gandhi writes 'After long study and experience, I have come to the conclusion that 1. All religions are true; 2) All religions have some errors in them' 3) All religions are almost as dear to m e as my own Hinduism. All religions are true because they contribute efficaciously to the spiritual progress of humanity' (Selected Works of Mahatma Gandhi, S Narayan (ed) Vol VI, p.269). For Sri Ramakrishna, 'it is the same universal God that assumes different shapes of incarnation: diving in the ocean of life he manifests himself as Rama, there as Krishna somewhere else as Christ!'[107]

6.   Tolerance Model (Avery Dulles) It endorses freedom of religious beliefs and practices. Dulles writes, we tolerate things that we find less than acceptable because we find ourselves unable to suppress them or because the suppression would itself be evil [Dulles 2002:5]. The Holy Qur'an is being quoted by a number of people for a dialogue on coexistence. Maulana Wahiduddin Khan[108] in his *Progress in Inter-Religious Dialogue* argues that the first and foremost principle for any dialogue is to strive on a mutual basis for peace co-existence [2000:1]. He quotes from the Holy Qur'an, "To you your religion and to me mine" (109:6). To each of you we have

appointed a right way and an open road. If God has willed He could have made you one community but that He may try you in what is given to you. So be you forward in good works; unto God shall you return all together and he will tell you of what wherein you were at variance (5:48).These are some examples that demand clearly the dialogue for coexistence as part of Islamic faith.

M Fethullah Gulen points out to the fact that religions share a few pillars of dialogue that are love, compassion, tolerance and forgiving. These are essential components of coexistence of different religious communities[109]. Dr Radhakrishnan points out that the spirit of tolerance must not spring from a vague feeling of sympathy or compassion for the faults of others, but from the belief that Truth always transcends human understanding; that God contains in Himself more than man knows. He affirms: Toleration is the homage which the finite mind pays to the inexhaustibility of the Infinite' [1969:317]. Sri Ramakrishna also advices as: 'As you remain firms in your faith and opinion, so leave the others the same freedom to remain firm in their faith and opinion' [S Ghanananda,1970:139.].

    7. Developmental Model[110] - To work together along with NGOs and other religious institutions in order to bring about development of the communities where dialogue is basically about how people can develop themselves and also how the religious institutions can serve in a better way the communities in terms of their development [Moses 1954:4].

I have selected a few writers and approaches that focus on Interfaith dialogue at various levels. A few models may overlap and may not be successful one. Other models can also be added to the above stated ones.

Towards a dialogue at grassroots level

Theologians have discussed the topic of dialogue for more than five decades as I have given some examples in the above section. The basic purpose is to develop a better relationship between different religious communities. It is to encourage them to critically engage with the mass media that at times provide sensational and manipulative information about particular religious groups so that such relationship would be affected. This cannot be done merely by having dialogue at leadership or intellectual levels only. If understanding and practice of interfaith dialogue can be brought to the communities at grassroots then they can critically engage with the media's content together and thus recognise the manipulative representations of different religious communities.

I see an urgent need for establishing dialogic groups and direct communication between different communities at a small scale to help people to understand each other. Dialogue at grassroots means communication between two persons, two communities, two caste groups, or people from two nations who are not intellectuals or leaders, but ordinary members of their group.

Such grassroots communication will begin to eliminate ignorance of the other to a great extent and also help people demythologize the myths promoted by fundamentalist groups of all religions. Dialogue at grassroots refers to establishing contact, communication, relationship and understanding between communities. This could enrich the process that already exists in many contexts such as 'tea shops' where dialogue between people of different faiths is already happening, and where it can become the means to address many areas of religious conflict and social unrest. Instead of confrontation communities may work together to find a way to live in harmony. In order to begin the process we need to encourage Christians to initiate small groups of dialogue in rural and urban centres or even strengthen and network the existing secular clubs and communities in this regard.

Dialogue means to establish contact, presence, communication, relationship and understanding between persons or communities. If this is the case it does not demand change in the persons or communities' attitude, religion or perception during or after the dialogue. The changes may occur in both sides during the interaction only after the relationship between the participants becomes strong. Such a dialogue affirms the life of each other person or community; enables people to share their basic resources; guides people to recognize each other's search for God and leads people to recognize common human values such as justice and dignity.

Every human being tries to search for God in his or her own way, using his or her own religious or non-religious or even anti-religious means and methods. Such a willingness to search for God should be recognized in all persons and thus engaging in each other's search can be seen as dialogue. Religious narratives are supposed to guide people to engage in search for meanings of life and of God in a particular way.

The need for a theology of dialogic Communication

There is a general level of ignorance about other religious communities which demands a need for a dialogue between different religious communities at grassroots level. Dialogue often takes place between the leaders of different communities and amongst the intellectuals. Once, at grassroots level there was frequent interaction between religious communities but because of fear and suspicion about other religious communities this interaction in many parts of India has been reduced or even stopped. At the same time, there is a spiritual search for meanings of life and of God among the masses which is often misguided by the evangelists in the mass and new media[111]. The popularity of charismatic religion, the propagation of prosperity ideologies and the exploitation of physical and psychological weaknesses of the audience at times are against the basic values of any religion and also often create a stereotypical negative image of the others who do not follow this version of the religion.

There is a need for Christians to initiate dialogue at grassroots level. Dialogue for me implies making contact with people of other faiths, establishing discussions and relationship for coexistence and enabling one to understand the other so that ignorance will not sever links between them. The purpose is to guide the communities to live together in peaceful coexistence, to eliminate misconceptions of the other, and to foster a better relationship among them. This does not demand anyone to change their faith nor their religion.

Nevertheless many Christians in the churches see dialogue as an intellectual exercise and an attempt to eliminate evangelism and proclamation of the gospel[112]. Those who support dialogue, often try to impose pluralism on others [Hocking 1932:47; 1940:249]. This creates a suspicion over the whole project of dialogue at an intellectual level. But without dialogue religious communities enter into conflicts with each other simply due to ignorance.

All religions do have teachers and followers who show interest in understanding other religious faith communities, who try to reinterpret their religious teachings to enable people to enter into dialogue. Within every religion in Asia there is a search for meanings of God and of life that would enable them to hold a dialogue with others. This spirit needs nurturing and therefore there needs to be a careful approach in identifying the fundamentalist groups with evangelicals or the neo-religious spiritual gurus, though many of them often side with fundamentalist ideology.

An interactive methodology

I would like to propose an 'interactive approach' through which the importance of dialogue at grassroots can be promoted among Christians and also among other religious communities. Theologians need to develop a public theology of dialogue for Christians at the grassroots in order to encourage them to engage in dialogue with other religious communities and also to recognize the human dignity of each other. Theologians are challenged to consider the uniqueness of Christ (of course, one need to accept other religious claims of uniqueness too) that the majority of Christians do not want to give up while discouraging too much emphasis on 'exclusive' and traditional

Christianity.

This approach is neither pluralistic nor exclusive nor inclusive; rather, it seeks to hold different perspectives together in a process which is constantly interactive. It is an interaction between those who try to those who do not want to listen and those who wish to listen to other religious communities. We need to learn to live and work together at grassroots level.

Christian mission is often understood in terms of evangelisation of non-Christians. But Jesus listened to his opponents such as Pharisees and Sadducees and thus has seen dialogue as part of his mission of God (Luke 10). He also showed solidarity with tax collectors and sinners by eating with them (Luke 1:1). He also touched the person with leprosy to heal him. Jesus' mission was holistic as he not only shared his own thoughts in a persuasive way but also listened to others and engaged in the liberative aspirations of the marginal communities of his time.

Jesus held the tension between these different aspects of God's mission. In this sense some aspects of evangelising aspect of mission may be corrected or nourished by dialogic and liberative aspects of God's mission. God's mission involves holding these aspects of mission in a creative tension [David Bosch]. It is essential to see interfaith dialogue as part and parcel of holistic mission of God. This is where our doing theology[113] should focus for the sake of promoting a culture of dialogue and thus replacing a culture of violence and confrontation.

In this methodology, theologians need to recognize people as they are and accept their faith in Christ, Great Commission and so on. What is basically argued here is that for the sake of dialogue neither Christians nor Hindus should be asked to change their faith or beliefs, though one may nourish the other faith at a later stage of interaction. For the sake of coexistence one community can listen to the other community and communicate with each other and establish a relationship. This would enable one to understand the other better and thus remove ignorance about the other.

I call this a dialogue for co-existence. This dialogue for co-existence begins with the dialogue within, by which I mean the establishing a contact and communication between the leadership, theologians and the lay Christians in order to engage in grassroots dialogue.

At this stage, they may not even talk but simply join together in some activities or community project. Even if they talk in small groups they may try to avoid talking about faith related matters. The basic purpose of dialogue at grassroots level is to reduce the suspicion that one community or person has about the other and also establish a relationship. Once a relationship has been established then the communities can share their faith experience and may find their faith being nourished or enriched or challenged by the faith of the other. Such relationships at small group levels would certainly help people to relate to one another. It will lessen the degree of tension and hostility that develops after violent encounters between different religious communities and their reports in the media.

Dialogue at grassroots level

Interactive dialogue at grassroots level is a new approach because this dialogue is for co-existence rather than trying to use high Indian philosophical language. It attempts to remove the ignorance and misunderstanding between communities at grassroots level. The revival of an ongoing dialogue is the need of the hour. The communication process between the participants of the dialogue can happen either through rational discourse (Habermas), I-Thou relationship (Buber), merging horizons of past and present (Gadamer[114]), dialogic-language (Bakhtin[115]) and through common consciousness (Bohm).

In the following sections I will elaborately but selectively discuss three main concepts of dialogue (Buber, Habermas and Bohm) between individual and communities at grassroots. Martin Buber conceives dialogue as a process in which the other is fully recognized. Martin Buber [1958, p 15] postulates two "primary words", 'I-Thou' and 'I-It', in accordance with our "twofold attitude" to the world. The former can only "be spoken with the whole being"; the latter can only be spoken with part of the being.

The 'I-Thou' expresses a relation with nature, persons and spiritual beings [p 18-19]. The 'I-It' expresses all other relations of "I" to material objects or depersonalised human beings. The 'I-It' necessarily reifies, making people a "thing among things" [p 21]. This is useful in relating to the material world but may be destructive of or place limitations upon relationships with people.

> "Thus human being neither is not *He* or *She*...nor is he a nature able to be experienced and described, a loose bundle of named qualities. But with no neighbour, and whole in himself, he is *Thou* and fills the heavens." [ibid]

The 'I-Thou' accepts the whole being of the other without awareness of the parts. It is unconditionally being there and being with the other. The "I" who speaks "Thou" takes a non-reductionist, unanalysed, inchoate, unconditional, unified, unselfconscious relation to the whole being of the other. This could be called a 'stance', an 'attitude', an 'orientation'.

It is not required for the 'I-Thou' relation that the whole person be available to the other but that "I" accept "Thou" in the completeness of her being. Above, Buber makes clear that the other is not experienced in the 'I-Thou' moment. [Batros, 1996]. In his renowned work *I and Thou*, Buber points to the two-fold attitude toward the world: the I-Thou and the I-It relationship. Neither the I nor the Thou lives apart, but exists only in the I-Thou context, which precedes both the I and the Thou realm. Similarly, neither the I nor the It exists separately, but only in the realm of I-It. The absolute I-Thou is only valid in regard to God—the Eternal Thou—and cannot be fully realized in other areas of life— including human relations which frequently tend to sink into the I-It sphere.

The real determinant of I-Thou and I-It attitude toward the world is not conditioned by the nature of the object, but by the way in which one relates to that object. A human being is transfigured into authentic

John Joshva Raja

life only by entering an I-Thou relationship, therewith confirming 'the otherness of the other'. Contrary to the sphere of I-It, the I-Thou relations demands total commitment: 'The primary word I-Thou can only be spoken with one's whole being, whereas the primary word I-It can never be spoken with the whole being'. At the centre of dialogue is a meeting between two sovereign persons, who do not intend to impress the other or to make use of him. Buber comments that one can live without dialogue, but the person who never met.

However, one who enters into the realm of dialogue takes upon himself considerable risk, since the I-Thou demands a total exposure of the I, which may be entirely denied and rejected. While the subjective I-Thou reality exists in the terrain of dialogue, the instrumental I-It relationship is anchored in monologue, which transforms world and mankind into an object. Within the monological domain, the other is regarded as a thing among things— experienced and used, whereas in the dialogical sphere the other is met, acknowledged and addressed as a particular being.

According to Martin Buber, an essential building block of community is the concept of dialogue. People often think of dialogue as merely script, or an exchange of words. Martin Buber has presented dialogue as being much more than the exchange of messages and talk that takes place in human interaction. He describes genuine dialogue as "...no matter whether spoken or silent...where each of the participants really has in mind the other or others in their present and particular being and turns to them with the intention of establishing a living mutual relation between himself and them" (Arnett, p.6, 1986).

Dialogue is unique because it evolves through a process and particular quality of communication whereby parties achieve a "connection." This connection between participants allows for each party to potentially change the other, or be changed by the other (lecture notes). A relationship that has the ability to produce dialogue is referred to as I-thou relationship. This means that one will relate to and experience another person **as** another person. It requires having regard for **both** self and other. The opposite type of relationship is

140

referred to as the I-it relationship. Parties relate to and experience each other as objects or means to achieving goals in an I-it relationship. This relation contains only regard for self. Buber does not suggest that we are to avoid this type of relationship; he merely claims that dialogue cannot occur in the I-it relation.

Dialogue takes place between conscience-oriented thinkers as opposed to strategists. The conscience-oriented thinker will think in terms of a "good" outcome that maintains values and ethics, whereas a strategist will think in terms of achieving individual goals without concern for ethical practices (Arnett, 1986). Persons who are engaged in dialogue will participate in what is called narrow ridge communication.

The narrow ridge refers to a common ground between parties. It is a point for participants to meet and share their views. The common ground in narrow ridge communication is a place where participants are open to and can see the others viewpoint, it is not a place where participants meet and compromise their beliefs to suit each other. The narrow ridge is viewed as "a guide for the development of community which emphasizes the need to search for genuine alternatives to extreme communicative positions" (Arnett, p. 43, 1986). The last characteristic of true dialogue involves meaning. Dialogue allows participants to create new meaning together and come to a mutual understanding. In dialogue, meaning is actually discovered between persons rather than owned by each individual. This concept encourages one to recognize that there is meaning beyond what is *inside* of him/her (Arnett, 1986).

For Habermas Dialogue is establishing a rational discourse between individuals in the public sphere. Such a dialogue should lead to a realization of enlightenment values. By identifying these essential presuppositions to argumentation, Habermas completes his argument for the universal principle (U). If, whenever discussing a claim to validity, one must follow the rules of logical sense, assume a hypothetical attitude toward the relevant facts, and ensure the free and equal status of all the participants in the dialogue, then Habermas can

John Joshva Raja

derive the principle of discourse ethics: a norm is valid only if it meets the free approval of every person that may be affected.

For Habermas, a norm is morally justified for a community only if it is agreed upon as a result of a free, rational discussion. With this argument, Habermas appears to have achieved his goal: a universal criterion for evaluating moral claims whose justification is based on the actual, pragmatic needs of people engaged in argument. Habermas' own argument avoids reference to abstract ideals by beginning with presuppositions that he believes to represent the natural intuitions involved in actual arguments.

The point of agreement between Habermas' theory and critical thinking theory is also the point of difficulty: decentring and the hypothetical attitude. In order for socially determined difference to be authentically recognized, while still providing the possibility of agreement, participants in dialogue must move beyond their own perspective. Accounts of critical thinking must struggle to meet Habermas' original goals: they must do justice to a diversity of socially defined perspectives while providing grounding for the evaluation of controversial problems.

If critical thinking is described too loosely, it fails to be a useful concept for educators; but defined too narrowly, it can undermine its own empowering intent by eclipsing valuable ways of thinking. By beginning his argument with the intuitions involved in actual dialogue, Habermas suggests an approach to grounding reason that avoids these extremes, and he shows that a commitment to decentre is a necessary presupposition of genuine communication.

Habermas' concept of decentring mirrors many accounts of critical thinking, and engages in a struggle that they both share: the attempt to gain a clarifying perspective in evaluating controversial claims without denying the socially defined character of human beings. By attempting to characterize what it means to decentre and critically reflect on personal and social norms in new and creative ways, I believe that educators and philosophers can address this challenge that reason poses for preserving human difference.

A physicist called David Bohm speculated that thought itself is not the result of an individual in isolation, but is largely a collective phenomenon. A story creates a dialogue-like space in a free flow of meaning that passes and moves through and between people, in the sense of a stream that flows between the banks. As in dialogue, a group accesses a large pool of common meaning which cannot be fully accessed individually.

Bohmian dialogue aims at the unfolding of collective intelligence. David Bohm maintained that if we could become conscious of our thinking process we might be able to create a different kind of culture, one based on a holographic view of the universe[116]. Such a culture would bridge the needs of the individual and the collective leading to increasingly deeper levels of community and adaptation to the environment. Two important challenges for us have been how to best facilitate people's ability to participate in dialogue and then how to help them continue the practice and experience all of the possible ways it can enhance the group.

Bohm proposed that we live in a holographic universe. Every part of the universe both contains and contributes to the whole. If one part is affected by something (some change), it affects the whole and vice versa. Thus, we live in a relational world where the individual impacts the collective and the collective impacts the individual. The difficulty is that our thinking causes us to behave as though the opposite were true: that we live in a fragmented world where individual parts are separate from each other. Our thinking process works against our ability to perceive the interconnections and the whole.

Bohm offers dialogue as a means to uncover and correct incoherence. By pooling our individual perspectives in an environment of non-judgment, a larger view of reality becomes possible. We can start to perceive the necessary linkages between our actions and the results we get. Through dialogue we can participate in collective thinking. We no longer have to take actions based on limited understanding.

In the following section I will engage with these views of dialogue critically and attempt to relate them to grassroots dialogue. The purpose is to create spaces against the mass media spaces through which such ignorance about each other can be reduced.

Comments on these approaches:
Their emphasis is on the dialogic relationship of one with the other and tends to answer how to develop a dialogic link between people. Without a person deciding whether to participate in the dialogue or not there is no possibility of developing dialogic relationship among the participants. The above definition highlights the process of dialogue between the self and the other and thus dialogue is explained in terms of relationship with the other. Their emphasis on the other is important and its role in shaping the self should also be recognized.

Without a dialogue within oneself from different perspectives it may be difficult to extend it to another. It is not essential to change any perspectives or the self in order to extend the dialogue with the other. Nevertheless one may have to recognize within oneself the presence of difference perspectives, beliefs and views that are in constant dialogue with each other. Though one holds one's own perspective strongly one can still attempt to listen to the voices of the other perspectives within oneself because it is the nature of God in human self. In such a belief one's life, dignity and faith become important and so dialogue with the other on this basis may become possible at any level including people at grassroots.

Dialogue and ignorance
From people's experience of God they construct their own religion to enable the future generation to have similar experience and relate themselves with God and also with other. Each religious narrative is a construction of human beings from their experience of God and of life. These narratives have limitations in terms of linguistic expressions, narration, semantic constructions, and historical accuracies and so on. Yet, this does not prevent people from believing and practicing them. When it is relating people to God and to neighbour the religions seem to be working within a particular religious community. But when it

is extended to other religions or cultural groups, then there are issues such as conversion and the problem comes only when we provide an adjective to God and neighbour such as Christian or Jewish or Hindu God or Christian or Jewish or Hindu neighbour. If God is universal, then there is no need for any adjective (Christian God or Hindu God or Muslim God) to be added.

If God is approachable by people, each one's faith in God can be recognized as the starting point rather than religion. Jesus often recognized people's faith in God and appreciated them for their belief in him. Even in the case of neighbours the same conclusion is applicable. There is no need to have adjectives for neighbours such as Christian sister or Hindu friends and Muslim brother and so on to share our love and care with others. When any neighbour regardless of his faith becomes our friend, partner or brother then a dialogic relationship brings God's reign here and now. It means one should be ready to accept any neighbour as friend and as fellow faith seeker, for it is then that we express the image of God to others and thus witness God's love to the whole world.

This takes us to the next step of theology where we discover ourselves in the light of God. Each one of us has multiple 'personalities' in ourselves. A person's attitude, speech and relationship are often shaped by the perspectives that he or she has. Such perspectives are shaped and formed by many social institutions including religion, family, peer group, school and media. If one holds more than two perspectives in oneself on a particular issue at a particular historical time then there is a dialogue possible within one's 'self'. If one holds only one perspective without having dialogue with another perspective then no dialogue is possible within oneself and with others.

Persons with such single perspectives do not mind giving up their lives for the sake of such perspectives. This may lead to martyrdom and also to suicide bombers. People may allow themselves to be persecuted or to be killed for the sake of establishing a relationship with God and with their neighbours. Such kinds of martyrdom may be interpreted positively. At the same time if the martyrdom is carried

145

out in the name of fixed doctrines or 'single' perspectives then such an act can be interpreted as an act of terror. Recognizing within ourselves God's images with their diversities is the process of understanding God and of engaging in our salvation. Without trying to understand the opposing views in our 'self's' we cannot recognize and activate the image of God in ourselves.

When we can engage in dialogue within ourselves, then it is easy for us to extend it to people of other religions and other perspectives. If we are in constant dialogue with 'others,' then ignorance about them may be reduced or clarified and thus a positive relationship can be established. This need to be done not only at individual level but also at group and mass level so that the popular ignorance can be lessened and the chances of conflicts between different communities are reduced. There is also a need to engage through the media and with media personnel to challenge, critically engage and correct some of the perceptions and images that they present about the 'others'. It may also lead to involving the media in this public dialogue.

Section E – The media and inter-religious dialogue

According to Dr. S. J Samartha [1991:59], Dialogue is between people and so it is much a matter of relationships, discussions and communication. There can be no dialogue between 'faiths' or 'religions' or 'ideologies' [Samartha, 1991]. Dialogue is communication between two persons or two communities. From an Islamic perspective, dialogue is a dimension of human consciousness (not sceptical), a category of the ethical sense (not cynical). It is the altruistic arm of Islam and Christianity, their reach beyond themselves. Dialogue in short is the only kind of inter-human relationship worthy of human beings [Ragi and Faruqi, 1992:1-22].

Different types and means of communication can enhance inter-religious dialogue. The words interfaith and inter-religious dialogue are often used by different groups (Catholic scholars refer to inter-religious dialogue and WCC often refers to interfaith dialogue) to mean at times the similar activities or concepts. In simple terms inter-religious dialogue may mean dialogue or discussion between religious communities or people and interfaith dialogue may refer to those discussions among those who share different faiths.

This is already recognized by Samartha in his writings. He argues that not only the symbols of religious life and practice, particularly music, art, devotion, meditation and the controlled use of silence but also verbal communication are an essential part of dialogue [Samartha, 1981:7]. It is essential that we use the media for enhancing the process of dialogue. One has to realize the fact that many people are yet to be convinced of the need for dialogue. When we talk about the role of different means of communication we need to identify multiple approaches. This will enable us to engage both in communication and also in interfaith dialogue with an open heart leading to wider possibilities.

I have grouped the approaches into a few ways: dialogue with the media, dialogue through the media, dialogue about the media, dialogue in the media, and dialogue and the media. But our dialogue is with the people. There are a number of attempts by many of the religious groups and institutions to initiate, sustain and nourish inter-religious dialogue among different religious communities. This is happening at the intellectual, leadership, representative and elite level. Organized inter-religious dialogues are familiar to many of us at this level. But informal dialogue is happening at grassroots level (interpersonal, group, community and mass level) everyday.

People talk about their religions or about their faiths in their everyday encounter either in a shop or in any other public spaces with people from other religions. As the countries increasingly become multicultural it is sometimes unavoidable to have discussions about religion or faith. Such encounters can also be seen as interfaith dialogue at grassroots. However, recent hate campaigns and ignorance have caused a setback with regard to inter-faith dialogue. There are not many organized dialogic groups or dialogic action groups.

The purpose of the grassroots dialogue is to enable people to come in contact with other religious communities, to communicate, to understand and to establish relationship with each other.

Our interaction with the media should enable us to nourish dialogue at the grassroots and find new ways of establishing contact, communication, relationship and thus understanding which I call inter-religious dialogue. But it is not only discussions but communication and relationship which involve action and also joining spiritual and intellectual journeys along with other religious communities. Any dialogue that is not bringing together people, enabling them to establish understanding and thus remove ignorance about each other and not spurring them to act together will only be short-lived.

My main aim in the inter-religious dialogue is to promote discussions at grassroots level even as we maintain dialogue at the intellectual and leadership level without which dialogue at grassroots becomes impossible. In this case, means of communication can mediate between different dialogic groups and enable them to network among themselves.

Dialogue with media-people – It means to hold dialogue with the media professionals, personal and media practitioners. The media play a major role in reflecting and shaping public opinion and have great potential to facilitate dialogue between religious communities. This potential is not automatically realised as the media operate under financial constraints, strong competition, commercial marketing considerations, a growing demand for visual material and a public demand for sensational and exotic news.

Media professionals need to become more aware of the vital role that the media play in informing the public, their potential to foster dialogue, mutual respect, peace and justice between different religious communities [Abdelnasser,[117] 2004:1]. Some of them need an orientation to different religions with a practical exposure and with certain ethical discussions about the representation of the other in the media.

Many of our religious leaders and academics need to realise the limitations of the mass media industries and practices. This often leads us to discover each other and understand the other. In this sense, we start dialogue for wisdom (Jnana Marga[118]). This is an intellectual discussion on representation, values and role of the media in establishing harmony and peace. This intellectual discussion needs to establish regular correspondence, access, space for each other and thus create an atmosphere of understanding between them. This may lead to a culture of participation, a constructive critique of each other, learning and working together towards peace and harmony of the society. Thus a dialogue is essential with the media personnel.

The 1992 pastoral instruction document, *Aetatis Novae*, issued by the Vatican encourages pastoral outreach to and dialogue with media professionals, with particular attention to their faith development and spiritual growth [Eilers, 1996: 135]. It continues saying, 'in seeking to enter into dialogue with the modern world, the Church necessarily desires honest and respectful dialogue with those responsible for the communications media... Such dialogue, therefore, requires that the Church be actively concerned with the secular media, and especially with the shaping of media policy. ...The dialogue involves support for media artists..." [Eilers, 1996:128]. It is thus clear that the church has recognized the media as a powerful means for dialogue.

First, it is essential that the churches hold dialogue with the media professionals and then through them extend our dialogue with other religious communities. Through our dialogue we may enable the media practitioners as mediating and reconciling agencies of dialogue. In the Criteria for Ecumenical and Inter-religious cooperation, it is clearly demanded of Christian communicators to cooperate with members of other religions working in the field of communications for the preservation, promotion and coordination of the expression of a religious viewpoint in the media [Eilers, 1996:157]. At times such reporting or representations is done with intentions where dialogue with the media should become a critical and prophetic engagement with them.

Dialogue through the media – This refers to having a dialogue with the audience through the media. It aims at using any media as technological means for promoting dialogue at grassroots. The purpose is to promote inter-religious dialogue among the audience using different means of communication. We are not talking about the content here rather the technological form of the media. It means to make the media as a platform for inter-religious dialogue. For example, the internet is known for its interactive technology. So our attempt is to make the technology available for different religious communities to interact among themselves.

The interactive programmes (such as 'phone calls') via radio and television can be specially produced in order to encourage the audience to engage in different types of interfaith dialogue among them. The basic purpose here is to act – to use the media to bring people together and talk which otherwise is unlikely to happen. Then the use of the media should lead to Dialogue for Life (Jeeva Marga[119]) – which means to enable people to come together through the media and thus try to establish a contact, communication, relationship and thus understanding between them. This is where the use of the media for inter-religious dialogue becomes vital.

Religious media can play a major role in enhancing dialogue between different communities. It is essential that we create a multi-religious public space. Our media often aim at meeting the needs of our denomination members though some of them reach to other audiences. The best way of promoting a multi-religious public space is to widen the scope of our media to meet the needs of different religious communities. We can also try to form multi-religious voluntary groups based on a variety of cultural and social interests like music, arts and drama and so on [Amaladoss, 2004:6].

We need to begin to create occasions for symbolic celebrations of different religions and other social and national festivals. In the Pastoral Instruction on the Means of Social Communication *Communio et Progressio* (114), issued by the Second Vatican Council, the Council clearly mentions the need for the churches to look for ways of multiplying and strengthening the bonds of union between the members. For this reason, communication and dialogue among Catholics is indispensable [Eilers, 1996:99].

It continues saying, 'the church does not speak and listen to her own members alone; her dialogue is with the whole world' (*Communio et Progressio* 122). This shows that dialogue between members should necessarily be extended to a dialogue with others. This means our understanding of community should not be an exclusive and narrow one, rather it should enable us to create, provide and access to an inter-religious space where we can listen and interact with others.

In the document of *Criteria for Ecumenical and Inter-religious Cooperation*[120] [1989:16, 17, 19], cooperation among different religions can be realised in every aspect of social communication. This is already in itself a witnessing before the world. Inter-religious cooperation will take into account the specific context of production and planning on the local, regional, national or international level. Joint projects aim to allow Christians and members of other religions to give a common witness to God, a reciprocal trust and understanding among Catholic, other Christians, and members of other religions, based on mutual respect, and with a view to doing things together in communication. Christians are called to give fair and objective information on other religions of humanity [Eilers, 1996:159]. Many are exploring the possibilities of using different means of communication in order to encourage dialogue at different levels.

New technologies embody a huge potential to facilitate inter-religious dialogue. The internet in particular provides lots of opportunities to easily communicate with members of other faiths. It breaks the borders and boundaries of nations, despite a few limitations. The new media contribute to increased, diversified and decentralized information flow [Abdelnasser, 2004:1]. Their accessibility, availability and affordability are still serious issues that have to be addressed if we are thinking of using these technologies. Though the best form of communication is face to face communication we may consider some of these technologies and their characteristics in enhancing the inter-religious dialogue.

The internet provides us a high speed exchange of information that can foster a good relationship among the users. It is also an interactive culture that has evolved in the net where the gap between sender and receiver has been reduced to an active participants' role. The net provides convergent and hypertext technology through which all the analogue means of communication are brought into one machine and the search is done according to what we need rather than according what is made available.

The net has also evolved with new questions of self such as (virtual self), the relationship between God and I (one of the popular searched subject is God on the Net[121] and God has 430 million website links in the Google search). It is also found out that 64 per cent of Americans have used the internet for spiritual or religious purposes [Hoover[122], 2004: iv]. These characteristics of the new net culture may help us to enhance the dialogue between different religious communities where some may want to engage in the dialogue without releasing their identity and so on. For example, my paper on 'Internet, Mission and Ecumenism' is published in a number of journals including *Mission Today* (2004, August) and placed by the EMS Stuttgart as documentation on the net both in English and Deutsch[123].

Dialogue about the media – This is an effort to engage with people in talking about the media. It focuses on the audiences' use of the means of communication. The audience will engage in discussions about different religious reports that are presented in the media. Often people use media for different purposes. At times different means of communication may provide them right knowledge and at times may not do so. This is a grassroots-level dialogue where people come together and use media as a source of discussions.

It leads to action – that means to act together to establish further relationship (friendship); understanding and thus the community's relationship will be strengthened. People will start critically reading the media; write to them and avoid that part of the media which are promoting communal tension and violence. It also enables people to work together towards helping and developing each other and bring about reconciliation where it is needed. This method leads people to carry out dialogue for action (Karma Marga[124]) – acting together to bring about communal harmony and peace. A critical and discriminatory engagement about the content and technique of the media and its practice will help the audience to use them constructively.

Communio et Progressio states that 'Reviews of radio and television broadcast, of films and illustrated magazines can be of help in cultural and religious education. They will also help those who wish to make a wise choice of what the media have to offer.' [Eilers, 1996:99]. In *Aetatis Novae*, the churches are asked to include media education in the pastoral plan for social communication with a special emphasis on the relationship of media and values [Eilers, 1996:24]. The Pontifical Council- a supreme body of the Catholic Church (which makes statements on various religious issues including social communication issues) encourages further efforts at cooperation with the members of other religions to promote religious and moral values in the field of social communication. Most of our dialogue today depends on the content of the media. It would be easy for the groups or representatives to talk about the media and their content and thus initiate an inter-religious dialogue.

People can start analysing how the religions, particular communities or poor people or marginalized communities are represented in the media. Through such deconstructive learning the people not only engage in the inter-religious dialogue but also become constructive and critical users of the media. There is a need to conscientize the religious communities in order to challenge and change the incorrect attitudes, prejudices and biases towards others and remove the ignorance of the masses [Amaladoss,[125] 2004:5]. We have to create new experiences of community through dialogue and common action for justice. A change of attitudes will take place not only through preaching, not through abstract argument, but by actually encountering the others in multi-religious groups. This is where dialogue has to go to the grassroots in order to nourish understanding and relationship between different religious communities.

It is essential that multi-religious communities are formed not only to engage with the media in a critical manner but also to act together to promote human dignity, justice, peace and equality in the non-religious sphere or politics and society [Amaladoss, 2004:6]. During the riots the arms of the government should be neutral. Such movements must be multi-religious and so media should give appropriate commentary that enables people to awaken and conscientize rather than provoking a mad collective frenzy [Amaladoss]. Coalitions are happening and some newspapers, magazines and tabloids are playing a major constructive and critical role in presenting the stories about clashes. Not only the media but also the audience should learn to be critical users and readers of the media.

Media critique can be a starting point of such dialogue – particularly in relation to discussions about the representation of religious communities. Hess [1999] writes about this in detail, how media literacy can become a support for development of a responsible imagination in religious community, enable us to recognise the multiple ways of knowing and constructing meanings and help us in deconstructing some of our liturgies and so on. We have similar programmes such as media awareness programmes which are increasingly becoming popular among school children and also becoming part of the school education system. Media-talk and God-talk can nourish each other while they can correct the other too from their respective perspectives. The critique of the media should go along with appreciation about their excellent contribution to society at large.

At the same time there is a need to democratize the media, promoting freedom of expression and information at various levels of society, releasing a free flow of information and ideas to all and transfer of communication technology for development of communities. The inter-religious dialogue can lead to discuss these issues while focussing on the religion- related issues. There should be an openness to listen to the critique of the media towards religious leaders. Many of the religious institutions do not have a constructive and continued relationship with the media and their personnel. This can generate a lot of discussions at all levels about why media construct realities in this way when it comes to religion. This is not only a starting point but can become a sustainable process of dialogue. Particularly talking about the media in relation to religion can initiate dialogue and also encourage even the younger generation to interact with others.

Dialogue in the media means to present inter-religious dialogue programmes to the media for reporting. It aims at developing the content of the media in order to promote the inter-religious dialogue among the public. Religious leaders have to come together to produce media programmes that will promote better understanding and relationship between different communities. Dialogue can also be promoted through other genres such as drama, or film. We need to develop strategies where spiritual exercises that are similar and converging in meanings can be done together. Interfaith liturgies could be organized or a presentation of such a liturgy in the media. This leads to both a discussion among intellectuals and also a sharing of spiritual exercises through common liturgy or some common performance or at least 'clipping together' some common demonstrations of different religious communities which is Dialogue for Spiritual Search (Bhakthi Marga[126]). We need to develop programmes of dialogue for the media and invite the media for reporting our dialogue programmes.

We need to make sure that even in our media we present a good image of inter-religious dialogue so that people might be convinced. The content should merely not reflect the wealth, education or political power. The right to communicate is the right of all. It calls for special efforts not only to give those who are poor and less powerful access to the information which they need for their individual and social development but to ensure that they are able to play an effective, responsible role in deciding media content (Aetatis Novae 15 – Eilers, 1996:131). It calls us to promote inter-religious dialogue as an essential aspect of public communication.

Inter-religious dialogue should be presented in the public media as basic information for all the communities. Without such efforts the content often becomes too negative in the media's presentation of religious communities in general and no space for the inter-religious messages in particular. If this is neglected then it is taking away certain people's right to inform others about themselves and thus clarify certain suspicion or misinformation provided about them. It is essential for all the religious communities not only to provide information about them but also to provide a dialogic approach towards others.

Dialogue and the media – This is where we need to be open to listen to what the media expecting from inter-religious groups. Those who are interested in or promote interreligious dialogue often remain at different levels such as the representatives or leaders of different religions or at small group or community level. They need to produce media programmes and even run interfaith radio or television network wherever possible. Only by engaging in the media they can promote such understanding among the public about interreligious issues. They need to create programmes that would suit the media or would create an interest among the media and so the public on interreligious issues. It means to shape our own dialogical initiatives and change according to the needs of the media.

It may be risky to compromise our ideals but for the sake of promoting interreligious dialogue we may consider some of the possibility of the media that would disseminate and spread an interest in the dialogue at grassroots-levels. For example, the media may ask for a story or drama rather than for a discussion to promote dialogue. This is where we may have to do accordingly to promote the concept and practice of dialogue at various levels. A new interactive culture is emerging in the new technological media. This may enable and help us to provide space for those who wish to interact and engage with them in their interactive search for meanings of life and of God. Our search would be how the dialogue at the grassroots can be nourished by the new emerging culture of the media.

In what ways can we interact and incorporate the culture of the new media which can enable the representatives, leaders, intellectuals and people at the grassroots to develop a culture of dialogue. The search for meanings of life often begins from oneself. Thus within every, person, culture and religion there is a search for meanings of life and of God. How far can one engage in other's search for meanings are an essential question in our dialogic adventure? This is known as 'Dhyana Marga' whereby one not only meditates on one's own self but also tries to engage with the other in his or her meditation and search for God. The dialogue begins by being self-retrospective in our approach and engaging in other cultural and religious search for meanings of life and of God. People use media in search of meanings of life and of God and we are called to share in this search and listen to them. Listening provides us a space for our own meanings to be presented to them among an array of meanings that are available to them.

Conclusion

The media present a number of challenges to theologians. In this chapter, I have highlighted the problem with the media and their practices in terms of presenting the 'others' in their content. The other can include minority or marginal or the differently able or women or refugees who are often given a stereotypical and negative image in the public by the media. Using two case studies, I have demonstrated that such practices are there both at local and at global level. The question about the 'other' has become a real challenge for doing theology today. Such questions have been well addressed among theological circles. It is essential to take such theological thoughts to be presented at the grassroots and also to the public in an acceptable manner.

By taking the audience very seriously as they are and by interacting with them using theological and intellectual concepts the dialogue at grassroots can be promoted. The direct contact between different religious communities may enable the audience to become a critique of the media as such interactions will reduce ignorance about each other. In this chapter, a theology of dialogue at grassroots has been developed to bring about changes in today's context and thus enable the religious communities to co-exist and engage in each other's search for meanings of life and of God. While developing theological input, this chapter also highlights the way theological encounter can happen with the media by engaging with them through dialogue. Such dialogic encounters can also be explored in the new technologies and new methods of communication.

4 Netizens – Wandering Self and Virtual God

Having developed interest in online webcasting and Web interactive networking I found young people's talents are used or abused in this wonderful media. When I come back to theological interactions about the Web related media, I begin to realise that the discussions are often at very primary level. I was introducing online or Web mediated communication to theological students. Very often they reflect their church leaders' sceptical questions about accessibility, availability and affordability of the technology in their rural parishes in 2006. But by this time most of the rural villages in India have got internet access (2010).

William Fore (a scholar in religion and media) and I held a conference at Hyderabad in 2007for the Bishops, pastors and church leaders at Hyderabad in order to train them to become aware of the challenges of new media technology. But their questions clearly revealed that they are still sceptical about the technology and its use for the churches. They were also sceptical about their ability to learn to use this technology. Some churches webcasted the same information from their magazines. I had to give a lot of training for our students to use this technology for various purposes and thus the understanding of mission and ministry itself began to change for many of our students due to the influence of this technology.

In this chapter I ask questions such as: Can we use the web media for our mission and ministry of the churches? If so in what ways we can use them? Does it change in anyways our ways of doing mission and ministry? If so how our understanding of mission and ministry also changes accordingly? Can internet be used for poverty elimination, interfaith relationship and social awareness of the communities at large?

159

Netizens, technology and culture

The technology of the web has introduced a new culture – a culture of communicating at high speed, a culture of interactivity and a culture of hypertexts, a culture of 'wandering self', and a new religious culture. It is a mediated communication – which one can identify as e-communication or Web Mediated Communication (WMC). Those who engage in such communication have allowed themselves to be influenced by the culture of the internet. Those who use the internet often are called netizens because on the internet they are globally connected and transcend their national identity.

At first, WMC influences people's perceptions, attitude, faith and worldview and enables each person to discover one's self in one's own way. Secondly, it makes an impact on the relationship between persons – at interpersonal level and enhances the relationship to grow at the speed of light or break it at the same speed. Through such interpersonal relationships people discover a virtual friendship, relationship and also communities with which they can affiliate themselves. Thirdly, WMC influences the social, economic and political status of people.

This chapter will discuss the way in which information technology and the internet have influenced the life and culture of their users. Then there will be a brief description of the use of this technology by Christian institutions. The challenges for theologians will also be highlighted. This chapter includes a study of the use of Information Communication Technology (ICT) for people's development. Many concerns are raised about the ICT's role in furthering the division between the rich and the poor. There will be an exploration of possibilities of using ICT as an alternative technology for promoting development of the poor and the marginalized.

Interactive Communication and Net

Recent research in the field of communication has focused on the audience's role in the construction of meanings. While recognising some degree of reciprocity between encoding and decoding moments,

Hall argues that decoding (of the communicator) and encoding (of the audiences) are not identical [1980:136]. He [1980:130] points out that before the message can have an 'effect', it must be appropriated as a meaningful discourse and be meaningfully decoded. His approach recognises the role of the audiences before the message is constructed. As this decoding and encoding occurs in a particular social and cultural context, meanings are constructed through various other processes besides the communication process.

Jensen and Rosengren [1990:212] note that for cultural studies, the centre of communication research is located outside the media. For them the media are embedded, along with the audiences, in broad social and cultural practices. The communication process needs to be seen within the wider cultural and social context that the communicator and the audience share. McQuail [1983:87] classifies the approach as an 'interactive alternative' in which communication takes place within the social and cultural context, and the old forms of communication exist with the new media forms. In this approach meanings are mediated through a wide range of media and can arise from the context in which communication takes place. From such a perspective communication can best be understood as a cultural interaction between the communicator and the audience.

The book highlights the importance of analysing communication as a cultural interaction within a community. The need for such a study arises from the very rapid increase in the use of new forms of media (e.g. Internet) and the interaction among them. Plude [1994, 1999A] points out the interactive characteristics of media technology and its impact on the practices of communication. For her they present an inevitable challenge for the churches to rethink their passive perspectives and search for a participatory approach [Plude 1994:180&195]. She develops her interactive approach from looking at the technological impact on the communication pattern and organisational structures of society [1999A:5].

In the computer era these interactive patterns of communication certainly emerge, but, without a theological perspective the churches will find it difficult to engage in such interaction. Neuman [1991:105] proposes a similar approach which arises from technological interactivity. For him this produces a new grammar and cultural genre. Instead of studying the inevitable interactive patterns that technology presents to culture, it is necessary to look at how the cultural and religious patterns can make present and future communication interactive. By pointing out the dramatic changes television has caused in radio programming McLuhan [1993:54] notices an increasing interactivity among different types of media. These interactive characteristics mediate a wide range of meanings (social and religious) to the audience while also encouraging them to participate in their construction.

By recognising these technological and cultural developments, Christian communicators can become aware of the plurality of possible meanings. They can participate in the communication process in order to provide their own meanings of the gospel amidst of other meanings. If the churches wish to communicate the meanings of the gospel, then they have to begin their communication from where the audiences are. By sharing the audience's belief and worldview and by taking part in their communication process, the Christian communicator may help them to interact with the meaning of the gospel.

If the churches and their media institutions consider this approach, they can effectively share and participate in the communication process of a wider audience. In this approach the churches are invited to present their meanings among the wide range of meanings that are available to the audience. The interaction among the churches, communication and culture does not always result in desired effect. Yet the churches need to participate because this is one of the ways to engage in the audience's communication process and to interact with their belief and worldview. If the context demands such interaction, then the churches need to take immediate steps to become involved in the audience's communication process.

This interactive perspective is different from the dialogic approach that Dominic Emmanuel [1999], an Indian colleague, is trying to develop in his study of the Catholic churches' approach to communication. His main emphasis is on the inter-religious dialogue. His perspective on dialogue highlights the need for the broadcaster to consider each member of the audience as an equal, and to duly respect his/her opinion. He concludes that there is a need for a change in the broadcaster's attitude towards the audience who precedes the broadcaster in the dialogue [1999:170].

In contrast to this my study emphasises the need for the communicator to engage in the audience's process of communication. By sharing the audience's beliefs, their communicative forms3 and their worldview, the Christian communicator not only participates but also interacts with the audience. As participants together in the process, each learns from the other's experience of religion and culture. This cannot be achieved without a change in the perspective of the communicator towards the audience. It requires a reinterpretation of the theological basis which supports previous perspectives.

While interacting with the audience, Christian communicators are called to bear witness to the meanings of the gospel. Thus it is essential to present the meanings of the gospel message among a wide range of other meanings. In this sense the interactive approach broadens the dialogic approach by highlighting the roles of the communicator and the audience in the construction of meanings. It is essential to recognise 'we' as part of the community which is shared by 'them'. Communication needs to be seen and studied within the social and cultural context in which the communicator and the audience live. In this sense interactive communication is more effective than dialogic communication. Plude and Neuman pointed out that the new interactive media such as internet and video-conferencing try to change the concept of culture and communication.

The use of the interactive media by a large number of people leads to an interactive culture in which communicator and audience are both learners and participants. This evolution of the interactive culture poses serious challenges for Christian communication. Plude has highlighted the need for identifying an alternative theological basis in order to meet the demands that arise out of this cultural interactivity. Communication has interactive characteristics even though well enhanced by the interactive media.

Communication is interactive because there are a large variety of media and forms available to communicators. The audience uses each media to satisfy their own interests. The audiences also share certain beliefs, certain worldviews and certain forms of communication even before the communicator participates in such methods. Because of the diversity of beliefs, forms and worldviews the audiences are exposed to different types of religious, cultural and social meanings among themselves through the media. Christian communicators are called to present the gospel meanings among a wide range of meanings that are available to their audience. By engaging in the audiences' communication process and by sharing their beliefs, a Christian communicator can interact with the audience. People have developed a culture using internet technology to interact among them. In this culture of interaction people are able to engage with each other with an open mind at all levels of life with an acceptance of each other as they are.

In this culture of interaction among different communities, people began to look at the way the religion itself began to change. People from different religious communities use the internet for different purposes. Their religious faith is also being influenced by what they read and experience 'on the net'. Fabio Pasqualetti[127] argues that internet culture is challenging the global and local discrimination of the people. It has moved the users from their institutional affiliation of a religion to seekers of personal spirituality. The Internet users have changed their affiliation from believing traditions to the affiliation of meanings. They are seekers of subjective truth rather than objective truth. Their language is of a cultural language rather than of a technocratic language. Thus users of the internet form their own relationship with others. They search for God and for meanings in their own way. People post many blogs on God and websites.

When one makes search for God in the Google search engine,

it gives nearly 300 million links to websites. In the Google list of top most searched words include god television as the second most searched word[128]. In this sense one may argue that God is one of the most popular searched subjects on the internet People engage online to search for God in one way or the other. They wish to criticise or question or search for meanings or speak against the word 'god' and its use in the net. It is essential for a Christian communicator to consider engaging in such search for meanings by finding the audiences' interest, expectations and their needs.

High speed and exchange of information

In the interaction between human beings and the internet we need to identify the way the new technology differs from the old media technology. People often emphasize the high speed with which they can access enormous quantities of information. With telephone facilities we speak with other person or send faxes, which depend on the availability of the other person the other person being available at a particular time and in a particular place.

But here we can send any texts with nearly the speed of light to the other person. We write and receive the reply at high speed. It brings people closer in terms of sharing information, resources and opinions. Through email and e-groups people interact with each other at great speed (chat mails are banned in some countries). At times major decisions are taken and many programmes are broadcast using fast interactive services. The communicators feel the presence of the other in the net, but virtually. Using File Transfer Protocol, one can change any text of their website at any place in the world if one has the username and password of the site. In fact, I myself have access to my e-group from any part of the world and moderate the discussions.

Interactive internet

Mail that can be sent in seconds from one part of the world to another includes material of all kinds: information, pictures, educational material, entertainment programmes, and knowledge banks, along with junk mail. It is proving difficult to screen or control unwanted

165

or unsolicited information. One can 'post' useful information on the websites. Instantaneously, one can have access to any government or non-government website and send mail to ministers about any issue. Because both the communicator and receiver can play an alternative role of sending and receiving, a new culture has evolved in the use of the Internet which is interactive in its nature. In such an interactive culture the gap between sender and receiver is reduced[129]. This interactivity encourages people to participate and to interact with each other in an easy manner and enables them to establish a new democratic and equal relationship[130]. The interactivity between the communicators increases due to the convergence of technology.

Convergence

Convergence means to bring technologically all the analogical operations such as voice, visual text, picture, data, telephony, text exchange, music and networks, that were done using different instruments, mechanisms and means into a single digital computerized system[131]. Technological advancement has thus extended people's ability to communicate and interact with each other. ICT can bring together different types of the analogical communication forms into a single digital system so that through a single digital system multiple operations have become possible. Such digital systems are more accurate than analogue systems. This convergence technology may be cheaper than other technologies of broadcasting or networking or interaction.

To some extent investment and operation costs are comparatively cheaper than the old broadcasting systems of communication. Convergence is a technological phenomenon through which telephone, radio, television, VCRs Cameras, and so on, are becoming an integral function of the multimedia personal computers[132]. Recent examples of convergence are: web casting of radio and TV programming, using the internet for voice telephony, email and chat mails through digital TV decoders and Internet services provided to TV sets via Web TV and cable networks.

166

Convergence and hypertext

Chandrasekar Vallath [2000:33-47] notes that the technological convergence is leading a fully digital network, capable of carrying any type of information, be it text, data, voice or video. This network will integrate all forms of wire-line and wireless media, allowing anyone to communicate with anyone else, at anytime, or to access to an infinite, globally-dispersed array of information and entertainment sources. Digital Technology is able to transcend some of the limitations of previous technologies. 'In cyberspace we can construct worlds that have no connection with physical reality.' [Lochhead, 1997:68]. Because of the availability of hypertext the exploration of multiple paths is made possible according to one's own interest. In the culture of the internet, there is a choice for the users to continue to search as they wish through hypertexts. There is no 'start' and 'end' point in one's search. The person becomes a 'wandering self' in the wilderness of information.

Networking

Manuel Castells, in his UN report on ICT, defines a network as a set of inter-connected webs of relationships between people or organisations[133]. It may have a hierarchy but is without a centre. Networks are the appropriate organization for the relentless adaptation and the extreme flexibility that is required by an interconnected, global economy by changing economic demand and constantly innovating technology. Networks have always existed in human organisations but with the new information technology the network is centralized as well as decentralized. It can be co-ordinated without a centre. I recently started an e-forum for Interfaith Interaction.

The purpose of this forum is to enable different religions to understand each other. If anyone sends an email to this group it is automatically sent to all the members without the consent of the moderator (of course there is an option for moderating the forum should this become necessary). Instead of instructions, we have interactions. With the help of convergence technology such network has created an interactive culture at all levels of life (but not with those who do not have access to ICTs).

Digital world and virtual self

The Internet provides a self-identity for many users. The self-identity refers to an identity that an individual develops using emails, blogs, YouTube, chat, face book, e-groups and Websites through which he or she shares his or her own ideas, pictures and concepts with people around the world. Such identities are often used for making friendship or for networking or for sharing information with people around the world. It helps individuals to form their real and virtual self with an interaction through and with the net. The internet provides a multiplicity of the self – by projecting oneself into a web and seeing a self without reflecting the self itself [Turkle, 1997].

At times, there is a gap between the projected self and the real self – highlighting the diversity of the character of the person. The internet not only provides a space for social relations to occur, but provides the tools needed to enter that space [Jones, 1995]. The net creates a desire for more interaction and information about anything and everything in a virtual community and virtual presence. Digital technology removes us from the physical experience of the other and from contact with the physical reality. There is an absence of physical language [Lochhead, 1997].

On the net, one surfs. This passage from one point to the other on the net is reflected sometimes, in this style of life, as the passage from one experience to another, but in its more positive and mature form it is experienced as a culture of separation, of non-affiliation to something specific. It favours the spirit of search. It is a culture that offers and is generous, although it can also be a place of abuse and embezzlement [Jones, 1995]. The user often tends to float the 'self' with strange identities and establish relationship within what he or she has created about herself or himself. Elizabeth M. Reid [1991] describes 'the formation of a new society out of Internet Relay Chat (IRC)'[134]. The users of IRC choose to join a channel and select a 'nickname' under which to interact. The users have created a whole set of written symbols that enable them to express feelings in a written form.

The widespread use of 'emoticons' is strong indication of the important role affections have on the internet. Users of IRC often develop strong friendships with a sense of responsibility to their fellows, and regard their electronic world with a great deal of seriousness. By detaching the virtual self from the real self the user often finds it earlier to communicate the way he wanted to. With the use of nickname, emoticons and non-affiliation there is a communication without transfer of any meanings from one person to the other but the presence of both in the net is what matters.

The other side of the web

In this culture, there is also a problem of spreading a virtual hatred about other religious or minority communities. In this interactive culture, such 'hate' texts should be identified and raised with the people concerned – moderators, hosts, or countries – so that such texts will no longer be available to the public. Online pornography is one of the major problems and a large number of visitors to internet cafes identify this as one of their primary purposes for using the internet. This has evolved into a culture of viewing porn, and both parents and teachers need to instruct children to avoid it. The intruders are often big problems in many of our nets [Lochhead, 1997].

While recognizing the positive elements of internet culture, we need to identify the way the digital divide is made between the rich and the poor. The discrimination is not explicit in the net but the access is easier to an urbanized middle class youth than a rural poor person. I find it difficult to argue against the fact that technology has widened the division between rich and poor. Yet, while recognizing this critically I find that there is a possibility of engaging in a positive way, in mission and ecumenical activities through the Internet.

John Joshva Raja

Section B – Challenges for Theological Engagement

Christian institutions and the internet

There are a variety of ways that the Christian institutions often use the internet for their mission and ministry. They essentially provide a website which gives basic information about their institutions, doctrines and activities[135]. Many of them have their own websites[136] and use the website as a means to inform the public. One needs to appreciate some of those institutions who are developing these websites and exploring new ways of communicating to the people within and outside the church. There is a need to use the internet in a proactive manner in which media literacy and development information are provided through an interactive way.

Netizens and Christians

We need to identify the kind of information that is being sought by people on the internet. It means that our website should be open for people to add their suggestions. It should provide a space for people to ask questions, and indicate how and where netizens can meet up with the churches. Some of the mission organizations[137] and individuals provide information and publicity about their activities in order to raise support for them. They do not create any space for interaction of the people in the web. Some of them have even developed online donation forms[138]. They see the internet as an extension of their pulpit. There are not many websites that present the gospel in the people's own languages (regional languages) and also in an interactive way. This is one of the major tasks facing theologians today; to make the theological concepts and ideas accessible to local people in simple language.

Christian institutions

Theological seminaries also have their own websites, as do other faith-based organizations and Christian institutions[139]. They provide basic information about their institutions and courses that they offer[140].

170

I have begun to see that the institutions are not in a position to provide an interactive website because of their effect-centred approaches. Many of them are told that the internet is part of globalization and will widen the gap between the rich and the poor. They fear that some of the information available will destroy the values of the society, and those children, and other vulnerable people, might have access to pornography or other undesirable material. Some of this could be true, but not all use the internet for these purposes.

Even those who are against this technology in public use it when it becomes essential for them. Such views have made the Christian institutions sceptical about the use of technology. Also, an unwarranted fear is being created by a few, who do not know the technology or of ways to protect the system, that people can intrude into their computer using their websites and infect their computers with viruses. Frequently, institutions have no clear idea about the copyright of documents and files, and this creates more uncertainty and confusion in providing online archives and libraries to the web public.

Dr William Fore, one of my former colleagues at United Theological College, Bangalore, started a website for scholarly religious writings to make them available for those who may not able to buy them (www.ReligionOnline.org). He asked me whether I could help him in collecting files which I did for him[141]. The purpose was to provide a number of books and articles on the website for the sake of the students, and other researchers from the developing nations, who cannot afford to buy expensive books from the West. Today it is one of the topmost visited websites in the area of religion.

Some individuals use websites for different purposes which are often ecumenical and dialogical, though limited in service, and not representative of their churches' or institutions' views. Some are doing mission in the sense of social networking: development-oriented websites and religious dialogue programmes which are helpful to communities at large[142]. Among them only a few are aware of the advanced technological capabilities, and culture of interaction

John Joshva Raja

and communication which is rapidly developing through the net. This knowledge would have enabled them to be more interactive, effective and participatory in their mission.

A few have email lists for religious discussion groups and their members[143]. These groups are seen as interactive groups where people express their views freely. Some of them are related to theological issues and other religious studies. Even though these e-groups help us to organise major conferences, seminars, dialogue and other projects, I do not receive any financial support to run these groups. There are other e-groups who network Christians, Churches and NGOs from all over the world. We need to network with those who are engaged in this networking ministry[144]. Those who are interested in doing mission have not come to grasp the culture of the net as they accustomed to sending and receiving mail by air or sea which takes days and at times months.

The internet and challenges to theologies

There are various ways with which the churches can engage in the culture of the internet. In this context, they can consider engaging with the innovative technological means, the interactive way of communication and the virtual communities. The interactive culture of the internet, Convergent technology and networking communities posit many challenges to theological thinking. These are a few examples of the changing culture of communication and technology and their impact on the public lives of the people. Theologians have to evolve with new paradigms of theology that would enable them to engage in people's search for meanings of life and of God in the new emerging contexts and cultures. In this section, I highlight certain possibilities of taking part in the culture of the Internet and discover new ways of doing mission and ecumenism.

Theology and technology

The digital technology, culture, space and virtual communities of the internet have provided a platform for theologians to share their thoughts to the public. The internet, as mentioned above, has changed the way people communicate among themselves and thereby their culture and way of life. It has become interactive where the roles between sender and receiver are changing and the communication is in both directions. This is one of the major challenges for theological thinking because most of the churches and theological practices are accustomed to the old style of unidirectional communication.

Such practices and perspectives of communication are developed on the basis of theological paradigms in which God is seen as a permanent sender and the people as receivers. Even though some of the practices and perspectives are challenged and changed, it is not accepted by many Christian institutions and churches because the theological paradigms are not challenged radically in this regard. God is seen as a participant in human beings' search for meanings of life and of religion [Raja, 2000].

It is also essential on the part of the theologians to engage in the search for human beings' search for meanings in a similar way God has engaged. One of the best ways is to engage with individuals who are seeking meanings of the Gospel through the net. Through the websites one can establish contact with those who search for the meanings of God and of life. At times we have to establish different types of websites for Christians and non-Christians and also cater to individual's questions. Websites There is a need to develop websites for different audiences, such as websites that develop theology for a wider public. For children, Christian-education oriented animated theological narratives and games can be developed in regional language. Our websites should present theological concepts and other arguments in a simple manner to the readers.

The digital technology, culture, space and virtual communities of the internet provide e-space for people and for theologians. Through e-groups, e-communities and websites theologians can establish contact with those who are searching for the meanings of the gospel. The kind of pseudo-identity of the participants helps people to ask genuine questions and try to find answers from others in the groups. The content of the discussion will differ according to individual's or community's interest.

These discussions can be widened to search for meanings of life and of religions. One can also establish different groups or communities in order to initiate discussions on different topics. One may share expertise in areas such as counselling, ministerial guidance, lay training, and mission studies. With their help one may be able to provide online counselling or answer theological questions or clarify some questions about Christianity itself.

For theologians, there is also a need to clarify some of the misconceptions about theological formation and to promote media literacy through the internet. Such attempts would educate the public to read critically the messages of television evangelists. The charismatic and ultra-evangelical groups have recognized the potential power of the internet and have already started placing their video on demand, their sermons (both text and audio files) besides providing any other information that the users want.

Some of these groups provide misinformation about Christians and Christianity by emphasizing the number of converts through their mission, by popularising the prosperity gospel and by highlighting their links to certain fundamentalist Christians in other parts of the world[145]. This creates a bad image for Christianity, and Christians, and is one of the main reasons for attacks on churches. The primary task of theologians is to provide moderate information about theology to all people through the net. It is essential to make our doctrines, tradition and gospel clear to the net users. But such activities are not possible if we do communicate in a simple direct and plain ways. We need to use indirect methods and interactive ways to engage with the netizens in their search for meanings of God and of life.

We can no more share the gospel message directly which means an open invitation to people through the methods of evangelism.

Different age groups respond differently to the direct methods, many find it irrelevant and non-understandable in its content. It is possibly only to start with an indirect method such as encouraging them to ask questions about the young people's interest and talents. Some have started with questions about their favourite football team and so on. This provides a theological challenge for us to explore any indirect ways of communicating with those who engage in this kind of media. I try to explore whether the concept of indirect communication as used by Kierkegaard can be helpful in such context.

Kierkegaard's concept of Indirect Communication

A need for a theological basis for such an alternative approach has already been noted in my critical study of the churches' documents. This section will focus on the three essential aspects in Kierkegaard's understanding of communication that contribute to the theological basis. The first is his emphasis on the indirect communication of Christ to his hearers through a 'sign of contradiction'. He speaks of the impossibility of communicating Christ directly or objectively. The second is that the teacher or the communicator needs to begin from the place where the learner or audience23 is. The third point is his emphasis on the ethical issues in which the need for sharing higher virtues is emphasised.

While enabling the learners to choose certain values, the teacher learns together with them. In this process, the teacher shares his message in order to enable the learner to realise his capability and to choose to live with virtues. Kierkegaard's three aspects of communication arise out of his theological concern for communicating the Christian faith. These principles and their applications in constructing an alternative paradigm will be noted in this section.

A. Indirect Communication

In his book *Training in Christianity,* Kierkegaard [(1850) 1941A] argues that by his very nature Jesus did not directly communicate himself to the world, even to those closest to him. Jesus' message,

175

John Joshva Raja

Kierkegaard notes, was indirect and his followers were asked to believe in it. Indirect communication is defined as the opposite of direct communication that can be produced by the art of reduplicating communication24 [1941A:132]. This means there is no objective way of communicating Christ. Kierkegaard states: If someone says directly 'I am God; the father and I are one, this is direct communication. But if the person who says it, the communicator, is this individual human being... just like others, then this communication is not quite entirely direct.... that an individual human being should be God - whereas what he says is entirely direct. Because of the communicator, communication contains a contradiction, it becomes indirect communication [(1850) 1991:134].

In Kierkegaard's concept of indirect communication, Christ did not communicate directly to his followers through his teachings. Those who believe in Christ could recognise the 'sign of contradiction' in him. For Kierkegaard [1941A:124] Christ is a sign, 'a sign of contradiction'. A sign of contradiction is a sign which contains in itself a contradiction. To be a sign of contradiction is to be another thing which stands in opposition to what one immediately is [1941A:124-5]. Christ is a sign of contradiction because on the one hand he says he is one with the Father and on the other he is an ordinary human being like others and thus contradicts himself.

The sign of contradiction that Christ offered was offensive, and so, too, the indirect communication of a Christian will also offend [Arbaugh and Arbaugh1968:274]. For Kierkegaard Christ places before individuals a choice, and while they choose, Christ himself is revealed to them [1941A:98]. Kierkegaard points out that Christ called on people to accept him as Lord by accepting rejection and by allowing himself to be crucified. It is in the form of an irony that attempts to persuade a learner to choose to believe that Jesus is God.

The second point that Kierkegaard makes in defence of indirect communication is that it exists only for faith. He argues: He (Christ) is the paradox, the object of faith, existing only for faith. But all historical communication is communication of 'knowledge'; hence

176

from history one can learn nothing about Christ. History makes out Christ to be other than He truly is [1941A:28]. For Kierkegaard faith is thus the response to a communication that is indirect and direct communication of Christ is an impossibility. He argues that the 'proofs' in Scripture for Christ's divinity, such as his miracles and his resurrection from the dead, are recognised through faith. The miracle stories prove that all these conflict with reason and therefore are objects of faith [1941A:29].

In Kierkegaard's theological understanding God is seen as one who has given freedom of choice to human beings; the choice whether or not to believe in him. In Kierkegaard's argument God chooses to participate in communication with his people through indirect communication. It is God who wants to communicate indirectly27. It brings a new understanding to the relationship between God and human beings, as communication does not simply flow from God to people. God enters the human level of understanding and uses the form through which he attempts to share his love and care for his people. Kierkegaard was critical of the Christendom28 that has transformed the whole of Christianity into direct communication [1941A:97].

For Kierkegaard, until now, people taught Christianity as knowledge that has triumphed over actuality and reduplication [Pattison 1992:74-6]. By making it a dogmatic and apologetic confession, the act of communicating faith becomes merely an imparting of knowledge and information about God, and about Christ, which for Kierkegaard, is a misunderstanding of Christianity. These criticisms are relevant to the theological basis of the present churches' approach to Christian communication.

By adopting the instrumental approach, Christian communication is made the equivalent of imparting information and knowledge about God and Christ by the churches to the people through a medium. Swenson [1941:238] argues that for Kierkegaard the nature of faith is distinctive and cannot be transferred from one person to another as a complete package. To communicate the faith, with all the questions neatly resolved in a planned programme that would lead the recipient

John Joshva Raja

to a full Christian faith, is not possible. Direct communication is a distortion of the truth. The truth is distorted because the subjective is objectified [Weber 1993:66].

If Christian communication is direct, then it denies choice to the audience. In order to participate in the process of communication, churches need to realise the contradiction within the content of their message and the inability to objectively communicate the gospel. On the one hand they would claim the presence of God's saving act in and through the church, and on the other hand they contradict this by choosing the way of the cross which is 'a sign of contradiction'. By enabling the audience to interpret their beliefs and relate them to their context, the churches can indirectly bear witness to the gospel. The churches can bear witness to the gospel through their indirect involvement in the audience's communication process.

The primary task of Christian communication is to offend with a sign of contradiction and enable the audience to choose the meanings of the gospel. This theological basis emphasises the freedom of the audience, and their choice to believe, while attempting to persuade them to believe. This communication cannot be direct because what is communicated cannot be provided with evidence [Pattison 1992:85]. Rather the purpose of Christian communication is to share the gospel through story forms with the audience in such a way that they might interpret their beliefs and relate them to their context.

The audience is provided with a choice to believe and to stand alone before God. The emphasis on indirect communication involves recognition of the complexity in sharing the gospel. By recognising the complexities in the audience's communication process Christian communicators need to realise that they can communicate the gospel indirectly while being a witness to it. By realising these complexities, they can interact with the audience as Christ interacted with the people indirectly in the process of communication in biblical times.

B. Midwife's Role of the Communicator
In order to enter into a communicative act with his audience,

Christ interacted with his audience by constructing a sign, a sign of contradiction to catch their attention and to challenge them. Kierkegaard argues that Christ did not communicate directly29 and his direct utterances can serve, like the miracles, to make people attentive [1941:131]. This Christological understanding of Kierkegaard highlights the basic principles of an indirect communication in which communicator and audience are seen as participants (learners) in the search for meanings of the gospel. This aspect of indirect communication is explained with the help of the mid-wife imagery. Kierkegaard borrows the midwifery image (*maieutic)* from Plato and uses it in his *Fragments.* The imagery appears in the dialogues of Plato where Socrates says, "I am so far like the midwife that I cannot give birth to wisdom… all who are favoured by heaven make progress at a rate seems surprising to others as well as to themselves, although it is clear that they have never learned from me. The many admirable truths they bring to birth have been discovered by themselves from within" [Hamilton and Cairns 1963:853-5]. The midwife's role is to help a woman in the process of delivering her child; it is the woman who delivers the child by herself with the help of the midwife.

For Kierkegaard the communicator's role, like a midwife, is to help the learners (audiences) to become free and to stand by themselves in the process of believing and entering into the God-relationship [(1847) 1995:276-78]. The communicator remains anonymous in the process. Arbaugh and Arbaugh [1968:274] point out that for Kierkegaard the teacher, like a midwife, should deal with the learner where the learner is, in whatever state he or she may be, and seek to progress from that point towards the eternal. Both are concerned with seeking eternal truth.

The purpose of indirect communication is not to bring the learner into a relationship with the teacher but rather into relationship with God. In an essentially aesthetic age if the teacher is to start where the learner is the teacher must start with the aesthetic – even though the aesthetic is incapable of expressing religious truth [Pattison 1992:72]. Kierkegaard defines aesthetic as a pleasure, which is more than an art, and as personal interest which is more than sheer pleasure. With an aesthetic attitude one is caught up in various attractive experiences of the moment, in a state of immediacy which does not reach beyond itself [Arbaugh and Arbaugh 1968:64].

In his *Training in Christianity,* he identified the learner as being in the age of aesthetics. The teacher has to go to the place where the learner is in order to communicate with him or her indirectly [Kierkegaard 1941]. The age in which the clergy of the established churches are derided as 'poets' and in which the sort of character portrayed in Heiberg's *A Soul After Death,* is also considered as aesthetic [Pattison 1992:62]. The aesthetic age means the age in which the audience engages often in the cultural practices that give them pleasure and entertainment. To make communication effective, there is a need to recognise and share their audience's medium and aesthetic interests. The primary task of the Christian communicator must be to find and to start from the place where the audience is.

C. Choice and not Code

Kierkegaard is also concerned with moral life that for him is learnt by practising the art of such living, together with observing this art as demonstrated by noble examples. In *Either/Or* he uses another metaphor of a judge who views the aesthetical, the ethical and the religious as three great allies [1959(2):150]. The ethical will not annihilate the aesthetical but transfigure it. In this way Kierkegaard combines indirect communication, Christology, aesthetic and ethical aspects together in the teacher (communicator) and learner (audience) relationship. In combining these aspects of communication, he sets out the goal and the role of the Christian communicator.

The goal of Christian communication should be to bring the audience not into an intellectual acceptance but to a personal acceptance of spiritual and ethical principles through aesthetic characteristics. Kierkegaard notes, "The ethical must be communicated as an art, simply because everyone knows it. The object of communication is consequently not a knowledge but a realisation" [1967 (4): 272].

The learner needs to be prodded into self-awareness in relation to these principles by means of irony, pathos, and dialectic. Such communication addresses an individual, a constituent of the audience, to help him/her to see inwardly and then to choose these principles in the light of his/her God-relationship. It is to enable the individual to seek for himself/herself these principles in communication.

In Christian communication it is essential to recognise the fact that the task is to help audiences to realise their capability and to persuade them to see in themselves these virtues. Pattison argues that the ethical teacher is not concerned to put knowledge into the learner but to draw out from him his own capability or potentiality [1992:74]. Kierkegaard notes, "It may be that science can be pounded into a person, as far as aesthetic capability is concerned and even more so with the ethical, one has to pound out of him" [1967 (4): 285].

He explains this using an analogy in which he illustrates the difference between pounding the soldier out of the farm boy by recognising the capability in him and the soldier studying a manual of field tactics in order to become a farm boy. It means that ethical communication does not require any kind of knowledge [1967(1):285]. This argument supports the fact that the audience shares certain ethical and social values even before they are communicated to them. The task of the communicator is to make them to realise these values in them.

It is important to note that in Kierkegaard's argument about indirect communication, the communicator should make it clear that he is not the teacher since only God bestows eternal truth on each individual. It leads to an act of recognition on the part of the communicator that the learner somehow already possesses the truth. He must acknowledge that everyone stands absolutely alone in his relationship to God. Arbaugh and Arbaugh argue that in Kierkegaard's understanding this ethical communication develops a response, but does not seek to inform [1968:272-3]. They interpret Kierkegaard's ethical communication as to coax the ethical out of the individual because it already exists inside him or her. They also point out that in

John Joshva Raja

ethical and religious communication the teacher is himself a learner who benefits from the response of his pupil [1968:272-4].

This characteristic of ethical communication, as explained, recognises those religious and social meanings as already present in the audience, waiting to be shared and interpreted through the communication process. It has been noted that a wide range of competing meanings is available to the audience through various social processes. In these circumstances the best way to communicate the ethical meanings is to present them among a wide range of social values that are available to the audience. It is vital to relate those ethical principles to religious beliefs through the aesthetic aspect of communication. This would enable audiences to read themselves and might make them more aware of the God-relationship.

The communicator's role is not simply to pass on information but, rather to enable the audience to realise the meanings in themselves. Communicators merge into the communication process and lose their identity in order to enable learners to live aesthetically with higher virtues. The Christian communicator, according to Kierkegaard, should also fade into the background leaving the hearers standing solitary in the presence of God. For him, Christ willed to be incognito [1941A:127]. Kierkegaard points out that Christian communication must end in witnessing which he identifies as direct communication [1967(2):1957]. For him witnessing expresses in the recipient's life what he or she has come to believe [1967(1):659]. When the communicators become one with their communication, they become witnesses and are then no longer engaged in indirect communication.

D. Reflection

Kierkegaard's understanding substantially shifts the theological basis of communication. God chooses to communicate with his people indirectly and Christ demonstrated it. Christian communication involves sharing the good news of God's involvement in the human communication process. On the one hand Christian communication is direct in stating that God is with us (Immanuel), and on the other hand there is no evidence provided for such a claim except asking people to believe in it. By engaging in the audience's communication process and by bearing witness to this belief, then the Christian communicator can interact with the audience. This makes Christian communication indirect.

The basic purpose of the indirect communication should be to enable the audience to 'read' themselves and to enable them to stand-alone before God. Kierkegaard's idea of indirect communication expects a Christian communicator to start from where the audience is. Christian communicators need to participate in the communication process where the audience is participating, by sharing the medium and the format and also their faith, and their world-view with the audience. In this indirect communication, the audience's preferences and tastes need to be taken into consideration and also their qualities of aesthetic appreciation. In Christian communication it is vital to capture the attention of his audience and to start from where the people are. If people prefer an aesthetic form of communication, then the Christian communicator should use such forms in their communication.

Forrester [1993:72-3] in his article on the 'Media and Theology' argues that Christianity belongs within a powerful medium such as television rubbing shoulders alongside other images, stories and instruction. There is a need for Christian communicators to share with the audience their aesthetic qualities and understanding, and to interpret their faith in order to persuade them to have a direct communicative relationship with God.

There is a strong recognition here of the audience role in Christian communication which gives credence to this study in establishing that Jesus himself participated in such a process of communication through parables. Christ interacts with his audience through aesthetic means. This shifts the concept of Christian communication from a sender receiver model to a model based on indirect communication. In indirect communication the audience does not consist of passive receivers but of active participants, seeking and sharing meanings of eternal truth, and of life, together with the communicator. In Kierkegaard's understanding of ethical communication there is an emphasis on the ethical capability of the individual.

The Christian communicator learns together with the audience by participating in the process of communication. It is essential to enable these individuals to see in themselves their potential to acquire higher virtues. This, for Kierkegaard, is possible through faith. In order to enable these individuals to see inwardly, the aesthetic aspect of communication should be used. Thus aesthetic aspect, Christian faith and ethical communication are related to each other in Christian communication. These principles in Kierkegaard's indirect communication have helped this study to develop a new theological basis for Christian communication. By identifying these principles in Kierkegaard's concept of indirect communication, a theological basis for an alternative paradigm of Christian communication can be developed. However Kierkegaard understands of indirect communication needs to be extended into an interactive paradigm.

Interactive Method in Theology:

Kierkegaard identified the theological necessity for the communicator to begin from the state of the audience. He also points out that both the communicator and the audience are in the process of coming into a God relationship. The ethical aspect of this indirect communication, for Kierkegaard, works on choices in which Christian values are shared with aesthetic elements. This forms the theological basis in which God is seen as an effective participant in human communication.

In the study of Freire's pedagogy, it was pointed out that the communicator is a co-worker and participant in the investigation of knowledge. His emphasis on concentization is relevant in the interactive communication because communicator's action follows his or her reflection. The freedom to think critically and to choose an appropriate action is emphasised in Freire's work. In the process of Christian communication, there is an interaction between people's faith, medium and their social-cultural contexts. Kierkegaard identifies communication as an interactive process in which communicator and audience help each other in the construction of meanings. The interaction between the communicator and the audience is essential not only to maintain the ritual order of other social processes but also to make it an effective and growth-oriented process. This perspective sees communication as an 'interactive process' within the wider social and cultural context in which it occurs.

A. Interactive Process

In this study communication is seen as an interactive cultural process in which communicators and the audience participate in sharing and constructing social and religious meanings. The communicator engages in the audiences' process of communication in order to interact with them. This perspective highlights the role of the audiences in communication even before the message is communicated. Interaction occurs not only in interpersonal and group communication but also at the mass level. Interaction is understood as a process of "linkages between or among countless factors, each functioning conjointly, so that changes in any one set of forces affect the operation of all other processes to produce a unique and total effect" [Sereno & Mortensen 1970:8]. The communicator can often interact more effectively if he/she is aware of the audience's meaning making, beliefs and worldviews. Two scholars in the field of communication have identified the significance of this approach. They are McCoroskey [1968] and Schramm [1973] whose work is a study of what happens after the message is communicated. The important features of McCoroskey's model are i. Communication is a circular process. ii. There is a linkage of encoding and decoding to the process prior to (investigation process) and after communication (communication effects). Thus it views encoding and decoding in the social context [McCoroskey 1968:25]. The social and cultural contexts are changing and so are the technologies in the communication process. These changes make communication into an ongoing spiral process which tends to influence other social processes and in turn is being influenced by them.

Schramm's model also visualises communication as a circular process. It has no starting point and no end. It is really endless. It also conceives of decoding and encoding as activities maintained by sender and receiver [1973:31]. Hall's study on 'encoding' and 'decoding' which was noted earlier in the introduction is relevant here. Hall argues: Events can only be signified within the aural-visual forms of discourse; it is subject to all the complex formal 'rules' by which language signifies. To put it paradoxically, the event must become a 'story' before it can become a communicative event [1980:129]. They put the emphasis mainly the decoding of audiences. They hold the view that decoding takes place when the communicator has communicated his message. They do not recognise the complexities in the process of 'encoding' of the communicator and the 'decoding' of audiences. In the interactive perspective, the process of encoding and decoding does not occur in isolation but within a particular historical context.

Plude argues that the communication patterns that arise from the new interactive technologies, such as teleconferencing and computers, begin to empower individuals and groups. For her in these Interactive Strategic Alliances, authority seems to move from 'the top' to 'the grass roots' [1994:193]. Her conclusions are derived from the perspective of the contextual necessity which is created by the use of interactive technology in communication. My own research highlights the interactive characteristics of communication from a cultural and religious perspective. In this interactive approach the communicator is part of an ongoing process. The communicator has to share in the existing media, faith and cultural systems in order to participate in this process together with the audience. The audience already shares these aspects and is also influenced by other processes. By entering into this ongoing process the Christian communicator can come to the place where the audience is. With the support of Carey, Freire and

Kierkegaard, this study places the communicator and the audience as participants in the ongoing communication process that occurs within the framework of their social and cultural context.

This interactive perspective is particularly relevant to Christian communication because the communicator is called upon to present the meanings of the gospel in the midst of a wide range of meanings. It is necessary for the Christian communicator to begin from the place where the audience is. One of the best ways of communicating the gospel is to interact with the audience's belief, their means and forms of communication, and worldview. By interacting with the audience, the Christian communicator realises that he/she too is a learner and enables them to realise the choice that God provides for them. In Christian communication there is an interaction between the communicator's and the audience's faith and between the media and their social realities. Both are involved in sharing and exchanging their religious understandings and social insights through the media. As it occurs within the particular framework of a society, the communication process reflects and reinforces the world-views and cultural attitudes of the audience. Christian communicators need to be aware of the numerous means of communication that compete for attracting the audience's attention.

In this interactive perspective, Christian communication is seen as part of the cultural process in which the communicator and the audience engage to share and construct meanings that are relevant to their belief and to their social context. It is essential for the Christian communicator to engage in the audiences' communication process because they are exposed to a wide range of meanings (both religious and social) through various processes (e.g. political and cultural). The meanings of the gospel need to be presented effectively among the wide range of meanings using aesthetic characteristics and forms that are familiar to the audience. Examples of the aesthetic forms of communication are the television entertainment programmes such as

quiz programmes. In short Christian
communicators need to engage in what their audiences share as
part of the communication process, in order to interact with them and
to present the meanings of the gospel.

B. Biblical Basis

In many biblical narratives, God is shown as one who is engaged
in the human communication process in a variety of ways (Heb
1:1). God shares his care and love within the limits of human
understanding, and expresses this within the framework of our
communicating abilities. At times he conceded to people's demands
in order to show them that he participates in their communication
process. For example, when the Israelites demanded a King, Yahweh
allowed Samuel to anoint a king for them even though he spoke about
the dangers of monarchy (1Sam 8:1-22). Even though the monarchy
was seen as a rejection of Yahweh's rule, he is portrayed as one who
accepts the demands of Israelites32. While allowing them to have a
king, Samuel presents 'the ways of the king' in verse 11. Commenting
on this passage (1Sam 8:1-22), Klein [1983:79] notes that by granting
Israel a king despite their sins, Yahweh demonstrated his generosity
to his people. Yahweh's involvement in his people's lives is thus seen
as an interactive participation. In this interactive perspective, there
is consideration for the audience's understanding and participation
on the same level as that of the communicator that is God. God and
human beings participated in the communication process in which
participant tried to understand each other. God is shown as one who
continued to interact through the monarchical institution with his
people. This clearly highlights the interactive characteristics with
which some of the biblical narratives portray

God's participation

God's involvement is presented in such a way that human
beings are able to understand him within their limitations and share
his concern through their forms of communication with others.

In this understanding there is a consideration for human interest and aesthetic taste, through which the messages and meanings are shared and exchanged among the participants. Even though the understanding and means do not completely picture or portray God or his activities in an objective way, yet, they attempt to persuade people to experience God's involvement in their lives by participating in this process together with others. In New Testament times, Jesus interacted in a similar way with his disciples and with his hearers. Some of his parables portray the way in which Jesus interacted with his hearers by sharing their faith, by reflecting their realities and by using their forms of communication. By identifying such an interaction, this study attempts to develop it as a theological model of communication. It can be inferred from the context of the parables that many conflicting and complex beliefs were redefined through these parables. Even though this study tends to apply all the modern understanding of communication to the parables, it does not assume that Jesus was aware of these issues.

Section C -Interactive Model for the churches

Even before the communicators share their message the audiences are engaged in a variety of cultural interactions. Sometimes they participate and interact through the media and this can enhance their cultural interactions. In the South Indian context the members of the village community used to gather together at the centre of the village for folk programmes. It has already been noted that cinema theatres replaced these centres but this meant that the people had to go to city centres to see a film in a theatre. The video cassette player brought the people back to the centre of the village and enhanced the cultural interaction among them. In this cultural interaction people gather together at the centre of the village during the night in order to participate in this ritual practice of gathering, join with other people in viewing the film and discuss the programme afterwards. In order to engage in such interaction, a communicator has to identify this

John Joshva Raja

ritual process of the village communities and participate in their interactive communication process. This perspective of interactive communication is different from the perspective that is developed from the interactive media by some of the scholars in the field of communication. Plude and Neuman pointed out that the new interactive media such as internet and video-conferencing try to change the concept of culture and communication.

The use of the interactive media by a large number of people leads to an interactive culture in which communicator and audience are both learners and participants. This evolution of the interactive culture poses serious challenges for Christian communication. Plude has highlighted the need for identifying an alternative theological basis in order to meet the demands that arise out of this cultural interactivity. Communication is interactive because there are a large variety of media and forms available to communicators. The audience uses each media to satisfy their own interests. The audiences also share certain beliefs, certain worldviews and certain forms of communication even before the communicator participates in such methods. Because of the diversity of beliefs, forms and worldviews the audiences are exposed to different types of religious, cultural and social meanings among themselves through the media. Christian communicators are called to present the gospel meanings among a wide range of meanings that are available to their audience. By engaging in the audiences' communication process and by sharing their beliefs, a Christian communicator can interact with the audience.

This perspective is particularly relevant for Christian communication in South India. Christian communication points towards engaging in a process where the communicator and the audience share and interpret their beliefs and worldviews. In order to interact with the audience the Christian communicator begins from where the audience is and continues to engage in the audience's process of communication until he or she chooses to stand alone before

God. Theologically God is portrayed in the Biblical narratives as one who continues to interact with his people despite their limitations. By recognising this perspective Christian communicators in India, particularly in Tirunelveli, should continue to engage in the Christian and non-Christian audience's communication process and present the meanings of the gospel indirectly.

Interactive characteristics of communication are important because they demand a Christian communicator to work with other communicators who have similar interests. These characteristics give importance to the equal status of the participants, particularly the communicator and the audience. In order to enable the churches to give importance to these characteristics of communication, a theological and hermeneutic basis for such perspective must be developed. By identifying such characteristics in the teachings of Jesus, this study argues that the churches should consider the importance of this interactive aspect of communication. This study has developed this interactive perspective by bringing together Carey's ritual view, Freire's liberation view and Kierkegaard's concept of indirect communication. The study of the parables and the video cassette ministry has shown that the principles of an interactive perspective would certainly enable Christian communicators to share and to participate in the construction of the gospel meanings together with their audiences.

Serving the Christian community

The internet provides a possibility of doing ministry and mission in a new way while raising new questions as well. For example the churches can cater for their members' needs by conducting online worship (for differently-able people or for those who cannot come to the church). Theologians need to think about the virtual body of Christ and explore the possibilities of serving virtual members. This also raises questions about the possibilities of replacing the presence of the community of members with the virtual presence.

John Joshva Raja

The virtual worshipping community can be present along with the real worshipping community rather than replacing one by the other. The virtual body of Christ can be universally present but, at times, members may hide their identity due to compulsion in their contexts.

More than five billion users are online everyday using the technology for various purposes[146]. One of the most popularly searched words is 'God' as said before and nearly 400 million websites are providing information about God in one way or the other (Google Search). In many cases, e-communities are created for discussions on the themes related to God. Theologians can also host discussion groups. Ministers can provide information about their members in the website and place their liturgies, sermons and devotional material for others to read. Today the segmentation of individuals and communities is increasingly becoming a reality in which the church can play a role by bringing people together virtually and thus establish a virtual Kingdom of God. We also need to place Christian educational material in our website so that it can be useful for others. For those who cannot come to the church the virtual online worship might enable them to worship along with others, even though virtual worship does not replace real worship. Then the theologians' task would be to bring separated people together in order to establish a community of God where broken relationships are restored and communities reconciled. One can make use of the modern technology of convergence such as video on demand or online radio that cost less than analogical broadcasting or even the narrowcasting.

New liturgies, attractive sermons and new songs can be placed on the churches' website so that others can use them. Many children are taught to use computers in their schools and when they come home they often play with computers and so we must also produce interactive animated Bible stories and value-oriented songs and stories and place them in our websites for children. As most of these are available in English we need to consider producing more of these in regional languages.

Training leaders

Internet technology provides a new hermeneutic space for interpreting the gospel and a new way of engaging with others in their search for meanings. The technology brings together the visuals, speech, and text and links them in a virtual convergent format. Theologians need to explore the **virtual hermeneutics** through which the e-gospel can be interpreted to the context of virtual communities using this convergent technology. Even theological online classes may be conducted through such technology to promote lay training. As McLuhan says, the medium shapes the message; internet technology shapes and interprets the gospel in a virtual way. Such interpretative characteristics of convergent technology need to be studied extensively. It needs to take into account the expectations of the virtual audience and their methods of searching for God.

We need to train lay pastors and theologians to use theological resources on the internet. Our approach to mission in using the internet should not divide us; rather we need to be in a position to accept other types of mission and evangelism along with our present efforts to carry out God's work. Seminaries should encourage pastors to continue their education using Distance Online Learning (DOL) which can be used for reducing the gap between theological seminaries and the public. Some of the misconceptions about the theological seminaries can also be reduced by making the theologies available to the public through the internet. It is also essential for ministers and other church leaders to become literate and critical users of the internet and provide useful and educative information about it. Children and teens are the regular users of internet which brings them a wide range of information and interaction on the one hand and violent, hatred and offensive material besides pornographic contents. Such inappropriate contents are available and accessible easily that it can affect many people psychologically, religiously and socially. Some become addicted to online gambling, web based games and other internet contents that can easily affect school education or even change behaviour radically. Pastors have to learn the technology and

193

sensitise the children and parents to become aware of the issues in the internet. The churches can also consider linking up with educative, entertaining and engaging websites and promote them among their members. It is essential to promote media literacy as part and parcel of the ministry of the church through which such awareness, education and positive engagement can be promoted among the members and also among non-members.

It is essential to promote internet literacy as part of general media literacy which means to make the net users critical readers (literate) of the net. In order to enable the children to use the net properly the churches need to provide interesting, creative and imaginative websites. The websites should be interactive and open ended to encourage asking questions of anyone, and the content should be edutainment and info-tainment oriented so that the young people, and others, will visit and use our websites. If such is the case we will certainly be able to transcend our doctrinal, denominational, religious and national boundaries and do a holistic mission and foster ecumenism on the internet. Training pastors and missionaries theologically online will be easily achieved and needs to be explored.

Ecumenical net

The internet also provides new radical spaces where people would find it easy to discuss some issues that they may not be able to do otherwise. There is a need to recognize local connectivity while the global relationship cannot be neglected in this new e-space. It is a challenge for theologians to recognize the importance of localness while interacting with global communities. This leads to a 'Theology of Global Space' which tends to maintain the tension between two concerned spaces, local as well as global. It is essential to engage in the internet to network people, organizations and churches who share different interests. Ecunet[147] is an example which brings together the churches ecumenically. The theologians' task is to network and serve churches and also to initiate an ecumenical dialogue among the churches.

Many ecumenical issues can be discussed and an ecumenical union might happen first at virtual level, and then in reality. This could also help us to transcend our borders and establish relationships with each other. Even online video conferencing facilities are possible to make congregations speak to each other in any language with a proper translator. Networking can also help the churches to work together via the Internet and to learn from each other the way to do mission. Even constructing a website together with another church needs courage and is a radical step. When the net helps people to break their barriers of language and border, then it can also help to eliminate the denominational barriers and other types of blocks that normally hinder us from coming close to one another.

Theologians often have looked critically at Information Technology (IT) and were very sceptical in using it for their communication. They argue that IT divides people and thus widens the gap between the rich and the poor. In a post-industrial world where knowledge and information has become a commodity IT has become part of the neo-liberal ideologies. Theologians have the option of two views, either to support it or to reject it. In this chapter, a third way is suggested in which the theologians are invited to interpret the technology for life rather than life for technology. For example many people tend to depend on technology often that they tend to replace their relationship with their mediated communication through internet, SMS or phone. Due to the demand from the pornography market, children's lives are abused and displayed in the websites and thus their lives are used as commodity to be displayed, bought and sold in the media market.

Such values are against the basic human values which need to be addressed and challenged. They are particularly against the values of the Gospel which emphasises the importance of life above everything in this world (Matthew 16:26). An alternative model of development and thereby an alternative way of using information technology should be explored.

For theologians it is essential to look for alternatives both theologically and theoretically in terms of developing human life. Theologians have done a lot of deconstruction work on the texts and thereby enabled their students to critically engage with the religious narratives. It is also essential that we reconstruct alternatives and make them available to the communities. The basic concepts of life and of God need to be reworked so that people might relate themselves with God and also with their neighbours. This is the way the alternative communities would be developed where both individual freedom and communitarian values will be nourished. Information technology has provided such challenges to theological thinking, some of which are identified in the above chapter. While we take the new technology and the new media seriously we need to focus on the traditional ways and methods of communication to engage in search for meanings with the audience.

5 Dancing for change – Community Media as an alternative

Introduction

The churches and theological colleges have a tradition of using any media as extension of their pulpit or intellectual rhetoric information to the audience. When our students were trained to become aware of HIV/AIDS issues they wished to do something in promoting such awareness to the slum dwellers in Bangalore. We took it up as a challenge and went to slums and provided information to the public, except a few children all elders left when we began to talk about HIV/AIDS. We felt it as our failures to communicate the awareness. But then our students began to write messages in the tune of popular cinema songs and with dances we performed such messages to the public in the slum areas. Then people came in large numbers to enjoy the dance, drama and also began to listen to our messages. We asked questions at the end to know whether they got our messages and realised that such an alternative method of communication worked very well. Some of our students began to develop concepts, ideas and practices in alternative methods and means of communication not only in the street theatres but also in magazines and radio messages which became popular among some local Christian radio stations in India. This raises many questions for theologians which are: Can church media become alternative media? What were the alternative media used by Jesus or Early Christians? Can theologians/minister dance in the church? How theology can respond to the challenges to counter media for liberation, development, renewal, reform and transformation of our communities and of the churches.

After studying various mass media and also new technologies and their relevance in theological thinking, it becomes essential for one to complete the book with alternative and community media.

John Joshva Raja

The concept of alternative and community media is often explained in binary opposition to the main stream media – horizontal/vertical; communication/information; democratic/authoritarian; dialogic/ monologue [Huesca and Dervin: 1994]. The community media are those media that play an alternative role in a community, often as alternative to the mass media, as means for social change, as agents of harmony and peace, as voice of the voiceless, as liberating agents and as counter, participatory and democratic methods. The community media are accessible, affordable and available to the people easily. This community media can include posters, pictures, charts, banners, postcards, letters, books, articles, journals, magazines, Internet, and so on that are shared by a community at local level and possibly a virtual community at global level. The community media do not refer to only to the above media or to the use of these media but points to the way these media are used as alternatives to the main stream media and also to bring about social changes in the society.

Community media act as alternative media and also as people's media in a way they are shared and operated by the communities themselves in different ways. The community media should be dialogic, intercultural, local and interpreting universal/global, promoting values, represents the voice of the voiceless and accept people as they are, engage in people search for meanings. Alternative views need to be aired. The Democratization of the media is the purpose of the community communication. The alternative media provide diverse views and perspectives alongside the mass media and do not try to replace the mass media. By developing community media one may be able to join in and enhance the development process of the community and also interact and explore new paradigms of community in terms of their relationship, understanding, structure and development. Through the community, members share these media; the individuals are allowed to express their own freedom and are encouraged to be in negotiation with the community values and development. This is what a reconstruction of the deconstructed media is[148]. It is essential to move beyond deconstruction that is to highlight the meanings and voices of the margins that were never heard before to a reconstruction. Reconstruction means to re-establish the centre at the margins where all would share their resources with others and might recognize each others' dignity. Thus the process leads the community where religion, race, caste, class or colour may not be barriers in relationship, communication and understanding. This is an ideal situation where multiple meta-narratives would coexist, nourish and correct each other continuously.

In spite of the differences, people would negotiate their values and worldviews while trying to accommodate and wrestle with the others'. Community media provide a platform for such practices where those who were at the margins would become the centre where all are welcome to express their views, values and opinions. They are supposed to facilitate the community members to move towards this ideal situation though it is not possible to bring this ideal situation into a reality. Rather, it is a freedom to negotiate between communities and individuals. Community media enable people to negotiate between technological determinism and social construction and find new local ways of interacting among themselves and also with other communities [Rheindorf, [149]2005].

The concept and practice of community media evolve from South America as the people use such media in their communicative and liberative experience. Originally the concept was countering the mass media that did not provide any space for the communities and to replace them with alternative media. Because of the profit motives the public sphere was not only shrinking but also was used by a few powerful people and the rich to manipulate the masses. In order to counter such activities, the alternative media activities were initiated that were trying to use grassroots and traditional types of media.

Community media have evolved from such types of alternative media considering not only traditional but also the new media technology that are shared by the community and thus engage in such media to bring about the social changes among them. In this way, community media are pragmatic in their approach and practice. This raises a number of issues for theological thinking. Particularly the concept of community within the churches and Christian communities which is often narrow and does not include other members in terms of working for social changes except through a Non-Governmental Organization or for doing charity work among them. This challenges our theological thinking of community as well as our perspective and theology of community communication. Our theology of community communication is challenged because theology will also be constructed from the people's experience, participation and interaction with the theological communities. Theological thinking becomes a community's struggle in the search for meanings of God and of life. It is no more kept within the campus of a theological college or seminary rather it is a communitarian theology that negotiates between community and individuals. This is not to go in a popular way of doing theology rather challenging, participating and having interaction with people's faith and their life struggles.

Theological paradigms are often provided by theologians and the public remain receivers. There needs to be theological public sphere where even the public can contribute, participate and challenge in order to bring about changes in their communities. With these questions in mind, I highlight the issues related to alternative media, community media and also traditional formats and then reflect on the issues related to theological paradigms. In the following sections, I will start with the alternative media, critiquing the old paradigms of communication and then highlight the characteristics of community media. Alternative and community media are not to replace the mainstream media – mass media. Rather they are to express the voices of the margins among the communities as well as among the public. They also attempt to correct and challenge the mass media, provide a platform for correcting themselves, and develop a public sphere for an open dialogue and interaction not necessarily on the basis of enlightenment values [Habermas] but on the values that are negotiated, applicable and acceptable to the members of the community.

Then the next section will focus on how the perspectives of communication within the community need to be changed in order to develop community media. To develop the concept of community media I use two examples from two different genres of communication – one is traditional art and another one new media. I use dance and drama as metaphors of bringing about changes in the perspectives on communication and thus make an attempt to enable people to see the importance of establishing community media. I also explore whether using information technology one can provide a platform for the communities to interact and develop themselves. IT is often blamed as a medium that divides people into rich and poor. The third section explores the possibilities of using information technology for community participation and development and thus finds whether this technology can be used as community media. This raises questions for theological thinking particularly the concept of community and the perspective of interaction with other meanings and truths that are in tension within communities. These issues will be discussed in the following sections.

Section 1 - Communicating towards an alternative community

A universal model or theory for communication is impossible, as the understanding of alternative community itself would vary from country to country. What is being analysed here in this section is one of the ways of studying a social process. It is also constrained within a particular context and history. These variables need to be kept in mind so that a blind generalization is not made in the minds of the readers. One of the oldest communication models is that if a person knows how to solve a particular issue or problem he or she must inform others of the way he solved that particular problem. This is what is called diffusion model.

If there are projects that would bring about social changes and so development among communities, then information about such projects should reach them. In order to reach out to the people, all

201

the available means and formats of communication should be used. In this sense radio, television and computers need to be used in order to bring about this information to the people. According to Everet Rogers in order to diffuse such information, it is essential to transfer technological innovations from development agencies to their clients and to create an appetite for change through raising a climate for modernisation among the members of the public [1986:49]. The modernization perspective identifies the problem within the developing nations.

Diffusion theory works on the model of Sender-Message-Channel-Receiver (SMCR) and implies that communication can make an impact on the lives of people. White [1982:30] argues that the above model perceives media information as 'an all powerful panacea for problems of human and socio-economic development'. In this way of thinking communication is primarily understood as transfer of information and so the emphasis is on the effects. Communication is important in spreading awareness of new possibilities and practices and should enable developers to bring about an attitude change in the audience that in turn would lead them towards a developed and civilized society. Such a society is identified as a real humanity according to modernity. In such a society, media and communication, according to Schramm [1964:263] should perform at least three functions which are that of: watchdogs, policy makers, and teachers for change and modernisation. For McLuhan, however, any technology gradually creates a totally new human environment and so the medium is the message [1994].

Modernization is understood as a process of moving away from the traditional way of life towards a westernized or modernized society which is supposed to be a developed way of life [Jan Servaes, 1993:24-39]. The communication technology becomes a means of communication to spread awareness of new possibilities and practices that would bring about changes in communities. From the perspective of modernity an alternative humanity is possible with the help of transfer of communication technology to spread the new innovative concepts and thus to bring about changes in society. In this sense, alternative community means to become like a developed and modernized country. Since the western countries are supposed to be developed countries the alternative humanity would refer to being 'westernized'. The changes are brought from outside and the local culture and social structure is seen as a block for development or changes. The external changes are brought by transferring capital, expertise and technology from the developed countries to developing countries. In terms of information, communication technology modernization means to promote awareness of innovative concepts through the present computer technology or through other microprocessor units.

Such a change in society will be a disaster because it will make sure that the underdeveloped countries remain dependent on those developed countries in terms of technology and expertise. Thus the underdeveloped country will remain underdeveloped by depending on others and thus the causes of underdevelopment remains external to the countries [Servaes, 1993:26]. This creates a culture of dependency. The dependency perspective identifies the problem of underdevelopment outside the developing nations.

The third model that exists is the participatory model of development which stresses the importance of cultural identity of local communities and of democratization and participation at all levels – international, local and individual. Listening to what the others say, respecting the counterpart's attitude, and having mutual trust are essential. Participation involves the more equitable sharing of both political and economic power, which often decreases the advantage of certain groups [Servaes 1993:30]. The change involves the redistribution of power. Thus the development of social trust precedes task trust.

There is a need for another way of communication which favours multiplicity, smallness of scale, locality, and de-institutionalization, interchange of sender-receiver roles and horizontality of communication links at all levels of society [D. McQuail, 1983:97].

John Joshva Raja

In this process meanings are shared and exchanged rather than transmitted or transferred from one person to the other. In Freire's approach, the oppressed should be treated as fully human subjects in any political process which implies dialogical communication. The second UNESCO approach is about self-management, access and participation. Access refers to the opportunities available to the public to choose varied and relevant programs and to have a means of feedback to transmit its reactions and demands to production organisations. Participation includes involvement of the public in the production process and also in the management and planning of communication systems. Self management means that the public exercises the power of decision-making within communication enterprises and is also fully involved in the formulation of communication policies and plans. Such types of participatory communication are possibly only if people have access to simple media technologies; if they are able to share and use such media and also if such media are sustainable technologically and economically. Such media are often identified as alternative media or community media. The following section will highlight the need for such media in any context to bring about social changes.

Mass media and neglected communities

The main stream media or the mass media are often controlled by a few professionals, by the rich owners, by the government, by the political groups or even by the industries or by the powerful people in any society. This main stream media often shape the public notion and attitude of the people and thus generate an impact on them either directly or indirectly. Though mass media cannot be blamed directly for many issues and problems in the society, they do not provide much space for any harmony or peace. At times, they themselves become source of misunderstanding between communities and thus create a culture of ignorance and confrontation. To a certain extent mass media or main stream media have failed in bringing harmony and reconciliation between communities and individuals.

At times, they do not provide access to critical intellectuals nor ordinary people but to the professionals, rich, political leaders, powerful, government officials. The mass media are no more a critique of the structures that discriminate people and are corrupted because their support come from them. They do not provide success stories of harmony and reconciliation. They often misrepresent and misinterpret reality. They are powerful and influential in terms of carrying information, spreading rumours, providing entertainment and persuading the consumers through advertisements.

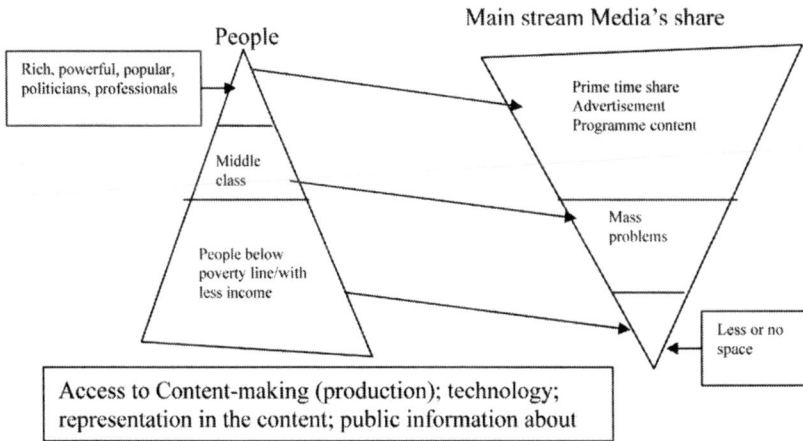

The picture shown above highlights the problems of the main stream media or mass media. To some extent, the mass media have become part and parcel of the hegemonic forces in the society though not all of them. Of course, there are other ways and means through which the homogenising forces are at work and so mass media alone cannot be blamed. Also mass media articulates certain values and ideologies that often create ignorance among the public about the minorities and others within the communities.

The narratives of the mass media are often constructed in favour of the ruling class, powerful institutions or of the rich ones and so on. There is no space in the public for the poor, minorities, women and people at the margins to express their views and opinions. There are not many means that would challenge the dominant values and ideologies that are projected by the mass media. Many of the other types of communication and other means are taken over by the mass media for the sake of increasing audience and thus add their revenue through advertisements. People tend to resist at times a few social processes or ideologies or tendencies that divide them or create conflicts among them. A few communities have resisted modernization and globalization and thus at times campaigned against the mass media which enhances such processes.

The mass media and other types of professional media began to widen the gap between the audiences and the communicators. There was less scope for a collective production in the media industries. The main purpose of the mass media industries was to make profit by widening the audience and turning them into consumers. The mass media increasingly move away from the everyday life and the ordinary needs of people [Enzenberger: 1976].

These issues and problems give rise to the need for an alternative methods and means of communication. Many of the concepts of alternative media are influenced by Gramscian notion of counter hegemony such as working class newspapers [Allen 1985; Sparks 1985]. The alternative media did work against the process of modernization, the process of hegemony and thus became alternative to the mass media. In the alternative media, there was an attempt to democratize, provide more interactivity between audiences and producers and thus reduce the gap between them.

In some alternative media, the audiences themselves become the producers. In the alternative media the role of audience is more important than the communicator. It is the people who communicate among themselves. Thus the alternative media favour 'horizontal patterns of interaction' where participation and interaction are key concepts' [McQuail, 1994:132]. The alternative media also includes artistic and literary media (video, music, creative writing) as well as to the newer cultural forms such as Zines and hybrid forms of electronic communication. The new technology of convergence and diverse cultural knowledge have brought out the heteroglossic (multi voiced) text [Gauntlett, 1996:91]. This gave raise to heterogeneity of the content and meanings in the alternative media.

Alternative Media for me means to enable people to have an access to the media to express their views, for which purpose it should be available in their place and also the access should be affordable for the people. Alternative media should enable people to participate and express their concerns among themselves and with others. Multiplicity of channels cannot be called as alternative media and also not all small media can become an alternative of kind. Though one of the major concerns of alternative media is development of the people but it is not the only concern.

We need alternative media for a number of reasons as stated above

- to challenge and counter some of the forces of hegemony
- to provide a media space for those who cannot express or communicate otherwise
- to bring out the alternative perspectives to the public
- to enable the audience to express themselves and thus reduce the gap between the communicators and the audience
- to provide access of new technology and its communication to the people/public
- to encourage different cultural groups and practices to share their views
- to bring people closer to realities which are often misrepresented in the mass media
- to train people to use alternative media for social change and harmony
- to popularize the stories of harmony through the alternative media.

Having highlighted the need for the alternative media, at this point I would like to define alternative media. This will help us to identify and recognize the different means and the methods of communication that can be used as alternative in our mission and ministry of the church.

Alternative media – a brief background

In the 1960s, alternative media was understood in the Latin American region as an indispensable weapon of political communication to combat disinformation and misinformation to connect members, and to spread political ideology [WACC, 2001:1]. Such media were basically inspired by the Leninist and Gramscian writings about the role of intellectuals in revolutionary action and thus were identified as revolutionary media. Taking Paulo Freire's concept of alternative communication some of the Catholic churches have supported and developed grassroots communication among poor communities [Huesca, 1995; O'Connor 1989]. In the 1970s, the oppressive regimes that tended to asphyxiate the public sphere and to let the state and the market rule made the people at the margins find their own alternative means of communication [Kucinski, 1991:xiii]. The alternative media operated as a corrective mechanism to the main stream media and became the expression of the public [Rodrigues, 1986:55-56]. It brought the alternatives and the oppositional groups together [Raymond Williams, 1977:55-56].

From the mid-eighties alternative media began to play the role of defending democracy and constitutional liberties in Latin America and thus represented the politically excluded interests [Atwood and McAnany, 1986; Reyes Matta, 1983; Simpson Grinberg, 1986]. The changes came in the form of freedom of speech and freedom of the press and thus moved away from the left-wing and Catholic organisations to different range of organizations and groups such as women's, indigenous, ethnic, youth and marginalized [Lopez Vigil, 1994]. However, at the same time the alternative media suffered major setbacks in terms of political demobilization, apathy and the ebbing of social movements and also economic problems. But the alternative media emerged with recognition of multiple publics as counter media. They tried to recognise the people's cultural and political differences and thus create counter-discourses of representative voices of different groups rather than merely an oppositional voice (Fraser, 1992:123).

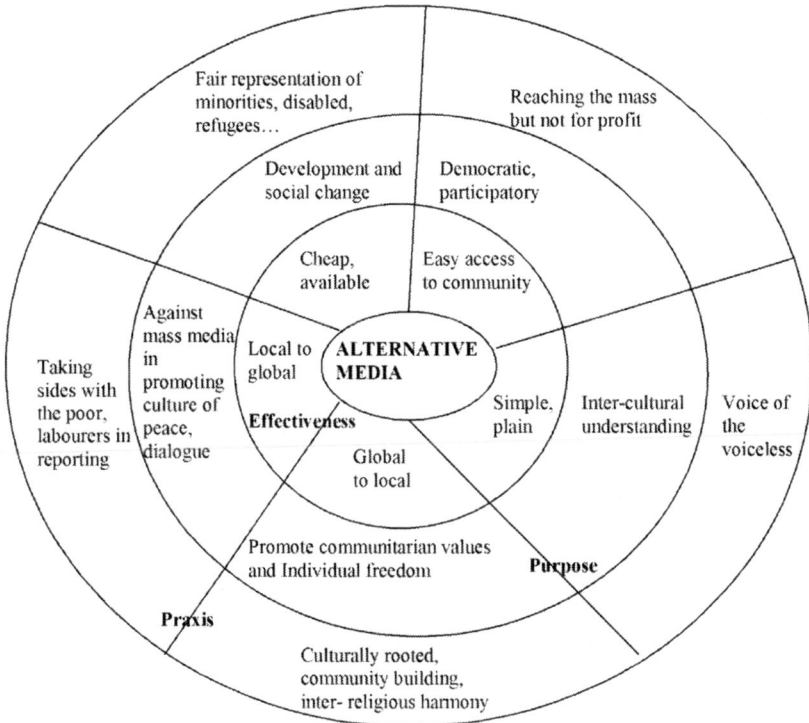

Alternative media are also known by various names such as: Radical Media [Downing, 2001]; Citizens' Media [Rodriguez, 2001]; People's Media, Community Media, Grassroots Media or Democratic Media. Having been used in diverse ways the alternative media have emerged as one of the recently discussed subjects and practice among many of the communication scholars and practitioners. We need to study the need for having such media in bringing peace and harmony in the society.

What are alternative media?

Though there is a significant difference between alternative use of media and alternative media as Traber has pointed out [1985:1], here, the two words include both the media that are alternatives to the main stream media and also the main stream media or any other media that are used to express the alternative voices and concerns that are not otherwise expressed in the main stream media. The concept of alternative media is often explained in binary opposition to the main stream media – horizontal/vertical; communication/information; democratic/authoritarian; dialogic/ monologic [Huesca and Dervin, 1994]. The alternative media are those media that play an alternative role in a community, often as alternative to the mass media, as means for social change, as agents of harmony and peace, as voice of the voiceless, as liberating agents and as counter, participatory and democratic methods. The alternative media are accessible, affordable and available to the people. An alternative medium does not necessarily meet all the aspects of the definition stated above. It means one medium can be called an alternative medium if it meets a few characteristics of being an alternative.

This media can include posters, pictures, charts, banners, postcards, letters, books, articles, journals, magazines, Internet, emails, websites, community radio, radio FM, cable television, local channels, street theatre, popular theatre, drama, songs, hymns, Bhajans (a genre of Indian songs), music, puppets, flannel graphs, dances, folk art, folk dances, house visits, interpersonal communication, Bible study groups, fellowship groups, cell phones, SMS, telephone, newspapers, pamphlets, tracts, newsletters, videocassettes, VCRs, VCDs, DVDs, players, computers, PowerPoint presentations, handouts, preaching, microphone, loud speakers, worship and teaching. Alternative media do not refer to only to the above media or to the use of these media but points to the way these media are used as alternatives to the main stream media and also to bring about social changes in the society.

Alternative media should be dialogic, intercultural, local and interpreting universal/global values, entertaining but not becoming pure entertainment, secular, democratized, development-oriented, promoting dignity of people, highlighting justice and ecological concerns, remaining cheap, both top-down and bottom-up. It should be culturally rooted, non-profiting but not at loss, promoting a culture of peace, reconciliation and harmony, involving people's participation, identifying and highlighting alternative issues, not merely accepting the public opinion but challenging them as well, entering the public or community's space or creating such a space, highlighting public concerns as well as minorities' concerns, simple and not professionally communicated, representing the voice of the voiceless and accepting people as they are. In short, it should engage in people's search for meanings.

Alternative views need to be aired. The democratization of the media is the purpose of the alternative communication. An increase in the number of channels also is part and parcel of the alternative methods of communication. It involves a technological transfer for those who do not have access and who cannot afford and for this reason it is also essential to subsidize the transmission of communication networks and means. It should challenge the monopoly of a few media moguls who try to take over the whole process of mass communication. The alternative media provides diverse views and perspectives alongside the mass media and does not try to replace the mass media.

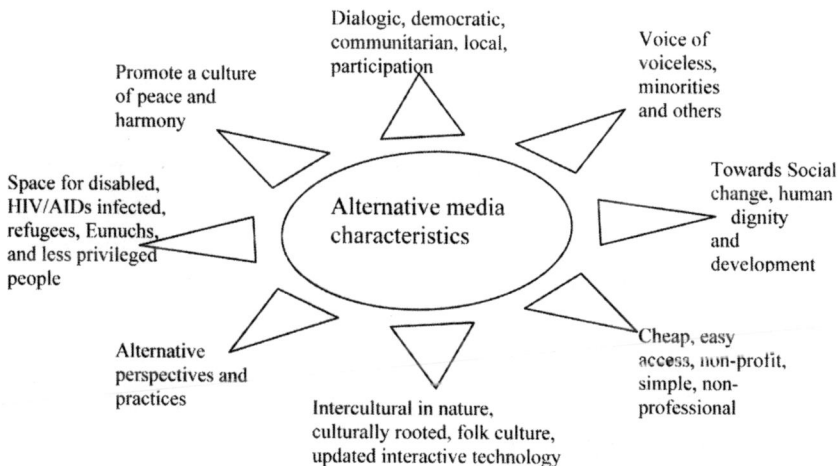

Alternative media also should take into account the concerns of ecology, refugees, disabled people and women. It should become the means of connecting and relating people at the margins and people at the centre. Alternative media refers to simple, small media such as folk types of communication to the highest technology. This enables the media to become community media by providing access to all the community members. It takes the content beyond our interests and thus breaks the regular barriers.

The above diagram describes the characteristics of the alternative media and thus establishes their role in a society. Such alternative media can help us in bringing harmony and peace among different communities in India. I will also now try to point out in what ways such media can be used by the church in enhancing peace. At times, alternative media may seem too idealistic to put into practice, as it calls for the participation of all in the content making and decision making processes that arise. Media have their own limitations. Alternative media can also become mass media such as Globe Television in South America or alternative media can become counter media in certain contexts for developing and liberating people from their poverty and from their undignified status. This is one of the reasons that the scholars and practitioners began to use the terms such as 'community media' and also 'citizens media'. There are numbers of examples of alternative community media such as *Indymedia, Malaysiakini, OurMedia group* and other media groups. For example the release of photos through the internet about the Tiananmen Square event in China brought criticism from all over the world and thus restricted the government from further actions.

Community media
Oepen [1993] argues that Community Communication (**COM COM**) can bridge the gap between these two models – transmission (this view defines communication in terms of sending, receiving) and participatory (this view defines communication in terms of sharing,

participating and interacting). Community communication is defined as a process of horizontal and vertical social interaction and networking through media regularly produced, managed and controlled by or in a close co-operation with people at the community level and at other levels of society of countervailing powers. It accepts the role of small as well as mass media in bringing about changes in society while recognizing the difficulties. It also recognizes the cultural diversity of development. Community communication promotes long term structural change, and allows participatory instruments of project monitoring[150]. In it technology is incorporated into the community communication in such a way that it is used for their daily life communication. This enables the system to be maintained, upgraded and used for other purposes such as disaster warning and so on. This is where many of the problems faced by the use of Information Communication Technology for rural development are addressed.

This changes the old paradigm of 'Media Technology driven Life' to 'Life driven Media Technology'. It means the human life should not be determined by the media and technological invention, use and advancement. In short, media technology should not determine the way of life of people. Rather, media technology should be shaped in order to serve our lives, our culture and our way of life. This means media technology should enable people to recognize each other's dignity, to share their resources and to participate in the decision making process. This in turn refers to a community-shaping media technology rather than media technology-shaping community. This concept differs from the technological determinism and social shaping of technology (social constructionist view). This means technological determinism is being challenged in the way that our lives need not be adjusted for the technology that we have adopted. Rather information technology can be adopted and invented in such a way that serves our life and even during the time of natural disasters prior public warning through such technologies can minimize the damages for human lives and property.

In this way, technology can save our lives by enhancing our

present ways of community communication rather than we shape our lives according to the technology. It must involve an open holistic approach in the praxis. The community at local, regional and national level needs to be strengthened while changes should be brought about by the internal as well as external factors. While the members of the community have equal chances in the decision making process they also need to work towards the community's growth.

Community media in the Church

At present the available media in the churches in India are slide projectors, preaching, Christian education, worship, access to schools, fellowship groups, street theatre, posters, loud speakers, pamphlets, tracts, notice-boards, notices, websites, VCDs, DVDs, Video, VCRs, television, house-visits, computers, internet, puppets, flannel boards, postcards, Christmas cards, cards, magazines, newspapers, festival programmes, radio and special training programs and seminars. Most of them are cheap, available and accessible to the members of the churches. Some of them are simple types of communication (interpersonal or fellowship group communications) or small media such as loud speakers, post cards and so on. The question is whether the churches should try to introduce new media as alternative media or make alternative use of the available media. The churches can make alternative use of the available media that are cheap and participatory in characteristics while exploring the possibilities of new alternative media. It is essential that present available media be made use of as alternative media if their characteristics are embedded into the content and practice.

Not only have the churches used their available media as alternative media but also Christian institutions, para-Church and mission organizations. Christians who own or run the media should also be encouraged and trained in introducing, engaging or using the alternative media in their mission. Even those who work in other media can be encouraged to challenge the present practices of the media and thus provide alternative practices of the mass or other media. The new media such as internet and digital cable local transmissions need expertise and training for the community members to make them an alternative at a wider level.

To start with there is a need for making alternative use of the present available church or other media to carry out Christ's mission. In order to do this not only our perspective of the communication process has to change but our theological understanding of mission and use of such media for mission needs to undergo radical changes. In this sense before we think about the alternative media we may have to consider an alternative mission of the church. There are two questions that arise here – how to convert our present media into an alternative media that can be used for mission and how to develop new alternative methods of communication to widen our scope of doing mission. Having identified the possibilities of using the existing media as community media within the church, I will use two examples to highlight developing concepts, practices and theology of community media. The first example is identified from the traditional media such as dance and drama and the second example is from the new media – the internet. With these two examples there will be a struggle to identify whether community media can really be a possibility to implement and in what ways they provide challenges to theological communities.

Section 2 - Example 1: drama and dance as community media

Drama and Dance are art forms of communication. Such art forms provide challenges to hermeneutics. They use oral, written and visual methods of communication to interpret stories and texts to people. Among Christians, such art forms are often neglected due to a negative attitude to the body and or a suspicion of anything that is not entirely based on the word. Though there are examples in the Bible celebrating God's liberation through dance and enactment of God's drama in the lives of his people, such art forms are often rejected, mainly by Protestant traditions, as part of worship or homiletics. There are many programmes and events in which children dance or perform in plays. Nevertheless, due to a few missionaries' attitude towards local dance forms both from a high cultural genre and folk traditions there is neither acceptance nor a systematic use of these art forms in Christian ministry and mission. This article attempts to highlight the importance of looking at these art forms in terms of doing hermeneutics for communities. This may provide a new perspective and theological insights for engaging in the dance and drama of God in our lives.

Drama and dance are two forms of artistic performances and are traditionally preserved by folk and professional cultural groups. Different parts of the world have different traditions of dance and drama. From Polynesian islands to Ireland, in South America and African countries people use varieties of dance and dramatic events to promote values, to engage in community events and to celebrate their religious, cultural and social festivities. Indians are proud of the traditional and systematic dances ranging from Poikuthirai Attam (horse dance in South India), Moatsu (community dance in Nagaland), to Bharathanatyam (professional dance). The dances in India vary from high culture dances such as Bharathnatyam (which is basically Brahminized); popular dance (film dance); village dances such as Poikal Kuthiraiyattam; folk dances such as Santali Tribal dances to Mass culture dance Sivarathri dances in Gujarat. Some of them have inbuilt values of participation, and are communitarian whereas some have enabled the dominant ideologies to flourish.

While I do not support the misuse of dances (certain professional dances in India) to dominate others I do consider the possibility of using such art forms for communicating, building relationship and establishing understanding between individuals, communities and nations. Dance and drama in our culture enables us to hold dialogue within our selves, within our culture and between different religious and cultural groups in the world of imagination and entertainment.

Thereby people are introduced to new concepts, values and ideologies indirectly and are challenged within the imaginative world. This is what Jesus does while narrating parables and also by acting dramatically at times as when he enacted humility by washing the disciples' feet.

The Bible and dance

The Bible provides a very good platform for us to understand dance and drama. People danced whenever they realized the presence or performance of God in their lives. Dance is a celebration of life together with God. When God liberated his people, they celebrated their liberation with dance (Judges 11.34; Ex. 15.20—21; 1 Sam 18.6–7). Miriam led the dance after the Israelites were liberated from their enemies (Exodus 15.20–21). When David brought the Ark of the Lord to the Temple at Jerusalem, he danced celebrating the presence of God in their midst (2 Samuel 6.14–23). People were invited to praise God by singing and dancing (Psalm 149 and 150). When Israel was to be restored there would be dancing (Jeremiah 31.4, 13). There were a number of dramatic performances in the Bible that reveals God's loving presence in our midst and God's continued communicative action amidst us. Jesus' miracles can be seen as dramatic performances of God's presence in our midst which goes well with proclamation of the gospel. The return of the repentant son in Luke 15 leads to celebration with dance in the house of the Father. Dancing is so common that in passages alluding to rejoicing without specific mention of dancing, it can be assumed that dance is implied [Gagne, 1984:24]. Although seemingly restrictive in these early centuries, the church actually created a context for new flowerings of social, theatrical and religious dance [Fallon and Wolbers, 1982:9]. Early Christian church fathers have referred to dance in their writings – particularly on Palm Sundays[151].

Dance is a celebration of our lives together with God. When God restores his relationship with his people, there is a celebration which is followed by dance. When people are returning to God and restore their relationship with others, there was also dance as part of

217

celebration. When God is present in worship, we celebrate our lives together with God. This celebration cannot be completed without the shout of joy, songs of praise and dancing in adoration of God. Drama is an enactment or demonstration of celebration of our lives in God. If it is the celebration of our lives with God then it is dialogic within one's self and with God and also with others. Dance and drama are the performances where God and human beings can meet each other. They bring happiness and joy in both of us. Happiness and joy are expressed through dance: the joy which comes from liberation or victory, arrival of an important person or an important occasion or season.

As we have seen above, in the Bible dance adds important visual elements to the worship. Dance is the fulfilment of prophesy (Jeremiah 31.4). Dance is the sign of restoration of the people of God (2 Samuel 6.13–14). Dance as sanctification of the people of God (1 Thessalonians 5.23; Romans 8.23)[152]. In Indian tradition, Gods are seen as the creators and experts in Dances (Natya). Siva is seen as the Lord of dance. Dance is the religious expression and experience of God. Even among the early Christians in India, disciples of Thomas, there was dance as part of the worship and celebration of their lives in God [Barboza, 1990[153]]. In a way, it can be argued that dance has been an integral part of Christian worship during biblical times and among the early Christians and early Indian Christians too.

Bhakthi and dance

Dance is an expression of Bhakthi in us. Dance refers to the movement of the body according to music and is related to emotions and spirituality. Spirituality cannot be expressed without the movement of the body. That is why people raise their hands, kneel down, sing loudly, move their bodies one way or the other while they dance. Dance demonstrates a story of the presence of God or God's involvement in human history where the movement goes with emotions in the story and thus enables the audience to imagine the presence of God more accurately within the self.

Thus the self identifies with the dancer and leads one to relate oneself with God and enables one to feel God's presence through the dance. Such performances are the meeting point not only for God and human beings but also for the human beings among themselves and also with other beings. The message of the gospel is to build a true relationship with God and also with one's neighbour. The true relationship consists in sharing our resources, giving human dignity, building communities, interacting with others, nourishing cultures and trusting each other. Dance and Drama thus bring about harmony within oneself, with God and with others too. Dance is an expression of our spirituality in which God can be realized both by the performer as well as by the audience. In a way, dance is a spiritual expression and joyful celebration of God's presence in one's body movements[154].

We all participate in the dances and drama of God which he has given as life. But when it is professionally performed, we recognize ourselves by identifying with the characters and thus participate in making meanings of our lives and also of God together with others. The theology of drama and dances disturbs our minds from time to time when dualist views come to dialogue and interact but the transition from one to the other view is easily possible. This reminds us of Theo-dramatik of Balthazar where he insisted that the God reveals himself as beauty and engages with human beings in a dramatic manner. In the series of *Theo-Drama* 'the good' has been the focus. In his book on *Theo-Drama* Volume V Balthasar [1998] maintains that it is in the theatre that man attempts a kind of transcendence to observe and to judge his own truth about himself. He sees the phenomenon of theatre as a source of fruitfulness for theological reflection on the cosmic drama that involves earth and heaven.

As Balthasar [1994, Vol 4] expresses in the conclusion to his preface: here we discern the unity of 'glory' and the 'dramatic'. God's glory, as it appears in the world supremely in Christ is not something static that could be observed by a neutral investigator. It manifests itself only through the personal involvement whereby God himself comes forth to do battle and is both victor and vanquished. If this glory is to come within our range at all, an analogous initiative is called for on our part. Revelation is a battlefield. Those who do battle on it can only be believers and theologians, provided they have equipped themselves with the whole armour of God (Eph 6.11) [Balthasar, 1994][155]. Such concepts also disturb us to think of God as one who acts in multiple ways including as negation to life in order to bring human beings closer to him. Such concepts can be recognised in Indian concept of 'Leela' of God that characterizes some of God's intervention in the Biblical stories. Leela means God enacts drama with human beings in order to show that he is powerful and human beings have to depend on him for their existence and thus have to relate themselves with God. Theo-drama enables us to recognise God as one who wants to engage with human beings dramatically. Such dramatic involvement of God depends on imagination and aesthetic characteristics. God at times engages with human beings as a dynamic and active God who dramatizes their liberation, sustenance, protection and destruction. Drama becomes an essential enactment of God through which he breaks down his own rules and norms in order to establish contact with human beings and wants them to establish relationship with him in turn. It is also essential to recognize the fact that such narratives of God enable us to relate to each other and thus guide us to relate with other Christians through dance and also with other faith seekers. We need to see how far dancing can be used for building relationship among communities of different denominations and different religions.

Dancing for ecumenism

Having pointed out the role of dance in the Bible and also in the Indian Tradition, I would like to argue that dance and drama can bring about changes in our community. They have intrinsic characteristics of building relationship, bringing about understanding, engaging everyone, challenging the old systems and thus bringing about changes within the community. It enables people to deconstruct as well as reconstruct the new community. I would like to use an example from a north eastern state of India where the majority people are Christians. In this state there are different Christian denominations living side by side.

In Nagaland, when different congregations come together in the churches they are at times told not to communicate with members from other churches. Denominations are conscious of their differences and make sure their members do not have contact, establish relationships and understand the other churches. While such segregations are happening inside the church the people in Nagaland come together through folk dances during festivals regardless of their denominations and other difference. During the festival of Moatsu all the Ao Naga communities come together and dance together regardless of their denominations and other distinctions. Thus Dance and Drama does create a new dialogical and communicative space for the people to come and share meanings of life and meanings of God. Dance and drama can bring the people together when religions may divide them.

One of the Seminaries in South India (United Theological College, Bangalore) has been running Street Theatre programme (Therukoothu) to promote awareness about HIV/AIDS. The street theatre performance has become so popular that regardless of religion and caste people come together and join in performing along with our students. The Therukoothu includes dance, drama in local folk art forms that are enjoyed by the public in villages and urban slums. This is another example where dance and drama can be used for promoting awareness, understanding and development networks among communities. Drama and dance provide us a visual and intercultural hermeneutics that enables us to bridge, have dialogue with, critique (constructively), address and liberate communities of God. In this article, I will stress the importance of changing our perspectives and attitude and thus recognise the ways in which such art forms can be used in ministry and mission of the churches today.

John Joshva Raja

Dancing for dialogue:

To bring about social changes among communities dialogue is the best means to engage with each other. Dialogue enables people to establish contact, relationship and understanding between two or more persons or communities involved. Dance and drama can be seen as arts of dialogue, cross-cultural interactions, critical hermeneutics, spiritual expression and a sharing of good news. One needs to go beyond the question of indigenising through dance and drama to embodying the Kingdom values and relating the gospel to the context. It means dance and drama can create a space of interpretations and expositions of the Gospel. It can also provide a space where a dialogue between the audience, interpreter and the ultimate truth (God) can also happen. Drama and dance provide a sphere where people not only identify or relate themselves with the characters displayed but also where their eyes and ears are open to critical imagination.

Their regular thinking and values are reiterated, confirmed yet also challenged. Such a critical engagement leads to reconstruction of their accepted systems and values at times. This sphere also provides a space for tension and interaction between communitarian values and individual freedom. Habermas' vision [1991] for a public critical sphere can be rediscovered through drama and dance. Dance and Drama can create a public space for critical dialogue through which people become aware of the enlightenment values but also engage actively in critical dialogue with others. For this it is not only the dancer who gets involved but also the participants, possible mostly in the folk or traditional village dances where mass participation is appreciated. Folk dances and theatres are known for their participatory characteristics and critical dialogic involvement of people [Appavoo, 1986]. In the mass mediated shrinking public space, dance and drama can enable us to rediscover the dialogic engagement of communication in public. Dance and drama may enable people to transcend their cultural and racial limitations and thus enable them to widen their spectrum of communication.

To bring about the social change, we need to deconstruct the structure, language and history of particular communities. Only political, cultural and social critics can enable the communities to look at their issues and problems systematically. We need courageous critics of the society today among communities. Dramatists and dancers can also play the role of 'organic intellectuals' [Gramsci, 1971; 1973] who engage in a constructive criticism of the social structures and practices that are oppressive and homogenizing in nature. They can also create an alternative space for communicating the silenced voices and enabling people to break their culture of silence. Thus dance and drama performances can be prophetic in constructing a world of imagination in which the audiences are brought in and their old concepts and ideologies challenged. It is essential that critical engagement of the dancers is recognized rather than substantiating, upholding and reiterating the existing structure and their barriers such as caste, regionalism and religious fanaticism. Dance and drama will certainly enable people to be in touch with any other person or community. By prophetically involving in society we can bring about changes – not only social but also cultural in the mindset of the people. This will enable us to establish the Kingdom of God through such activities in terms of its values and principles.

There is a need to change the perspectives on Communication so that there might be a change in praxis. Theological bases for the dances were highlighted in the previous sections. In the following sections a shift in the concept of perspective on communication as a process, spectators and also characters of the story performed through dance or drama. There is a shift in the paradigm because ultimately the audience are given much more importance and accordingly one chooses to be in the media industry. In this paradigm shift a communicator becomes a communi-actor and spectator becomes spec-actor where the perspective and the practice changes in order enable the communication as an action of community and of relationship rather than an individual's possession. Friedland [2001:358-391] argues a community is necessary for the democratic function of the society and dialogic communication is essential for the reproduction of community. The concept of communi-action becomes relevant to the context of media saturated society because we translate our act of communication into an act of community.

Communi-action

In and through dance and drama in order to build authentic Christian communicators we need to communi-act while we communicate. **Communi-action** is an extension of communication, by which I mean we translate our communication into a community action. Dance is an act of communication. Communication is an action in relationship. Without the other being present and recognised there is no communication. Dance being an act of communication is also a public performance and can be performed in relationship. It can create Hetroglossia through imagination and relationship. Dance and drama are acts that can happen only in relationship with the other. They can build communities and nourish culture.

Dance and drama lead to action in community. Such action brings about changes because it is not an act of an individual artist and his or her own concerns and not merely for the gratification of the audience rather such act takes the audiences and their context seriously. Thus drama and dance convert the communication into an act for social change through the changed perspectives and attitude. These acts cannot occur in isolation or just for earning money; rather being a public act becomes praxis for building relationship and enriching people's culture. It is the praxis of Christian communication through which we not only build communities but also transform them into authentic Christian Communities. We do not communicate anything that is not public in characteristics and thus drama and dance are public in characteristics and have an obligation to serve the public as well [Bhaktin, 1982]. As performers, writers and directors we need to take this suggestion seriously, in order to translate our concepts into action the primary task is to hold a negotiation between entertainment, imagination, artistic performance, values or awareness, audiences' ability to understand and act.

Imagination, aesthetics and visual Hermeneutics

The performance itself becomes an imaginative act which was not anticipated and is as spontaneous as Jesus' washing of his disciples' feet. Sudden twists and turns are given in the story so that the horizon of the past and the horizon of the present merge into a visual hermeneutic where old thoughts and old paradigms are challenged whenever needed. Communi-actors need to realize the fact that they are recognized as community persons who speak or dance or perform that which belongs to the communities. Thus they hold the dialogic action with the community and its concerns. In this manner whatever the concerns and language of the community they are not only used as they are but also are acted out for the sake of interpreting and promoting faith and values. One of my graduate students Mr Charles, who was a magician, used magic not only for entertainment but also for value and faith formation of children in his locality. His graduate thesis focussed on this theme in which he realised that both value formation and entertainment can interpret the other through magic. He has been promoting such activities professionally as a pastor among the churches in South India.

Spect-actors:

Every dance and drama needs to develop this concept of communi-action which is also a participation of the audiences in which spectators would become spect-actors. Augusto Boal's [1982] model of enabling the spect-actors to complete the drama is an example for us to make the audience imagine and act out an alternative in the story and in the reality. Bridging the separation between actor (the one who acts) and spectator (the one who observes but is not permitted to intervene in the theatrical situation), the Theatre of the Oppressed' is practised by 'spect-actors' who have the opportunity to both act and observe, and who engage in self-empowering processes of dialogue that help foster critical thinking. The theatrical act is thus experienced as conscious intervention, as a rehearsal for social action rooted in a collective analysis of shared problems[156].

Members of the audience are urged to intervene by stopping the action, coming on stage to replace actors, and enacting their own ideas. The drama is not completed by the actors alone but by the spectators who engage in completing the drama. In this way the liberative praxis is not only communicated but also acted out. Thus characters in the performances become care-actors who care for the betterment of the society at large and for building authentic Christian communities in India. The enactment of drama is completed by the audiences and then is continued in their real context as well. Such a model raises a lot of questions in our way of worship and preaching. Dance and Drama may help us to attempt new options of open ended stories or drama where people can imagine further and complete the story or engage partly at the end to complete the story in the way they want. Such acts can also be attempted in preaching, in which the audience can be asked to complete the sermon or prayer and so on.

Drama for Social Change

What therefore needs to be dramatically changed in our performances? We need to bring about change of attitudes, perspectives, practices towards Dance and drama among Christian communities. It is only by promoting Kingdom values through dance and drama that we can bring about changes among the Christian communities. We need to move from entertaining and interpreting to action oriented and open ended drama and dance. Once we attempt to promote and activate human value among the audiences then dance and drama will have their own places in the people's mind and culture. The dialogic and participatory characteristics of any dance and drama enable the performers to bring about not only changes but also reinforce and educate the audience with values.

We need to promote Christian Education through this dance and drama. The concept of using theatre for education should be cherished.

One of my friends and colleague in Kerala, Rev Dr George Kuruvilla [2002] has argued in his book 'From Street Theatre to Eucharist' that these characteristics can be brought into our worship. Thus worship will become indigenized and nourished with such characteristics of the street theatre.

Dancing for Change:
Recently NGO's such as Association for Rural Poor and a few other churches tried to explore using drama to provide counselling for the Tsunami affected people. Folk drama genres are also used for promoting awareness about various issues such as foeticide in Dharmapuri (Tamil Nadu, India) and HIV/AIDs awareness in other communities. In the case of folk dance (such as dances among Santhalis and Oraons – Tribal communities in North India) and drama (Therukoothu and Pavaikoothu – Tamil genres of street and puppet theatres) people have readily participated. This is an inexpensive form and brings people into theatre; and theatre to people with concepts and ideas. Participation and critical interaction are common in such dances. Other professional dances too can communicate systematically such deep values. Drama can provide counselling, can enhance dialogue between different cultural and religious groups, can widen interaction within communities and can motivate people for bringing about changes and development in churches and societies.

Breaking Dualism
Drama and Dance create in us imagination, create a world of entertainment, and create a world where we allow ourselves to wander freely. Suddenly we are given a shock or surprise using different artistic techniques such as tragedy, colour, odour, joy, beauty and so on. A dualistic world is created and then transition between these dual worlds is easily possible because it is an imagined world. Thus light is contrasted with darkness, evil with good, beauty with ugly, holy with unholy, white with black, clean with uncleanness, and lies with truth. Thus stereotypical images of the opposite are often broken in

the imaginary world of dance and drama. Suddenly the characters change in such a way that the transition between these dual worlds happens to communicate a message through tragedy, success, joy or gladness. This enables the characters to challenge and reinterpret the stereotypical perceptions of oneself and of other. Such actions enable all our receptive senses to receive exactly what is communicated through every movement of the characters and the story. Because of imagination and entertainment people do not mind being challenged and are thus guided to change their exploitative and discriminatory structure and behaviour.

Drama-activate

To bring about changes the dramatist has to become drama-activist where the audiences are activated to imagine an alternative world which otherwise is difficult to construct. Taking the imaginary world to the real world is the process of drama-activism where the performer and the performance activate the spectator to join and complete the drama. This creates an inescapable and imaginary world where inescapable realities and values are shared in the midst of wide ranging realities and values. Drama and dance do not eliminate or condemn other values but evaluate them. They present their own values amidst other values as an inescapable system of thought.

In the churches today we need to bring about many changes to make them an authentic Christian community. An ecumenical, dialogical and liberative community has to be imagined, envisioned, performed and enacted both by the artists as well as by the spectators. Our worship itself is a drama and our life is a dance. If so, in what way can we incorporate the value and faith interpreting dances and drama into our worship and preaching practices? Besides these conventional practices we need to use such methods for our mission, Christian ministry, and street performances and so on. Through such activities we will build an authentic Christian community through which we will also bring other communities closer to God in our ministry and mission. The church needs to rediscover its tradition of dance and drama in their ministry and mission. As I highlighted these art forms have communicative, dialogic and liberative elements within themselves and can create space for people to change themselves and others. As the Christian mission is increasingly becoming people-centred, the cultural art forms that would enable us to worship God better and establish relationship with others should be included in doing mission and also ministry within and outside the churches.

Theological Response
Community media provide challenges for the theological community in various ways. First of all the concept of community is being challenged and secondly the social changes that are suggested are also challenging. According to Paul's term the church is the body of Christ. The body of Christ has the community of believers. The question arises whether the other can also be seen as part of the community in terms of transformation and social change. The social change means changes that are brought both by community and by individuals to find a negotiated space for Individual freedom and community values. The changes are brought to eliminate poverty, to make people respect the other's dignity and to involve them in the decision making process of the community. These changes also provide a space for expressing and listening to different views within the community. It provides a challenge for the understanding of the body of Christ for theologians.

Unless the body of Christ becomes inclusive of all, the genuine social change may not happen where each religious group would see themselves only as community. The Christians should transcend their community in order to bring about social change among all the community members regardless of their religion, caste and race which means all the members are seen as the body of Christ regardless of their identities. Dance and Drama can enable us to see through their construction of imaginary realities of performances. Christians do not see the other as the other but as part of their own community and thus serve them as catalysts to bring about social change. Often Christians see the other in terms of doing mission and service in order to attract them towards the Gospel. We need to go beyond this idea of relating ourselves to other only through mission, rather they should also be seen as part of the Body of Christ and thus we are part of a 'community' in general that needs to work together to liberate, to educate and to develop each other within the community. It is not only the idea of community but also there are theological issues related to using traditional media such as dance and drama.

A few missionaries who brought Christianity along with modernity as part of their missions created a negative attitude towards traditional media such as folk dances and cultural drama, particularly in developing countries. Though people cannot stop dancing during the worship services in Kenya, the Western mission theologies that often depend on establishing an 'order' in the context of 'disorder', do find dance and drama as part of disorderly culture of the local people [Kabasele Lumbala, 1995]. But for such contexts in Kenya, dance and drama are part of their cultural order that they cannot eliminate as 'disorder'. In a way without dance and drama there is no religious expression found either in the Bible or in the early Christian communities. They are also part of every cultural expression. Only by bringing them into our act of worship and sharing we may be able to transcend the barriers that we have erected through our religion and ideologies.

Section 2 - Example 2: Information Technology as Community Media

After highlighting the importance of traditional media in the community communication using the examples of drama and dance, I will explore in this section the possibilities of using new media to bring about social change among the communities. The simple question is whether we can use the new media technology as community media. This question raises a number of issues for theologians who have often looked at new media technology from a critical perspective. A technological determinist would argue that technology shapes and affects culture and the way of thinking of people. Media scholars have looked at this process from different perspectives that are helpful for theologians to understand the characteristics of information society and thus do hermeneutics in such a context.

Hamelink[157] identifies two major perspectives in this area which are: Utopian (Optimistic) and Dystopian (Pessimistic) perspectives. For him those who support Utopian perspectives highlight the positive development that is brought about by information technology. Those who support Dystopian perspective argue that the Information Technology (IT - includes computers and Internet) deployment will simply reinforce historical trends toward economic disparities, inequality in political power and gaps between the knowledge disfranchised.

Utopian Perspective

This perspective refers to the present time as the 'ICE age', 'media saturated age', 'new civilisation', 'information revolution', 'knowledge society' and "age of 'info-tainment'. It derives its image from a techno-centric perspective[158] that is characterised by an emphasis on historical discontinuity[159]. Information technology is seen as a process of bringing positive developments in society which would introduce new social values, will develop new social relations and offer widespread access to crucial resources. This perspective predicts radical changes in economics[160], politics[161] and culture[162]. Hamelink notes that in a 'Zero sum society' new social values will evolve, new social relations will develop and widespread access to the crucial resources will be possible. All the traditional borderlines and barriers will disappear in the new virtual communities. Those who support this perspective hold the view that the technology has come to stay and can be used for good purposes of human society. Many oppose such views and share a common ground which is identified as Dystopian.

John Joshva Raja

Dystopian perspective

In this perspective it is argued IT deployment will simply reinforce historical trends toward social-economic disparities, inequality in political power and gaps between information rich (knowledge elites) and the information poor (knowledge disfranchised). This perspective also predicts continuation and changes in the present economic[163], political[164] and cultural[165] systems. One has to understand that technology creates dependency of the developing nations on the developed nations. By denying access and dividing people into 'have's and 'have not's such technology is seen as widening the existing gap between the rich and the poor. Some Dystopians are Herbert I. Schiller, Ian Reinecke, Kevin Robins, Neil Postman and Mark Dery.

Both perspectives have failed to recognise the fundamental impossibility of foreseeing the future social and economic implications of technological innovation. For Hamelink, it is not possible to predict the future social impact of any technology and so social choices about the future can be made under conditions of uncertainty [1998:6]. Hamelink supports an approach focusing on 'social shaping of technology'. This approach emphasises the dynamic interaction between social forces that shape technological development[166] and technological innovations that affect social relations (which was originally suggested by MacKenzie and Wajcman, 1985). For Hamelink it is essential for those who wish to influence the course of change in IT, in directions that might support social development, to understand what forces shape the evolution of IT's, and how these forces interact.

Technology for Alternative Humanity

An alternative humanity does not refer to a technocratic or technologically saturated society nor point to a technologically powerful or superior humanity. But it suggests a community that allows everyone to have access to resources in general and communication resources in particular. In this sense communication as a process can serve humanity to bring about changes where it is needed. It can also support and uphold those elements of development and advancement in every society. In order to bring about changes people should be able to recognise and communicate among themselves their life related issues and problems. Communication as a process should enable people to participate in their own life struggles and in their development by sharing their knowledge and wisdom among themselves as well as drawing from other communities.

Communication can build relationships and thereby build communities. In the process of building relationships, it can also bring about social changes and development among the communities so that their lives become better than before. The present humanity is facing tension, confrontation, conflicts and violence in the name of religion, identities and culture. Some of the issues like poverty, corruption and disease have become a reality everywhere. In such contexts to bring an alternative humanity some of these issues should be addressed and those problems need to be reduced or eliminated. If the communication process could be developed to eliminate some of these social problems, there is a possibility of bringing about alternative humanity among different communities. Let me limit myself to Information Technology (IT) rather than technology in general, and to the present attempts by NGO's and Governments as examples.

Technology as a medium can bring about changes in humanity in two or more ways. It can bring about behavioural change, social engineering, productivity increase and status quo stabilisation through a mass mediated vertical model or self-expression, conscientization, emancipatory action, social and political competence and structural change through a communicative participatory horizontal model. Mass media usually prevents social interaction whereas small community or group media usually foster it. Without such interaction there is no social change and without social change there is no alternative humanity. The vertical mass mediated model has failed to bring about development whereas the horizontal participatory model has allowed the NGOs to play the roles of mediator or external agency. The decisions are often made for the people and the information is given to the people. There is a need to bridge the gap between these two models.

Third way

Both Utopian and Dystopian perspectives emphasise the role of IT (means) or of the developing organisation in bringing about development (communicator). I mean, IT is placed between a communicator and the audience and so becomes an instrument for bringing about development of the people. In these two views the main emphases are on how effectively the means (IT) can be used to bring about development among the people or how best the NGOs or the communicator use the means (IT) in order to develop the communities. These perspectives have an implicit assumption that people do not have any ideas to develop themselves nor possess any innovative concepts to bring about social change. Thus the development has to be brought by an external instrument or organisation. One should not try to see IT from a Scooby-Doo Model where the cartoon characters Scooby and Shaggy magically get their burgers by clicking the mouse of a computer. IT cannot directly eliminate poverty or hunger. However it alone cannot be blamed for such social problems.

Social problems such as poverty, starvation deaths and water scarcity are part of our everyday reality for many people in India. IT is neither a cause nor can solve this problem completely. The concept of development should not be narrowed down only to economic development. People in India cannot solve the above stated problems unless there is a co-ordinated and organised effort. Population explosion and less investment on people (more investment on missiles and nuclear arsenals), non-availability of resources, mass exploitation of wealth by a few, natural disasters and conflicts and mismanagement are a few factors that also contribute to problems such as poverty and starvation deaths. By organizing communities together and by bringing awareness among them these problems may be reduced to some extent though they have to be addressed at national and regional levels. IT can play a major role in bringing people together by establishing networks among the communities.

Old Model for Development and Means of Communication

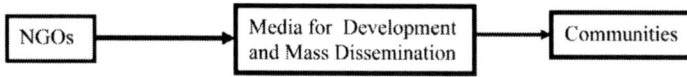

```
┌─────────┐      ┌──────────────────────┐      ┌──────────────┐
│  NGOs   │─────▶│ Media for Development │─────▶│ Communities  │
└─────────┘      │ and Mass Dissemination│     └──────────────┘
                 └──────────────────────┘
```

Proposed Model for Development and IT

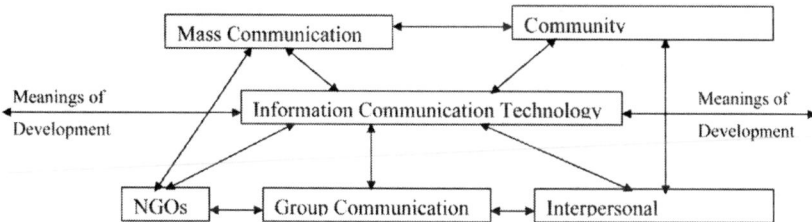

```
        ┌────────────────────┐          ┌──────────────┐
        │ Mass Communication │◀────────▶│  Community    │
        └────────────────────┘          └──────────────┘
Meanings of         ┌──────────────────────────────────────┐        Meanings of
Development ◀────────│ Information Communication Technology  │◀──────▶ Development
                    └──────────────────────────────────────┘
        ┌─────────┐   ┌─────────────────────┐   ┌──────────────┐
        │  NGOs   │◀─▶│ Group Communication │◀─▶│ Interpersonal│
        └─────────┘   └─────────────────────┘   └──────────────┘
```

IT and development

Any development perspective, to be holistic and sustainable, to some extent, should begin from the people, their understanding of development, their communication process and their context. In this sense, people are already engaged in a communication process (by using different means that are available to them), in a socio-cultural and political process (in order to develop themselves) and thus in search for meanings of life and faith that would enable them to bring about social change and development among them. It is essential for the NGOs and communicators to find ways to participate in such an ongoing process of the people and thus become participants or catalysts in the people's process of development using the available modern technology. From this understanding communication needs to be defined as a process in which the communicator (NGO's) participates, shares and interacts with the audience (people)[167]. The role of those who wish to use IT is to engage in those communities' communication process in order to find a way to enable them to use IT. Unless audiences share such means of communication (IT), the communicator cannot communicate with the audience. Unless computers become their medium, people cannot use it for their development and so our attempt to introduce information technologies would become an attractive but vain instrument that does not contribute to the process of development.

First, those of us who are interested in IT and development need to identify the way in which IT could become an integral part of their communication practice and remain a useful instrument for their daily purposes. We need to start enabling people to use IT as a platform where they can express their expectations and their meanings etcetera. It is essential that we engage in people's search for development oriented meanings. We need to first recognize such meanings and use their means of communication to disseminate among them. Using IT, such meanings can be disseminated not only among themselves but also to other communities that are struggling with similar issues and problems. Our attempts should not only be limited in bringing a particular community together and developing them but also networking communities together in order that they may share among themselves their innovative ideas and help each other addressing their problems.

Using the internet, we need to explore the possible ways of serving the many sidelined communities: refugees, prisoners, oppressed communities, HIV/AIDS-infected, farmers, fishermen, labourers and people below the poverty line (BPL). The area of internet and development is a subject which I have already dwelled on at major conferences in India and elsewhere. I wish to point to a few models that I proposed in that elsewhere - web-cafe model[168], web radio model[169] and multicasting model[170]. These models have been studied by the local governments in India to explore the possibilities of using Information Communication Technology for development. People at the margins should be given a chance to communicate their own problems, among themselves, and to the public. We have successful stories of such communication in Gujarat where SEWA has done this with a video camera. Information technology can provide information to these people at the margins about useful Government programmes. At the same time, they can express themselves to the outside world and bring their problems, and other issues, to the notice of the government. Some NGOs are already involved in the net for such development[171]. Making a video clip or an audio file in these systems is very easy, and then placing or sending it from one place to another place is also made easy through convergence technology.

Convergent technology and development

Recently by pointing out strong cases Bhatnagar [2000:17-32][172] argued that Information Communication Technology can be used to improve and operate mechanical works automatically, to empower citizens to access information and knowledge, to decentralize planning, to address bureaucratic problems, to monitor government development programmes. Convergence technology in the Information Technology (IT) provides opportunities to work towards people-centred development. Unless the perceptions on the role of IT in the process of development change are understood by all, this technology may not be useful either for the NGOs or for the people. Information Technology provides a new culture – a culture of interactivity among different communities. Unless it becomes part of people's communication process, NGOs attempt to use IT may not be successful. The enormous wisdom, information and knowledge that the village communities in India have, could be used, shared and sold through Information Technology. Such communities become powerful when they come to know their rights and government makes special provisions for them. By using IT, they can provide information about themselves and develop their daily business or any other dealings. Thus people become content makers of IT and become active participants in their own development processes.

With a single multimedia station in a village we may be able to integrate the people's needs by using the convergence technology and also an interactive web. In the age of computers, information, communication and knowledge are three essential elements that do address the specific issue of development in rural people. In some rural places, people should be informed about their rights and government programmes in their own language. In some parts, people are familiar with herbal medicine which could be collected and recorded in a web site. People who wish to communicate to their relatives from villages to towns could easily be made possible through Information Technology.

Through the convergence of technology the farmer may be able to speak face to face with the retailers and can sell his goods from his place itself. He may also be able to advertise in his web site about the variety and the price of his produce. He can collect information about loans, fertilizers, pesticides and government facilities through Internet facilities. These are some possibilities for the farmer to make use of in IT. There are people who can pay and use such facilities whereas there are many who cannot afford such technology either on their own or through the web-cafes. In such a context flexibility in terms of access is essential while using Information Technology. For those who are below the poverty line or daily labourers such technology could be provided with information about jobs and resources. They can find out government provisions and special programmes for such people below the poverty line. The relationship with the government could be made through the internet, videophone or through any other programmes through IT. Multiple functions of the media should be made known to people who can use IT for their own use in their own language. Here people become active partners in development rather than passive receivers of government largesse.

The internet as alternative media

The internet can also play a role of alternative media and so an alternative mission. It is an alternative because some of the news or information through other media can be censored or blocked by the government or powerful people whereas on the internet it is not possible. The incidents in Tiananmen Square were informed to the outside world first through the television in June 1989[173]. It is essential to expose at times certain events and incidents which otherwise go unreported, particularly the persecution of Christians in Pakistan[174], of Muslims in Gujarat and of democratic forces in Burma .These are a few examples which cannot be reported through a main stream media. Internet is the best medium to report these problems to the world. At times it is also essential to expose certain practices such as separate cups in teashops of South India (discrimination against Dalits – marginalised and other lower castes and others), hunger deaths of Adhivasis (a Hindi term for aborigines) in Orissa (a state in India) and secret deaths of Tribal community members in North East India. It is only by networking with people, churches and NGO's that we can inform such incident to the outside world authentically. Exposing poverty itself is part of mission as the Indian government claims to have become self-reliant in food production whereas people sometimes do not once get food grains from the public distribution system (PDS). Such activities are to be seen as part of mission.

Banking knowledge

A. K. Gupta, Brij Kothari and Krit Patel [2000:117-131][175] argue that knowledge can become a means of power if coalitions or networks of relevant actors evolve. They suggest taking people as resources of knowledge. Knowledge systems that enable people to survive, particularly in high risk environments have involved blending the secular with the sacred, reductionism with holism, short term options with long term ones, specialised with diversified strategies, involving individuals or collective material or non-material pursuits.

People possess different types of knowledge (about herbal medicines and about their innovative way of living under difficult circumstances) which could be shared after registering with the Intellectual Property Rights; ICT provides pages of information about the ways to get it registered. To do this we need to have knowledge of the network that connects innovators, enterprises and investments to bring about a sustainable development. NGOs can play a catalytic role in this networking of different communities.

Another way of engaging in liberative theology is to provide space for knowledge banks where archives, hypertexts of information sources, and research materials in any language are made available. If all the archive material in India can be made into CDs, the books can be preserved both in microfiche and digital text forms and also copyright can be sold to different universities around the world. Even the theses of the Senate of Serampore College can be made into a CD so that this could be available for others who are doing research in related areas. It would be good if the theological libraries and colleges can be networked together sharing similar information[176]. The internet helps to create a knowledge bank. Preservation and sharing of the knowledge bank bring income for the local communities. There is a need to protect certain cultural traditions of the people such as oral and written history and medical knowledge. The net can be a channel of preserving such traditions. Thus the voice of the voiceless – not often heard in the mainstream media - can be projected to the outside world.

Not only texts but also audio and visual material can be preserved through such technology and made available to people. Some people have lost their identities because they have lost their history. It is often argued that some people's history was intentionally eliminated by destroying their written historical documents and by taking away their traditions. The remaining element is the oral culture of a people. This, too, can be preserved through the net and be made available on the websites. In many places the rural and marginalised communities have maintained their oral traditions – stories, songs and music. Of course some of them are recorded on audio cassettes. These can be preserved and shared by making them available to other people. The way some of the communities solve their own problems can also be narrated and recorded in the net. Particularly the traditional medical, agricultural knowledge, information about animals and other traditional wisdom can be brought together and preserved without exploiting the people. This knowledge could be sold and the income shared with the people who provided such wisdom to others. In this way our mission will be genuine in the sense that we are engaged in the liberative process of the people. The process of development is also enhanced due to the enormous quantity of information that is available in the internet, exposure of the authentic issues to the public, people's participation in their own developmental process and a liberative experience in accessing the net.

Networking different communities

Networking can go beyond the process of bringing together the churches of different traditions; it can also attempt to bring together different religious communities. The internet provides a platform, and also the space, for people of different faiths to express themselves openly in a way which might not be possible otherwise. In certain contexts, people of different faiths cannot come together because of their doctrinal or ideological affiliations. Seeing a leader making a statement publicly about religious dialogue can be misinterpreted or misunderstood by followers of the same tradition; whereas the interactive nature of the net allows concepts to be freely expressed. The networking of NGOs will certainly help in the sharing of experiences, or best practice, from one area to another. When I do refugee networking, the information is very important because the next day it becomes part of a published newsletter for many NGOs who are working among the refugees.

As this message is spread to the top level leaders some kind of action is taken either in its favour or against it. Recently we ended up pressurising the Indian government to talk to the Bhutan government regarding the return of their Nepali Refugees. Networking Christian NGOs is important because many of them do not know what others are doing and repeat the same development programmes, which is a waste of precious resources. Mission is more effective if ideas and resources can be shared. Through networking, and information sharing, the sponsoring agencies would know what progress NGOs are making and of any problems to be addressed.

Church, technology and alternative humanity

Christianity is a religion of hope and expectation without losing sight of the present. The kingdom of God is both realised here and expected to come in future. In this sense eternal life is available to all here and now while its continuity is there even after death. The life here and now becomes very important and a new creation is possible on earth. The community values are very similar to the kingdom values without losing individual freedom. An expected alternative humanity is what Christianity proclaims as the Kingdom here and now.

As the theologians are involved in bringing about changes in the present society to bring about God's kingdom here and now in its limited form, they need to consider seriously the community communication in order to fulfil God's mission on earth. The present humanity lacks its vision in achieving any changes because of the failure of modernisation and other reforms. It becomes the task of the churches, as part of their mission, to carry out the transformation using Information Communication Technology to bring about changes in the society. Theologically, this idea of using information technology as alternative media challenges the conventional ways of critiquing technology. Regardless of the limitations of the technology we need to create a community where social changes would be negotiated between community and individuals and also between communities. This also takes us beyond the instrumental use of information technology for our mission and ministry and raises wider questions about using it for community building. In this manner, our hermeneutics is not merely determined by the content of Christianity but also our presence and engagement in the community communication. We will discover fullness of our humanity by engaging in the community's search for God and for life.

This enables to see the communitarian aspect of God. The Bible depicts God as one who is also living within a community where he listens to other voices even if they are opposed to his voice (Chapter 3). The concept of Trinity is ultimately presenting the communitarian element of God in which there is a possibility of human participation.

The concept of Trinity is presented in terms of absoluteness (Father), humane (Jesus) and presence (Holy Spirit) [Kaufman, 1981:271-2]. It give us the picture of the community of God in which there is an interaction, participation and sharing of the three in one. God is one who interacts within his community, participates with others in the dialogue and thus shares their views at times.

Section 2: Example 3 – Eucharist as an alternative space

The basic question here is whether the church can transform its own means and spaces into an alternative spaces for the people at the margins. The global media and other powerful communication industries do not provide space for the people at times to express their concerns against social, political and cultural institutions as they are powerful and rich in the society. Church needs to consider providing space for people to communicate for bringing about social changes within their community and also speak against those powerful centres of exploitation and oppression. The following sections will discuss the ways in which the churches can attempt using the Eucharistic space for bringing about such social changes within and outside their Christian community in the context of caste, racial, economic and political marginalisation.

Eucharist as Alternative Space

One cannot reconstruct an alternative without deconstructing the ideologies and concepts that tend to monopolise and promote false consciousness among the people. Can churches provide an alternative space where the voices that are not heard through the mass media can be heard? Can the practice of Eucharist where human dignity and life are affirmed provide a counter and alternative space for global media dominated public space? These are a few questions with which I struggle in this article. In this article I give a historical background of new world order which set base for globalisation of the neo-liberal values particularly in the media markets. Then I will also point out the need for alternative media to counter such values and the process of globalisation that are promoted through the mass media[177]. At the end I will argue that churches can redefine the rituals of Eucharist as the community space to counter the values and ideologies that are promoted by the process of globalisation. Secular initiatives on alternative models have often failed as they could not bring people on a platform that would bind them through a particular faith or worldview system.

For me globalization[178] refers to the inevitable interconnectedness of the cultures, economies, communities, societies, nations and races at international level. Thus globalization of the media means internationalization of the process of information and communication through huge media corporations and cultural industries in every part of the world. Before we analyse the effect of globalization we need to look at the background of globalization of media. Globalization is an escalating reality of global interdependence. If globalization is one of interdependence, we need to address the issue of internationalisation, universality of values, emerging multi-polar values and meanings, intercultural communication and so on. Globalisation of media particularly eliminated all other small, alternative and counter voices and spaces by using power, money and neo-liberal ideology. The voices of people who lost their dignity, power, values of life and resources were silenced by the global communication system.

To counter the globalisation one needs to create alternative space where human dignity of all would be recognised and respected. In this space life would not be commoditised rather celebrated as part of the community. Eucharist provides an alternative space with the concept of the body of Christ where not only life is affirmed and resources are shared but also the human dignity of all the participants are accepted and respected. Eucharist can be an alternative space where not only dignity is shared but communicated, reiterated and voiced. It is the place where the voice of the silenced can be heard by all. First one has to highlight the rise of globalisation as a process. In the following section I will highlight how the global public space was taken over by those who supported the New World Order and thus commoditised the public space where even life is identified as a commodity. Before identifying and recognising Eucharist as an alternative communicative space, it is essential to highlight how the global space enhanced and furthered marginalisation of the poor, victims, differently able people, minorities and people living with HIV/AIDS. The global network of communication reinforced the local exploitation and strengthened through a neo-liberal ideology. Thus the process of communication eliminated all the other voices even from the local community space by providing a negative image of such voices altogether.

Background of Globalization of Communication

In 1973 the fourth summit of Non Aligned Movement (NAM) in Algiers called for more cooperation in the field of mass media among the developing countries [Gerbner, Mowlana and Nodenstreng 1993]. The member countries established Non-Aligned New Agencies Pool (NANAP), regional news agencies and the Broadcasting Organisation of Non-Aligned Countries (BONAC). NAM wanted such cooperative efforts to operate at international level through the United Nations. The New International Information and Communication Order (NIIO) was accepted by NAM countries and was brought to UNESCO in 1976 in Nairobi and was accepted as New World Information and Communication Order (NWICO) resolution. A commission was set up in 1977 under Sean MacBride. The MacBride Report was accepted in 1978 in the 20th General Conference of UNESCO. In 1978 the UN General Assembly adopted this resolution. It was in 1981 Reagan Administration began to interpret NWICO as a threat to press freedom and asked UNESCO to stop and eliminate NWICO from UNESCO. This was one of the reasons for the withdrawal of the US and UK from UNESCO in 1987. From this time the NWICO lost its momentum. The US President Ronald Reagan and UK Prime Minister Margaret Thatcher came up with new ideas for a New World Order in which

John Joshva Raja

intellectual property rights and patent issues were brought up. Thus new world bodies such as International Monetary Fund (IMF), World Bank (WB), World Trade Organisation (WTO) and G-6/8 nations are introduced to bring about this New World Order.

The NWICO movement highlighted the problems with the old international information order that are [Kleinwatcher 1993:13-14]:
     a.   the big gap in the world-wide distribution of the means of communication
     b.   the imbalance in the world-wide information flow
     c.   the one-sided and distorted coverage of the developing world by the dominating Western Mass Media.

Against the above problems the NWICO emphasised five major objectives in communication development that are [White 1993:22-5]:
     a.   There should be equity and autonomy within Global Communication. It emphasises a vision of national self-reliance in communication and reaffirms national cultural identity within an expanding system of international news agencies and other transnational cultural industries.
     b.   There is a need for establishing national communication policies that would support the developing countries communication systems.
     c.   A more participatory communication institution within every nation needs to be promoted.
     d.   There is a need to stimulate indigenous cultural expression and local culture industries in the midst of transnational marketing of the media.
     e.   Major non-governmental and autonomous institutions should be encouraged to provide free expressions and raise the voice of the voiceless people within and outside the nation.

These are the five major objectives of NWICO movement in bringing about changes in communication and media systems around the world. It aims at eliminating the imbalances and inequalities of information and communication, eliminating the negative effects of certain monopolies, public or private, removal of internal and external obstacles to a free flow and wider and better balanced dissemination of information and ideas, plurality of sources and channels of information, freedom of the press and of information, the freedom of journalists and all professionals in the media. Respect of each people's cultural identity, respect for the right of all peoples to participate in international exchanges of information on the basis of equality, justice and mutual benefit, respect for right of the public to have access to information sources and to participate actively in the communication process [Sean MacBride and Roach 1993: 5]. If these are the aims and objectives then it was unfortunate that NWICO movement was stopped by a few powerful countries with the clear intention to dominate and control the process of communication. I will try to highlight the ways in which the globalization of the media has evolved after the NWICO movement and made an impact on the lives of the people.

New World Order with its new organisations such as IMF (International Monetary Fund), World Bank and WTO (World Trade Organisation) have brought five monopolies into the world. They are technological monopoly; Control of Worldwide access to the planet's natural resources; Media and Communication monopolies; monopolies over weapons of mass destruction [Oommen 1998:19]. George Cheriyan [1998:63-74] clearly shows how globalization has evolved through the new world order that was brought about by the Reagan and Thatcher administrations. The purpose of Globalization is the free flow of goods and services between countries in an unhindered manner says Varadhan[179]. The ultimate purpose is to give the customer the benefit of having the choice of goods and services from anywhere in the world to suit his needs and tastes.

John Joshva Raja

Global Public Space and No People
The first impact of globalization is internationalization of communication. The internationalization of communication is seen by some as a means of bringing nations and peoples together, and as a power to assist international organizations in the exercise of their services to the world community [Mowlana 1997:6-7]. Secondly, this international communication is also called political proselytization and is seen as propaganda, ideological confrontation, advertising and the source of myths and clichés. They are usually one way communication systems. They are imbued with a certain authoritarian, totalitarian character which allows the manipulation of people. Thirdly, international communication and information in the global context leads to growth in economic power. Local transformation is as much a part of globalizations as the lateral extension of social connections across time and space [Giddens 1990, p.64]. Homogenization is provoked by differentiation and pluralisation, yet both mutually influence each other. Broadcasting Institutions at a National Level held together the divergence and convergence which later becomes a continuity of globalization[180].

In economic terms globalization creates wants yet does not satisfy the needs of the majority of poor people. It stimulates dispersal of the production process under the centralised control of corporate owners and technocrat-managers. Socially globalization divides the people, explodes the ethnic and cultural values and breeds corruptive practices[181]. Most of the international organisations have used this to their advantage and thus continued to dominate the weaker and peripheral nations which are referred to as 'Westoxification' (converting people to adopt non-indigenous forms of behaviour that could result in a certain schizophrenic paralysis of creative power). Fourthly, information at the international level is seen as political power. There is a concentration of the means of international communication in a few countries. When the information flows it? the cultural content of the source is often conveyed and their interests are often protected [Mowlana 1997:7].

248

Media technology, content, messages; professionals are all controlled by a few multinational corporations (star agencies/Microsoft industries) or owners such as Rupert Murdoch and Bill Gates. Thus the globalization process has created new global media giants who can influence and change the political, social and cultural lives of the masses with their media industries (Time Warner, Walt Disney Co. Sony - Smith 1991:21-37). Information, like other indices of wealth, tends to cluster around the already rich and powerful. It is far from being a common resource available to all on an equal basis. The heavy influence of commodities and communications, with advertising seeking aggressively to forge in consumers ever stronger links of product-related desire and purchase, lead many to fear that cultural diversity will be lost. Others tend to rejoice in the new diversities – of race, diet, language, music and religion which they see blossoming in our cities [Arthur 1998:6]. The international communication systems are controlled by a few elite individuals who are primarily motivated by profit-based or political interests. Many of these systems are entwined contours of entertainment and commerce rather than related to education, environmental awareness, good citizenship or material development. Globalization has seen information become a carefully controlled commodity rather than a freely available resource and thus media facilitate commerce [Bagdikian 1992:247 – Arthur, 1998:9-10].

There is information deprivation in an information rich society. Schiller argues that today the power of huge, private economic enterprises is extended across national and international boundaries, influencing and directing economic resource decisions, political choices and the production and dissemination of messages and images. Corporate speech has become a dominant discourse, nationally and internationally and has changed dramatically the context in which the concepts of freedom of speech, a free press and democratic expression have to be considered. In this sense there is no public sphere -rather a sphere which is divided, bought and sold by the private companies and used for profit making, at times even at the cost of people's lives. There is no space that exists for the people - or the public - to share or express their concerns unless a counter means is established. It becomes very difficult to survive in the world of media market and competition. In this way the media often are used as Weapons of Mass Distractions (WMD) to divert people's interest towards a desire for material goods and possessions, thus creating artificial needs. This often leads to misrepresentation of other people in the media, thus polluting the information itself.

The pollution of information raises questions about values and priorities that are inbuilt in the practices of the media leading to the construction of media myths where poor people are blamed for their poverty, and so on. Thus sweeping moral generalizations are made that ignore the diversity of the media and audience and blame some else for the problems. Large numbers of people are involved in this process: directors of violent films, authors of depraved computer games, schedulers who allow unsuitable material to appear in children's' programmes, editors of tabloids who connive at the casual daily provision of pornography and the stereotyping of women, journalists who focus on the trivial and advertisers who press anything into service to sell a product, media tycoons whose monopoly threatens freedom of expression and diversity of opinion and commentators whose sound-bite analyses result in grotesque over-simplifications [Arthur 1998:31]. In this process the media's representation of minority and vulnerable religions is often negative and shows articulated ignorance of the professionals who work in them.

Silencing and Eliminating People's Voices
With the new world order concept of Intellectual Property Rights and neo-liberal values are also embedded and promoted around the world. Mass Media played a major role in promoting neo-liberal values of the markets as many of them were bought by the global media moguls. It is about free flow of goods, resources and enterprises across the borders of the world. There should be competition between

enterprises that make goods available at cheap prices and with high quality. The five basic tenets of the neo-liberalism are: there should be greater openness for the international trade and market and thus allow the rule of the market; the government should cut the public expenditure such as for education and social security system for the pensioners; the government should reduce the regulations on social conditions of the people such as working environment of the labourers; state owned companies should be privatised; and finally eliminate the concept of public good or existence of community by replacing it with individual responsibility. These are the core values of neo-liberalism. In simple terms for a company or business institution to survive one has to compete with the other and thus provide quality goods to succeed in the market at cheap price.

In the media market, neo-liberal values found easy way in and thus eliminating all other voices that would not bring in money to the owners of the media industry. Those things that can be sold can only be shown or broadcast. This led to degradation of the quality of the programmes and focus mainly on profit making of the media industry. If anything good is done by the churches or by the community at large it cannot be a newsworthy issue rather mass murderer or a rapist can easily fill in the front page. More negative the news is it becomes worthy of being published in the newspaper or in the television or in any other media. The industrialists and the rich owners have bought the shares of the media industries and thus eliminated the concept of public service from such cultural industries. Thus the media industries survive today as merely entertainment agencies or private means to sell good via media. They not only do not show any interest in the public service but also tend to highlight only the problems and mistakes of those institutions that are trying to provide service to the public. Of course there are still a few public broadcasting institutions that provide service to the people with the help of the support from the government.

John Joshva Raja

This provides challenges for the nations, communities, Non-Governmental organisations and Faith based organisations that try to communicate to the public through various means and methods their basic values. Because the mass mediated public space is bought and sold for huge money only those who can convert religious values into a package that can be attractive and sold like soaps can only find space in space. Otherwise religious, social service organisations and particularly those whose voices are never heard in public are silenced, rejected and negated. It becomes very essential for the churches and other socially motivated organisations to use the existing space or create new spaces among communities where they can enable the voices of poor, differently able people and HIV/AIDs infected and other marginalised communities.

The next section will discuss about the way an alternative space can be created or an alternative use of media can be found among the churches, Non Governmental Organisations (NGOs) and Faith Based Organisations (FBOs). This will counter the neo-liberal ideology that degrades human life into a commodity by affirming human life at the centre of one's faith and by respecting the dignity of all human beings. The basic values of many religious communities are questioned due to the commercialisation of human life in the public sphere. Communities find it hard to express an alternative views among themselves in many contexts and so dragged into a passive acceptance of this neo-liberal views. Here the religious institutions and also social service organisations can play a major role by creating an alternative community sphere where people can communicate to themselves. This is not to return to old values without being critique of them and not to maintain the status quo of the structure of the society where some people's dignity is not respected. But it is an attempt to develop an alternative space where human life is not commoditized and where human dignity is affirmed regardless of gender, caste, colour and class. In the next section I will discuss about the possibilities of such an alternative communicative space within communities local and global.

252

Let My People Speak - Eucharist as Alternative Space!

Though New World Information and Communication Order was not again given importance by the UNESCO under the pressure of a few rich countries, the concepts have remained in the mind of many communication scholars and practitioners who were committed for the cause of the poor and marginal communities. This enabled many to identify alternatives to the New World Order and the Global Media that works in favour of such order. Alternatives were developed in many ways including concepts, perspectives and practices. But alternative types of communication existed already in may South American countries. From the mid of 1980s the alternative communication began to play the role of defending democracy and constitutional liberties in Latin America and thus represented the political excluded interests (Atwood and McAnany 1986; Reyes Matta 1983; Simpson Grinberg 1986)[182]. Alternative communication is also known as Radical communication (Downing 2001); Citizens Media (Rodriguez 2001); People's Media or Community Media or Grassroots Media or Democratic Media. Having been used in diverse ways the alternative media have emerged as one of the recently discussed subjects and practice among many of the communication scholars and practitioners. We need to study the need for having such types of communication in bringing peace and harmony in the society.

Our question here is Can Eucharist be an alternative? It means – Can Eucharist provide an alternative space for people to think, imagine and communicate in dignified and life-affirming ways. This is not possible either through the mass communication or through any other communication that divide people and communities. Eucharist is celebrating the life in Christ. It is also an act of affirming our being in part of the body of Christ. In Christ there is no male and no female and there is no Jew and Greek. It does not eliminate the difference and does not make all into one race or colour. Rather Eucharist invites us to accept each other's dignity and importantly accepting each other as they are. Of course the denominationalism and religious narrowness of many of the Christian traditions tend to eliminate or reject others from being part of this wider body of Christ. But in its real sense the Eucharist provides a space for all people to come together and share the body and blood of Jesus Christ. Those who affirm life and who accept others dignity are to be invited to be part of this celebration of life in God. This is in continuity with what Christ did and so the body of Christ becomes inclusive of all those who affirm life in God and respect others' dignity. If this is the case then Eucharist can be a counter space where dialogue can happen between people who affirm human life and dignity of all.

Thus Eucharist becomes dialogic, intercultural, local and interpreting universal/global, promoting values, entertain but not become pure entertainment, secular, democratized, development-oriented, promotes dignity of people, highlights justice and ecological concerns, remains cheap, both top-down and down-top, culturally rooted, non-profit but not at loss, promotes a culture of peace, reconciliation and harmony, involves people's participation, identifies and highlights alternative issues, not merely accepting the public opinion but challenging them as well, enter the public or community's space or create such a space, highlights public concerns as well as minorities' concerns, simple and not professionally communicated, represents the voice of the voiceless and accept people as they are, engage in people search for meanings.

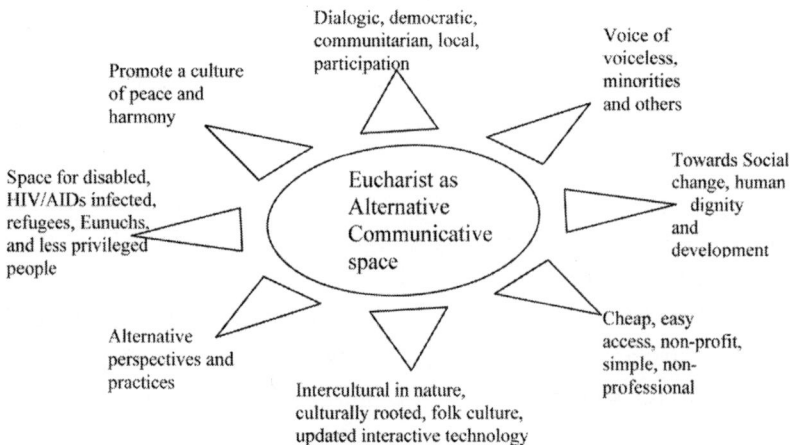

Dialogic, democratic, communitarian, local, participation

Voice of voiceless, minorities and others

Promote a culture of peace and harmony

Space for disabled, HIV/AIDs infected, refugees, Eunuchs, and less privileged people

Eucharist as Alternative Communicative space

Towards Social change, human dignity and development

Alternative perspectives and practices

Cheap, easy access, non-profit, simple, non-professional

Intercultural in nature, culturally rooted, folk culture, updated interactive technology

One may ask question 'why should Eucharist provide alternative communicative space?' Rather this is a Christian ritual celebration of the body and blood of Jesus Christ which are given only to those who belong to a particular denomination and also to those who are confirmed through a certain process of education. Eucharist is originally a celebration of life in God and being the body of Christ. It is intended as a space for inviting people to join and experience the body of Christ which is the Church. Having made it into an exclusive gathering such an act of celebration together led Christian not only to a separation from others, but also to conflicts within Christian community. In a way it sets a model for widening the reign of God to all. It is particular for Christians in so far as it points to universal and thus invites all to share this body and blood of Christ and thus to be part of the celebrating act of the Church.

The Eucharistic communication also should take into account the concerns of ecology, refugees, disabled people and women. It should become the means of connecting and relating people at the margins and people at the centre. It provides access to all the community members. This also involves enabling the media to become a community based media or have access to the existing media and enter the space as well. It is also taking the content beyond our interests and thus breaking the regular barriers.

Eucharistic space can be used as an alternative method of communication where human dignity is assured and all are considered to be part of the body of Christ. In my example I have pointed out that the ideologies have failed in their attempt to bring about radical changes among these communities. Such concepts divided people and led them to violence among themselves. This led to the suffering of the marginal communities in multiple ways. It is the community's gathering before, during and after the Eucharist that bring about radical changes and enable them to think of an alternative community where people's dignity is restored and where everyone is invited to share this dignity and share their resources as well. I strongly argue that without such faith centred approach a critical engagement alone will not bring about any social change among the communities. Eucharist provides a space for communities to share their issues and facilitate discussions on the issues of globalisation. Thus it becomes a reconstructed alternative space where not only faith is expressed and experience but also the experience and social realities are communicated and discussed among the communities. Such communication does not happen otherwise at the public or community sphere through the mass media or any other mediated public communication.

The churches' mission is to provide an alternative space where values affirming human lives are discussed together with other religious communities. In a way the churches can use their communication methods and practices to create, sustain and develop such space where globalisation is critically discussed and alternatives are developed locally and globally. In my case study I suggested Eucharist as an alternative space. In order to create an alternative community space the churches have to widen the present practices of communication that serves only Christian community. The churches need to use the available methods and means of communication for this purpose or invest on new media to create such space for critical engagement of the community with the process of globalisation. Without theologically sustaining such alternative communication the churches may find it difficult to provide an alternative space for the communities at large.

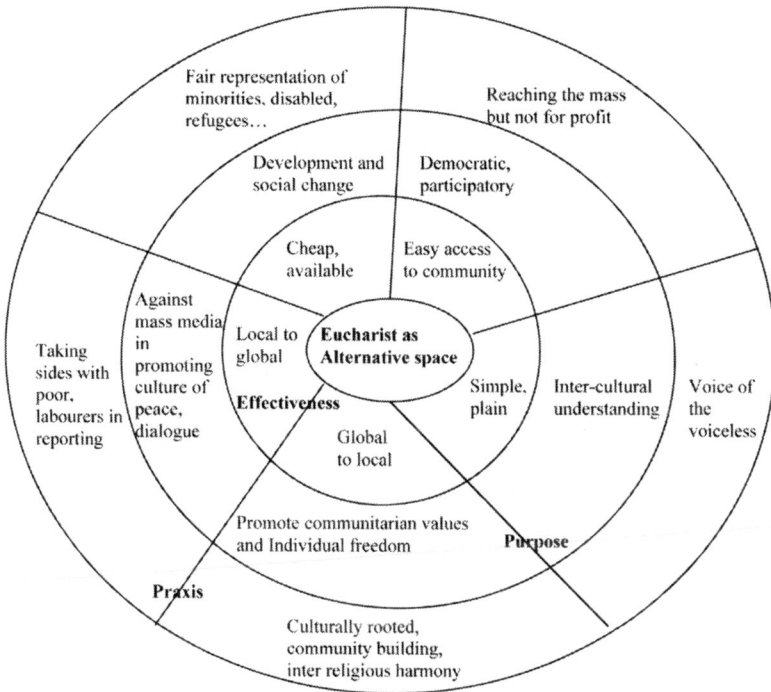

Fair representation of minorities, disabled, refugees…

Reaching the mass but not for profit

Development and social change

Democratic, participatory

Cheap, available

Easy access to community

Against mass media in promoting culture of peace, dialogue

Local to global

Eucharist as Alternative space

Effectiveness

Taking sides with poor, labourers in reporting

Simple, plain

Inter-cultural understanding

Voice of the voiceless

Global to local

Promote communitarian values and Individual freedom

Purpose

Praxis

Culturally rooted, community building, inter religious harmony

Conclusion

The media pose many challenges to the audiences' faith, worldviews and attitude. At times, they do hermeneutics through their content and tend to play the role of theologians in public. They often use imagination as well as deviational imagination as their method of approaching, attracting and buying the mass audience. Theologians need to engage with the media not only critically and academically but also empathetically in a way that would establish an interactive relationship with the media practitioners. Media practitioners on the other hand, tend to recognize the popular search for meanings of life and of religion and blend them with their own imagination and tend to provide answers to those questions raised in the public in their own way among many other answers available to the mass audience. Because the mass media, particularly films, tend to make people imagine a new world and play to their emotions and thus identify themselves with such struggles of faith, they can be called 'modern parables'. Theologians have to recognise and learn from the roles of the media in the use of imagination and also the display of religious faith in the public. Theologians need to look for a theology of public imagination and thus recognise the tension between the role of imagination in bringing out the counter voices and in respecting other voices too which are contrary to the marginal voices. This is going to be an ideal and a tough task to go forward in building communities.

Tele-evangelists engage in the popular search for meanings in strange ways. In the context where science and rational thinkers are looking for proofs and demonstrations the tele-gurus have come up with their own demonstrations and proofs for their claims about God and about miracles in front of the camera. They entertain people through their messages, demonstrations and their music groups. They have their own fundamentalist doctrines and perspectives. Their value systems coincide with neo-liberal values such as survival, competition and success. In a way their theologies are popular because they assure everything to the people. They sell religion and God like any other goods in the media market taking advantage of the physical and psychological weakness of the audience. Their interest is not in poverty and in conflicts rather their interest is on prosperity theology. These tele-gurus engage through the media in search for meanings along with the audience. While doing so they are submerged into the values and policies of the media market forgetting the realities that are faced by the people in their everyday life. This distracts people clearly away from the reality in which they live in. Such popular mediatised doctrines of tele-gurus provide a challenge to other theologians to educate the public to use television creatively and critically. Thus there is a need to develop a theology of entertainment and also a theology for media literacy programme through which theologians would also be present in the public with their theologies and literacy programmes.

The realities at national and international level are at times misinterpreted and misrepresented by the media in the public. Thus they become a Weapons of Mass Distraction (WMD) by producing and reproducing the stereotypical images of the 'other', often minorities in their country or at an international level. Such representations lead to a mythical image of fundamentalism and terrorism in the mind of the public who come to know about the other only through the media. To a great extent one may argue that mass media are responsible for the conflicts between religious communities. I have used two case studies to show that this is possibly the case. This raises serious questions about dialogue at grassroots. Often religious dialogue is held between religious leaders or intellectuals. It is essential to think about taking the dialogue to the grassroots with a new approach. Such approaches may seem contradictory or compromising but will be pragmatic in their implementation. The suspicions about the dialogue and relationship with people of other religions need to be removed from the minds of the public. This would enable us to have a major breakthrough by establishing a direct contact, relationship and understanding between different religious communities and thus reduce ignorance, conflicts and misunderstanding that are created by the mass media.

Such interactions are possible through the new technology called Internet and Information Technology. Theologians are confronted with the new culture (hypertext, online chat), new language (convergent) and new methods (blogs) that are changing the way people behave and communicate among themselves. It is a high-speed transfer of information, interactive between the communicators and is user based in their search and applications. At times, such practices change the perception and attitude of the internet user to avoid any other practices or perceptions that are contrary to these. For example, the church services are uni-directional and monotonous in their communication methods. Young people may not like such kind of communicative serves because of their changing perceptions and activities due to their engagement with the internet. It questions theologians to see and find ways of changing or relating the unidirectional and monotonous methods of preaching to the context and culture of the young people.

By blaming technology for all the problems, theologians and the churches may isolate themselves in the race to provide meanings to the public. Using this technology, theologians cannot only cater to the spiritual needs but also interact with those who are in search of God and life through the internet and online connections.

This also raises the question about using net for the theological specifications. Technology is a challenge for the people and for the theologians for often people, who are using technology and are fascinated by their use, adjust their lives and heavily depend on technology, even shaping their lives according to technological expectations. Theologians need to raise serious concerns about this in the public and emphasize the importance of life over the technology. It is life that should determine the way technology can be used. If that is the case theologians need to explore alternative methods and means of communication that would enable people to retrace their relationship within the community while maintaining their individual freedom. Each community should develop their public sphere in stark contrast to the mass media that shrinks such spheres by selling it for their profit. Theologians need to highlight the importance of communities in a wider sense and thus encourage people to find their own community medium to express themselves in the public. This would enable the theologians too to be present in the public and also educate the public theologically and provide meanings alongside the meanings that are provided by the mass media. It would be presenting their meanings among the market of meanings that are available to the public in an attractive and compelling way.

This book has attempted to highlight a few issues between theology and media. It is essential to see the media and their practice within the hermeneutic process of search for meanings of God and of Life by the audience. It is also essential for the theologians to engage in the mass media and thus with the public in their search for meanings. While critically engaging with the media, theologians need to appreciate, learn and develop theologies that may help some of the media practitioners to relate their work to the mission and ministry of the church. I hope that my attempt to highlight a few theological issues that emerge in the interaction between theology and media will prove to be relevant for theologians, pastors and mission workers around the world.

John Joshva Raja

Bibliography

Abu-Amr, Z. 1994 *Islamic Fundamentalism in the West Bank and Gaza: Muslim Brotherhood and Islamic Jihad.* Bloomington, IN: Indiana University Press.

Aggarwal, S, K. 1989 *Media Credibility.* New Delhi: Mittal Publications.

Allen, P. 1985 'Socialist Worker – Paper with a purpose', *Media, Culture and Society.* Journal 7: 205–32.

Andreas G. 2000 'A Brief Survey of Mission Discussions and Its Importance for the Theme', in V. Premsagar, ed., *New Horizons in Christian Mission: A Theological Exploration,* Chennai: Gurukul Lutheran Theological College.

Appavoo, J. T. 1986 *Folklore for Change.* Madurai: Tamil Nadu Theological Seminary.

Arbaugh G E and Arbaugh G B 1968.*Kierkegaard Authorship: A Guide to the Writings of Kierkegaard.* London: Allen and Unwin Ltd.

Ariarajah, S. W. 1991 'Interfaith Dialogue', in N. Lossky, J. M. Bonino, J. Pobee, T. Stransky, G. Wainwright & P. Webb (eds., *The Dictionary of the Ecumenical Movement,* Grand Rapids: W. B. Eerdmans Publishing Co.

Ariarajah, S. W. 1999 *Not Without My Neighbor: Issues in Interfaith Relations.* Geneva: World Council of Churches.

Armstong, K. 2000 *The Battle for God .* New York: Alfred A. Knopf.

Arnett, R. C. 1986 *Communication and Community*. Carbondale: Southern Illinois University Press.

Arthur, C. 1993 *Religion and the Media: An Introductory Reader*. Cardiff: University of Wales Press.

Arthur, C. 1998The *Globalization of Communications Some Religious Implications*, Geneva: WCC..

Ascroft, J. & Sipho M. 1989 *From Top-down to Co-equal Communication: Popular Participation in Development Decision-making*. A Paper presented at the Seminar on Participation: A Key Concept in Communication and Change in Atton, C. 2002, *Alternative Media*. London: Sage.

Atton, C. 2002 *Alternative Media*. London: Sage.

Atton, C and Couldry, Nick 2003 'Introduction' *Media, Culture and Society*, 25:579-586.

Atwood, R. & McAnany E. 1986 *Communication and Latin American Society*. Madison, WI: University of Wisconsin Press.

Avis, P, 1999 *God and the Creative Imagination: Metaphor, Religion and Myth in Religion and Theology* Routledge.

Babin, P, 1991. *The New Era in Religious Communication*. Translated by D Smith, Minneapolis: Fortress Press.

Bakhtin, M. 1984b. *Problems of Dostoevsky's poetics*. C. Emerson, Ed. and Trans., Minneapolis, MN: University of Minnesota Press.

Bakhtin, M. 1981a *The Dialogical Imagination*. M. Holquist, (ed.

Austin: University of Texas Press.

Bakhtin, M. 1982 Holquist, Michael Liapunov, Vadim Brostrom. Kenneth Trans., *The Dialogic Imagination : Four Essays*. Texas: University of Texas Press Slavic Series.

Bakhtin, M. 1986. *Speech genres and other late essays*. V. McGee, Trans. Austin: University of Texas Press.

Bakhtin, M. 1982 'Discourse in the novel'. In M. Holquist (Ed., *The Dialogic Imagination: Four Essays*. C. Emerson & M. Holquist, Trans. Austin: University of Texas Press.

Bakhtin, M. 1984 *Rabelais and his world*. H. Iswolsky, Trans. Bloomington: Indiana University Press.

Balasuriya, T. 1998 Recolonization and Debt Crisis, p8-12, in *Globalization: A Challenge to the Church* edited by Jagadish Gandhi and George Cheriyan, Chennai, Association of Christian institutes for Social Concern in Asia.

Balthasar H U (1901-88) 1982. *The Glory of God: A Theological Aesthetics –Seeing the Form.* Vol 1 tr by E Leiva-Merikakis and ed by J Fessis and J Riches Edinburgh T & T Clark.

Balthasar H U (1901-88) 1986. *The Glory of God: A Theological Aesthetics – Studies in Theological Style – Lay styles.* Vol 3, Tr by A Louth and ed by J Riches Edinburgh T & T Clark.

Balthasar H. U. (1901-88) 1991. *The Glory of God: A Theological Aesthetics – The Old Covenant.* Vol 6 tr by B McNeil and E Leiva Merikakais and ed by J Riches Edinburgh T & T Clark.

Balthasar H U (1901-88) 1991.*The Glory of God: A Theological*

Aesthetics – The realm of Metaphysics in the Modern Age. Vol 5 tr by O Davies and ed by B McNeil and J Riches. Edinburgh: T & T Clark.

Balthazar, H. U. 1994 *Theo Drama: Theological Dramatic Theory : The Dramatis Personae Man in God.* San Francisco: Ignatius Press, Trans. by Graham Harrison. Volume 4.

Balthazar, H. U. 1998 *Theo Drama: Theological Dramatic Theory : The Dramatis Personae Man in God.* San Francisco: Ignatius Press, Trans. by Graham Harrison. Volume 5.

Barboza, F. 1990 *Christianity in Indian Dance Forms.* Delhi: Sat Guru Publications.

Bausch W. I. 1986 *Story Telling: Imagination and Faith.* Connecticut: Twenty-Third Publications.

Beale, D. O. 1986 *In Pursuit of Purity: American Fundamentalism Since 1850.* Greenville, SC: Unusual Publications.

Belsey A. & Chadwick, R 1992 *Ethical Issues in Journalism and the Media.* London: Routledge.

Beltrán, L.R. 1993 'Communication for development in Latin America: a forty-year appraisal' in Nostbakken, D. & Morrow, C. (eds. *Cultural expression in the global village.* Penang, Malaysia: Southbound. 10–11.

Bhatnagar, S. 2000, 'Information Technology and Development: Foundation and Key Issues' in *Information and Communication Technology in Development – Cases from India, et al by Subhash Bhatagar and Robert Schware, New Delhi:* Sage.

Boal, A. 1982 *The Theatre of the Oppressed.* New York/London:

John Joshva Raja

Routledge Press.

Boersma, H. 2005 *Imagination and Interpretation: Christian Perspectives.* Vancouver: Regent College Publishing.

Bohm, D 1998 *On Creativity.* Routledge: London.

Bohm, D. 1996 *On Dialogue.* Routledge: London.

Borsch, F. H. 1988 *Many Things in Parables: Extravagant Stories of New Community.* Philadelphia: Fortress Press.

Bosch, D. 1991 *Transforming mission. Paradigm shifts in theology of mission.* American Society of Missiology Series, no.16. New York: Maryknoll Orbis Books.

Bosten, R. 1996 *The Most Dangerous Man in America?: Pat Robertson and the Rise of the Christian Coalition.* New York: Prometheus Books.

Bowen, W. 1996 Citizens for Media Literacy, Asheville: NC.

Brasted, H. V. 1997, 'The Politics of Stereotyping: Western Images of Islam', *Manushi*, Journal Issue no. 98, January-February 1997, pp.1–11,

Buber, M. 1958 *I and Thou*, 2nd edn. Southampton: Camelot Press

Bunsa, D. 2002 Peddling Hate: The Role of the Dominant Gujarati Language Media during the Genocidal Anti-Muslim Pogrom was Chillingly Communal and Provocative. August, *Frontline,* 2, pp.13–14.

Carey, J. W. 1989 *Communication as Culture. Essays on Media and Society.* New York/London: Routledge.

Carpenter, J. A. 1997. *Revive Us Again* . New York: Oxford University Press.

Carr, W.1990 *Ministry and the media.* London : SPCK.

Castells, M. 1998 "Information Technology, Globalization and Social Development." Papers presented at the *UNRISD Conference on Information Technologies and Social Development.* Geneva, 22-23 June.

Cheriyan, G. 1998 Globalization – A Conspiracy of the Rich Against the Poor – p.63-74, *Globalization: A Challenge to the* Church edited by Jagadish Gandhi and George Cheriyan, Chennai, Association of Christian institutes for Social Concern in Asia, 1998.

Chomsky, N. 2002 "Clash of Civilizations?" *Seminar*, Vol.509, January, pp.100-102.

Christians, C. and Traber, M. (Eds) 1997 *The Ethics of Being in a Communications Context, Communications Ethics and Universal Values.* Thousand Oaks, CAL, London, New Delhi: Sage.

Christians, C. Mark, F and Rotzoll K. B. 1995 *Media Ethics: Cases and Moral Reasoning.* London: Longman.

Christopher, R, 2007 'The Impact of Television Evangelists on the Church-Going habit of Christians in Tuticorin District.' An Unpublished *M Th Thesis*, Bangalore: United Theological College.

Coleman, L. 1995 'Worship God in Dance *Renewal Journal* 6, 2, Brisbane, Australia, pp. 35-44.

John Joshva Raja

Crossan J. D. 1973 *In Parables: The Challenge of Historical Jesus.* New York: Harper and Row.

Crossan J. D. 1974 A. 'Parable and Example in the Teaching of Jesus', *Semeia.* 1,63-104.

D'Costa. G. 1986 *Theology and Religious Pluralism,* Oxford: Basil Blackwell.

Dalhouse, M T. 1996. *An Island in the Lake of Fire: Bob Jones University, Fundamentalism, and the Separatism Movement.* Athens, GA: University of Georgia Press.

David, C.R.W., ed. 1986 *Communication in Theological Education: A Curriculum.* Bangalore: Asian Trading Corporation.

De Vries, H. 2001 "In Media Res: Global Religions, Public Spheres and the Task of Contemporary Comparative Religious Studies" in De Vries and Weber, eds *Religion and Media.* Stanford: Stanford University Press. 3-42.

DeBerg Betty A. 1998 "Response to Sam Hill, 'Fundamentalism in Recent Southern Culture.'" *Journal of Southern Religion.* 1:1

Derrida, J 2001 Above All, No Journalists" in De Vries and Weber, eds 2001, *Religion and Media.* Stanford: Stanford University Press. 56-93.

Dodd, C. H. 1935 *Parables of the Kingdom* London: Nisbet & Co.

Downing, J. 2001 with Tamara Villareal Ford, Geneve Gil and Laura Stein *Radical Media: Rebellious Communication and Social Movements.* Thousand Oaks: Sage.

Edappilly, John.2003, *The Emerging Electronic Church.* Bangalore: Asian Trading Corporation, 2003.

Eilers, F-J. 1993a *Communicating between Cultures: An Introduction to Intercultural Communication.*
Indore: Staprakashan Sanchar Kendra.

Eilers, F-J. 1993b *Church and Social Communication: Basic Documents.* Manila: Logos Publications, 1993.

Engineer, A.A. 2002a *Media and Minorities.* Mumbai: Centre for Study of Society and Secularism.

Engineer, A A. 2002b Clash of Terrors, *Secular Perspective,* 16-31.

Entman, R.M. 1989 *Democracy without Citizens: Media and Decay of American Politics.* New York: OUP.

Enzenberger, H M 1976 'Constituents of a Theory of the Media'. *In Raids and Reconstructions: Essays on Politics, Crime and Culture.* London: Pluto Press.

Fallon, D. J. & Wolbers, M. J.eds 1982, *Focus on Dance X: Religion and Dance.* Virginia: A.A.H.P.E.R.D.

Fishbane, M. 1985 *Biblical Interpretation in Ancient Israel.* Oxford: Clarendon Press.

Fiske, J. 1982 *Introduction to Communication Studies.* London: Methuen.

Fiske, J. 1989 *Understanding Popular Culture.* Boston: Unwin Hyman.

Fitzmyer J.A. 1985 *The Gospel according to Luke X-XXIV.* The Anchor Bible. V28 A, New York: Double Day.

Flanders, L. 2002 *Real Majority, Media Minority: The Costs of Sidelining Women in Reporting.* Common Courage Press.

Fore, W.F. 1987 *Television and Religion: The Shaping of Faith, Values and Culture.* Minneapolis: Augsburg.

Fore, W.F. 1990 *Myth Makers: Gospel, Culture and the Media.* New York: Friendship Press.

Fraser, N.1992 'Rethinking the Public Sphere: *A* Contribution to the Critique of Actually Existing Democracy', in C. Calhoun, ed *Habermas and the Public Sphere.* Cambridge: MIT Press.109-142.

Freire, P and Shor, I. 1987 *A Pedagogy for Liberation. Dialogues on Transforming Education.* London: Macmillan.

Freire, P. 1972, *Pedagogy of the Oppressed.* Harmondsworth: Penguin.

Friedland L. A. *2001,* Communication, Community, and Democracy: Toward a Theory of the Communicatively Integrated Community, *Communication Research Journal*, Vol. 28, No. 4, 358-391.

Funk R W 1974 A. 'Critical Note', *Semeia.* 1, 182-191.

Funk R W 1974 B. 'Structure in the Narrative Parables of Jesus, Semeia. 2, 51-73.

Funk R W 1974 C *'The Good Samaritan as Metaphor',* Semeia. 2, 74,81.

Gabriel, A. Sivan, E. and Appleby. R. S. 1995. "Fundamentalism: Genus and Species." in *Fundamentalisms Comprehended* . ed Martin E. Marty and R. Scott Appleby. Chicago: University. 399-424.

Gadamer, H-G. 1979. *Truth and Method.* London: Sheed and Ward.

Gagne, R., Kane, T. & Ver Eecke, R. 1984, *Dance in Christian Worship.* Washington: Pastoral.

Galeano Eduardo. Clowns for the Market Circus: The Media and Globalization, *Media Channel February 3,* 2000, p1-3 www. mediachannel.org/views/oped/galeano.shtml.

Gauntlett, D. 1996, *Video Critical: Children, The Environment and Media Power.* Luton: John Libbey media.

Gerbner, G, Mowlana, H, Nordenstreng, K. 1993 *The Global Media Debate, Its Rise, Fall and Renewal*, Norwood: blex Publishing Corporation.

Giddens, A. 1990 *The consequences of modernity*, Cambridge: Polity.

Giuseppe, S. 2001 Spirituality in inter-religious Dialogue: Challenge and Promise. In *Encounter,* 274, April.

Goethals, G. T. *1990, The Electronic Golden Calf: Images, Religion, and the Making of Meaning.* Cambridge: Cowley.

Goethals, G T. *The Electronic Golden Calf: Images, Religion, and the Making of Meaning.* Cowley 1990.

Gramsci, *A.* 1971 *Selections from the Prison Notebooks.* Edited and translated by Q. Hoare and G. Nowell-Smith. "General Introduction" by Q. Hoare. London and New York: Lawrence & Wishart; International Publishers.

John Joshva Raja

Gramsci, A. 1973 *Letters from Prison.* Selected, translated from the Italian, and Introduced by Lynne Lawner. New York: Harper & Row.

Green G, 1998 *Imagining God: Theology and Religious Imagination.* William B Eerdman's publishing.

Gunewardena, V. 1997 'Communication Ethics and the Role of the State', AMIC, *Communication Ethics: A South Asian Perspective.* Singapore: AMIC.

Gunter, B. 2002 *Media Research Methods.* London: Sage.

Gupta, A.K. Kothari, B. and Patel, K. 2000 Knowledge, Network for Recognising, Respecting and Rewarding Grassroots Innovation! – in *Information and Communication Technology in Development - Cases from India, et al by Subhash Bhatagar and Robert Schware, New Delhi:* Sage,.

Gupta, K. 2004 *Hindu Tele-Evangelists.* New Delhi: Sunday Pioneer.

Habermas, J. 1987 *The Theory of Communicative Action vol. 2 Life world and System: A Critique of Functionalist Reason.* Boston: Beacon Press.

Habermas, J. 1990 *Moral Consciousness and Communicative Action.* Cambridge: MIT Press.

Habermas, J. 1991 *The Structural Transformation of the Public Sphere: An Inquiry into a category of Bourgeois Society.* Translated. Thomas Burger with Frederick Lawrence. Cambridge, MA: MIT Press.

Habermas, J. 1996 'The Public Sphere', in *Media Studies: A Reader.* Et.al., Marris,P. and Thornham,S. Edinburgh: Edinburgh University Press. 109-122.

Hadden, J. K. 1992. "Religious Fundamentalism," in Borgatta, Edgar F. and Marie Borgatta, eds. *Encyclopaedia of Sociology* . New York: Macmillan Publishing. Vol 3. 1637-1642.

Hadden, J. K. and Anson S. 1989 "Is There Such A Thing As Global Fundamentalism?" in *Secularization and Fundamentalism Reconsidered.* Jeffrey K.

Hall, S. H, D. and McGrew, T. *1992 Modernity and Its Futures.* Cambridge: Polity Press.

Hall, S.1977 Culture, Media and the 'Ideological Effect', in James Curran, M. Gurevitch, and J. Woollacott (eds., *Culture, Media, Language.* London: Hutchinson.

Hall, S. Et.al.,1980 'Encoding/Decoding', *Culture, Media and Language.* London: Hutchinson.

Hamelink C. J. 1997 "New Information and Communication Technologies, Social Development and Cultural Change." *Discussion Paper No. 86, June 1997, United Nations Research Institute for Social Development,* Geneva, Switzerland.

Hamelink, C. 1975 *Perspectives of Public Communication: A Study of the Churches Participation in Public Communication.* Baarn: Ten Have.

Hamelink, C.J. 1994 *The Politics of World Communication.* London: Sage.

John Joshva Raja

Hamelink, C. J. 1995, *World communication: Disempowerment and self-empowerment* London: Penang : Zed Books.

Hamelink, C. J. 1998, "ICTs and Social Development: The Global Policy Context." *Papers presented at the UNRISD Conference on Information Technologies and Social Development.* Geneva, 22-23 June.

Hamilton. E. and Cairns. H. 1963. *The collected Dialogues of Plato including Letters.* Princeton: PUP.

Hankins, B. 1996 *God's rascal: J. Frank Norris & the beginnings of Southern Fundamentalism.* Lexington, KY: University Press of Kentucky.

Heather C, 1999 Cultural Implications of the Internet & Postmodernity, pp39-47, in *Interactions: Theology Meets Film, TV and the Internet.* Edited by Heidi Campbell and Jolyon Mitchell Edinburgh: CTPI, 9.

Hess, M. E. 1999 *Media Literacy as a Support for the Development of a responsible Imagination in Religious Community,* Presented to the Media Religion and Culture Conference, Edinburgh, Scotland.

Hick, J. 1980 *God has Many Names.* London: Macmillan.

Hill, S. 1998 "Fundamentalism in Recent Southern Culture: Has it Done What the Civil Rights Movement Couldn't Do?" *Journal of Southern Religion* . 1:1.

Hippler, J and Andrea L. Ed, 1995 *The Next Threat - Western Perceptions of Islam* Pluto Press, London.

Hocking, E. W.1947 *Freedom of the Press: A Frame Work of*

Principle. Chicago: University of Chicago Press.

Hocking, W E. 1932 *Rethinking Missions.* New York: Harper and Row.

Hocking, W E. 1940 Living *Religions and a World Faith*, London: Allen and Unwin.

Hoover, S.M. 1988 *Mass Media Religion: The Social Sources of the Electronic Church.* Newsbury Park: Sage.

Hoover, S M. and Lundby, K. 1997 *Rethinking Media, Religion and Culture.* London: Sage.

Horsfield, P G. 1984 *Religious Television, The American Experience.* New York: Longman Inc.

Huesca, R. 1995 'A Procedural View of Participatory Communication: Lessons from Bolivian Tin Miners' Radio,' *Media, Culture & Society*, Vol. 17, 101-119.

Huesca, R. and Dervin, B. 1994 'Theory and Practice in Latin American Alternative Communication', *Journal of Communication*, vol. 44, No. 4 53-73.

Kucinski, B. 1991 *Jornalistas e Revolucionarios nos Tempos da Imprensa Alternativa.* Sao Paulo: Scritta editorial.

Lopez V, J. I. 1994 *Rebel Radio: The Story of El Salvador's Radio Venceremos.* Willimantic, CT: Curbstone Press.

Huntington, S. P.1993 The Clash of Civilizations?, *Foreign Affairs, Summer Issue.* v.72, n3, pp.22–28.

Hunt, R. A. E. 1993 'Story Telling is the Basis of Religious Communication', *Media Development.* 3, 16-18.

Huntington, S. P. 1996 *The Clash of Civilizations and the Remaking of the World Orders*. Delhi: Viking.

Ismail Ragi A. A, 1992`'Islam and Christianity: Diatribe or Dialogue', in *Muslims in Dialogue: The Evolution of a Dialogue*. L Swidler, ed The Edwn Mellen Press, Lewiston, NY, pp.1-22.

Jayaweera, N and Amunugama S. eds, 1987 *Rethinking Development Communication,* Singapore: Asian Mass Communication Research and Information Centre.

Jeremias, J. 1954 *The Parables of Jesus.* London: SCM.

Jones, G V 1964 The Art and Truth of the Parables: A study in their Literary form and Modern Interpretation. London: SPCK.

Jones, S. ed., 1995 *Cybersociety*. London: Sage.

Juergensmeyer, M. 1993. "Why Religious Nationalists are not Fundamentalists." *Religion*. 23, 85–92.

Juergensmeyer, M. 1996. "Fundaphobia--The Irrational Fear of Fundamentalism." *Contention.* 5: 3. Spring 127-32.

Jung C G. 1969 *The Structure and Dynamics of the Psyche*, **C.W.** 8. Princeton University Press.

Jung C G. 1969 *Psychology and Religion: West and East,* **C.W.** 11. Princeton University Press.

Jung C G. 1971 *Psychological Types, C.W. 6.* Princeton University Press.

Jung, C.G. 1961 *Memories, Dreams, Reflections.* Vintage Books.

Kalipeni, E. & Kamlongera, C. 1996 The role of 'theatre for development' in mobilizing rural communities for primary health care: The case of Liwonde PHC Unit in Southern Malawi, *Journal of social development in Africa,* 11 (1, 53-78.

Katovsky, B. and Carlson T. 2004 *Embedded: The Media at War in Iraq, An Oral History.* The Lyons Press.

Kaufman G. D. 1981 *Constructing the Concept of God: The Theological Imagination.* Philadelphia: The Westminster Press.

Kierkegaard. S. (1813-55) 1959. *Either/Or: A Fragment of Life.* V1 & 2, tr by W Lowrie Princeton: PUP.

Kierkegaard. S. (1847) 1995. *Works of Love.* ed and tr by H V Hong, and E H Hong. Princeton: PUP.

Kierkegaard. S. (1850) 1941A. *Training in Christianity and the Edifying Discourse which 'accompanied it'* tr by W Lowrie. London: OUP.

King, D. B, and Wertheimer, M, 2005 *Max Wertheimer and Gestalt Theory.* New Jersey: Transaction Publishers.

Kleinwachter, W. 1993 Three Waves of the Debate, 13-20, in *The Global Media Debate: Its Rise, Fall and Renewal,* edited by George Gerbner, Hamid Mowlana, Kaarle Nordenstreng, Norwood: Ablex Publishing Corporation.

John Joshva Raja

Kraemer, H. 1938 *The Christian Message in a Non-Christian World*, London: Edinburgh House Press.

Kraemer, H. 1956, Religion and the Christian Faith, London: Lutterworth Press.

Kraemer, H. 1962, *Why Christianity of All Religions?*. London: Lutterworth Press.

Krippendorf, K. 1980 *Content Analysis*. Beverly Hills: Sage, 1980.

Kucinski, B. 1991 *Jornalistas e Revolucionarios nos Tempos da Imprensa Alternativa*. Sao Paulo: Scritta editorial.

Kumar, K. 2002 *Representation of Islam in the Mass Media: An Analysis from a Reception Studies' Perspective*, UTC Seminar on 'Perceptions of Islam in the   Media', Bangalore, January 25.

Kurien K P 2003 *Pentecostals Attitude and Use of the Television*, Unpublished M Th thesis, Bangalore: UTC.

Kuruvilla, G. 2002 *From People's Theatre to People's Eucharist: Recovering the Drama of Christian Worship*. New Delhi: ISPCK.

Lambeth, E B. 1992 *Committed Journalism: An Ethic for the Profession*. Bloomington: Indiana University Press, 1992.

Larson, E J. 1997. *Summer for the Gods: The Scopes Trial and America's Continuing Debate Over Science and Religion*. Cambridge, MA: Harvard University Press.

Larson, E J. 2000. "Inherit the Monkey Trial," *Christianity Today*. May 22, Vol 44, No 6.

Lawrence, B.1989 *Defenders of God: The Fundamentalist Revolt*

Against the Modern Age . San Francisco: Harper & Row Publishers.

Lochhead, D. 1997 *Shifting Realities: Information Technology and the Church.* Geneva: WCC.

Lopez V, J. I. 1994 *Rebel Radio: The Story of El Salvador's Radio Venceremos.* Willimantic, CT: Curbstone Press. 1994.

Lynch, G. 2005 *Understanding Theology and Popular Culture.* Malden: Blackwell pub.
Mac Bride, Sean. 1978, *Interim Report on Communication Problems in Modern Society.* Paris: UNESCO.

MacBride, S. 1980 Many Voices, One World. Towards a new, more just and more efficient world information and communication order, London: Kogan Page. UNESCO.

MacBride, S and Roach, C. 1993 'The New International Information Order' 3-12 in *The Global Media Debate: Its Rise, Fall and Renewal,* edited by George Gerbner, Hamid Mowlana, K Nordenstreng, Norwood: Ablex Publishing Corporation, 1993.

Magnuson, N. A. and William G. T. 1990 *American evangelicalism II: first bibliographical supplement, 1990-1996.* West Cornwall, CT: Locust Hill Press.

Manuel C. 1998 Information *Technology, Globalization and Social Development*, Papers presented at the UNRISD Conference on Information Technologies and Social Development. Geneva.

Manuel, A and Boyd – B. O. eds. 1992, *Media Education. An Introduction.* London: BFI.

Marsden, George. 1980 *Fundamentalism and American Culture.*

John Joshva Raja

New York: Oxford University Press.

Marsden, George. 1987 *Reforming Fundamentalism.* Grand Rapids: Eerdmans.

Martin, J. 1998 "All that is Solid (and Southern Melts into Air: A Response to Sam Hill's Fundamental Argument Regarding Fundamentalism," *Journal of Southern Religion* 1:1

Martin, W. 1996 *With God on Our Side: The Rise of the Religious Right in America.* New York: Broadway Books.

Marty, M and Appleby. R. S. 1991 *Fundamentalisms Observed.* The Fundamentalism Project. Volume 1. Martin R. Marty and R. Scott Appleby. eds. Chicago: University of Chicago Press.

Marty, M and Appleby. R. S. 1993 *Fundamentalisms and Society.* The Fundamentalism Project. Volume 2 & 3. Martin R. Marty and R. Scott Appleby. eds. Chicago: University of Chicago Press.

Marty, Martin and Appleby. R. S. 1994. *Accounting for Fundamentalisms.* The Fundamentalism Project. Volume 4. Martin R. Marty and R. Scott Appleby. eds. Chicago: University of Chicago Press.

Marty, Martin and Appleby. R. S. 1995. *Fundamentalisms Comprehended.* The Fundamentalism Project. Volume 5. Martin R. Marty and R. Scott Appleby. eds. Chicago: University of Chicago Press.

McIntyre, J. 1987 *Faith, Theology and Imagination.* Edinburgh: The Handsell Press.

McLaughlin, R. W. 1968 *Communication for the Church.* Michigan: Zondervan Publishing House.

McLuhan, M.1994 *Understanding Media: The Extensions of Man.* Cambridge: The MIT Press.

McQuail, D. 1994 Mass Communication Theory: An Introduction, 3rd Ed, London: Sage.

Gauntlett, D. 1996 *Video Critical: Children, The Environment and Media Power.* Luton: John Libbey media.

McQuail, D. 1994 *Mass Communication Theory: An Introduction,* 3rd Ed, London: Sage, 1994.

Melkote, S. R. 1991 *Communication for Development in the Third World – Theory and Practice.* New Delhi: Sage Publications.

Melling, P. H. 1999 *Fundamentalism in America: Millennialism, Identity and Militant Religion Tendencies: Identities, Texts, Cultures.* Edinburgh: Edinburgh University.

Meshack, S. 1995, "Communication in Theological Education." Madras: GLTC. An Unpublished Paper.

Michale K. and Brian E. C. ed. 1997, *The Ecumenical Movement. An Anthology of Key Texts and Voices.* WCC Publications, Geneva.

Richard M. J. and Walsh B. J. 1995 *Truth is Stranger than it used to be: Biblical Faith in a Postmodern Age.* London: SPCK.

Mitra, A. 1994 *Television and Popular Culture in India: A Study of Mahabharat.* Delhi: Sage.

Mlama, P.M. 1991 "Women's participation in "communication for development": *The popular Theatre Alternative in Africa, Research in African Literatures*, 22 (3, 41-53.

Mohammadi, A. ed., 1997 *International Communication and Globalization*, London, Sage.

Morris, C.1990 *Wrestling with an Angel: reflections on Christian communication.* London: Fount.

Mowlana, H. 1996 *Global Communication in Transition: The End of Diversity?* Thousand Oaks, CA, Sage.

Newbigin, L. 1958 *One Body, One Gospel, One World.* London: International Missionary Council.

Nielsen, N. S. 1993 *Fundamentalism, Mythos, and World Religions.* Albany, NY: State University of New York Press.

Noll, M. 1992 *A History of Christianity in the United States and Canada* . Grand Rapids: Eerdmans.

Nolland J 1993 'Luke 9:21-18:34', *Word Biblical Commentary Series. V35B,* Dallas: Word Books.

O'Connor, A. 1989 'People's radio in Latin America: A New Assessment', *Media Development*, 2, 47-53.

Rodriguez, C. 2001 *Fissures in the Mediascape: An International Study of Citizens' Media.* Cresskill: Hampton Press.

O'Connor, A. 1989 'People's Radio in Latin America: A New Assessment', *Media Development*, 2, 47-53.

Oepen, M. 1993 'Community Communication – The Missing Link between the Old and the New Paradigm?' in Oepen, Manfred, Ed *Media Support and Development Communication in a World of Change.* B Berlin: Freie Universitat.

Oomen, M A. 1998 *Globalization and Decolonization: The Contemporary Challenges, in the book Globalization: A Challenge to the Church* ed by P Jagadish Gandhi and George Cheriyan, Chennai: ACISCA.

Patterson, P. and Wilkins L. *1991 Media Ethics: Issues and Cases.* Madison: WCB Brown and Benchmark.

Pattison. G 1992 *Kierkegaard: The Aesthetic and the Religious: From the Theatre to the Crucifixion of the Image.* Houndmills: Macmillan.

Peter K. 2001 *Towards A Dialogue of Learning and Criticism*, A Paper presented at the International Conference on the Dialogue of Civilizations, United Nations University, 3rd August, Kyoto: UN.

Petersen, N. R. 1974 'On the Notion of Genre in Via's Parable and Example Story: A Literary-Structuralist Approach', *Semeia.* 1, 134-181.

Pillai, M. 1984 'Communication of the Bible Message in India: To the Poorly Educated Masses', *Indian Theological Studies*, 21, 3-4, 269-295.

Postman, N. 1986 *Amusing Ourselves to Death.* London: Methuen, 1986.

Prabhat, P. 2002 Market, Moral and The Media, *Frontline*, pp.128-134.

John Joshva Raja

Race, A. 1983 *Christians and Religious Pluralism: Patterns in Christian Theology of Religions*, London: SCM Press, 1983.

Rahner, K. 1961-84, *Theological Investigations*. Vol 6. London: Darton, Longman and Todd.

Raja, J. 2002 *Communication, Reconciliation and the Culture of Dialogue*, a paper presented at Kualalumpur for Asia Region WACC Congress, Kualalumpur: WACC.

Raja, J. 2001 *Facing the Reality of Communication: Culture, Church and Communication*. New Delhi: ISPCK, 2001.

Raja, J. 2003 'Relevant and Effective Theological Education in the Twenty First Century India. January, *Ministerial Formation* Geneva: WCC's Publications.

Raja, J. 2005 *Internet, Mission and Ecumenism*, Published as Document of EMS, presented for Mission societies in Stuttgart, November, 2002.

Reid, E. M.1994 *Cultural Formations in Text-Based Virtual Realities*, M.A. Thesis at University of Melbourne, Melbourne: University of Australia.

Report of the Citizen's Commission on Persecution of Christians in Gujarat, 1999, *Hindu jago Christy bhago – Violence in Gujarat: Test Case for A Larger Fundamentalist Agenda.–* an Initiative of the National Alliance of Women. Print Media: April, 1-25.

Reyes M. F. ed 1983 Comunicación Alternativa y Búsquedas Democráticas. Mexico City: Instituto Latinoamericano de Estudios Transnacionales.

Simpson Grinberg, M. (ed 1986 Comunicación Alternativa y Cambio Social. Mexico: Premia.

Rodriguez, C. 2001 "Fissures in the Mediascape": *An International Study of Citizens' Media.* Cresskill: Hampton Press.

Reyes M. F.1983 ed *Comunicación Alternativa y Búsquedas Democráticas.* Mexico City: Instituto Latinoamericano de Estudios Transnacionales.

Ricoeur. P Ed, by Wallace. M. I. 1995 *Figuring the Sacred: Religion, Narrative, and Imagination.* Translated from the French by David Pellauer. Minneapolis: Fortress.

Woodberry R. D. and Smith. C. S. 1998 "Fundamentalism et.al: Conservative Protestants in America," *Annual Review of Sociology* 24:25-56.

Robinson, G. 1986 *Harmony Among Religions: Is it necessary? Is it acceptable? What is it for?* Nagercoil: KJPP.

Rodrigues, P. R. 1986 Vive a Imprensa Alternativa. Viva a Imprensa Alternativa in R Festa and C E Lins Da Silva eds Comuncacao Popular e Alternativa no Brazil 53-76. Sao Paulo: Paulinas.

Rodriguez, C. 2001 *Fissures in the Mediascape: An International Study of Citizens' Media.* Cresskill: Hampton Press.

Rogers E.M. ed. 1976 *Communication and Development: Critical Perspectives.* Beverly Hills: Sage Publications.

Rogers, E.M. 1969 *Modernization among Peasants.* New York: Holt, Rinehart and Winston.

John Joshva Raja

Rogers, E. M. 1985 *Communication Theory: The New Media in Society.* New York: The Free Press.

Rogers, E. M. 1976 'Communication and Development: The Passing of a Dominant Paradigm', *Communication Research.* 3, pp. 213-240.

Roozen, D. A Alice Frazer Evans, and Robber A Evans, 1996 *Changing the Way Seminaries Teach: Globalization and Theological Education*, Hartford: Centre for Social and Religious Research.

Rosengren, K.E.1981, ' Mass Media and Social Change : Some Current Approaches', in E. Katz and T. Szecsko (eds, *Mass Media and Social Change*. London: Sage.

Roxborogh, J. 2000, Persecution: Interpreting the information on the Internet, Evangelical Review of Theology, 24:1, 31-40.

Ruesch, J. 1957, *Technology and Social Communication. In Communication Theory and Research.* Ed. Lee Thayer. Springfield, Ill.

Ghanananda, S. 1970 *Sri Ramakrishna and His Unique Message,* London.

Radhakrishnan, S. 1969 Eastern Religions and Western Thought, New York.

Said, E. 1997, *Covering Islam: How the Media and the Experts determine how we see the Rest of the World.* New York: Amazon.

Samartha, S. J. 1981 *Courage for Dialogue: Ecumenical Issues in Inter-religious Relationships.* Geneva: WCC.

Samartha, S J. 1991 "Inter-religious Relationships in the Secular State' in *Interfaith Dialogue and World Community* edited by Mr Ch Sreenivasa Rao, Madras:CLS.

Samartha, S.J. 2000 *One Christ - Many Religions: Toward a Revised Christology.* Bangalore: SATHRI, 2000.

Saussy, H. 2001 "In the Workshop of Equivalences, Translation, Institutions and Media: The Jesuit Re-Formation of China", In De Vries and Weber 2001: *Religion and Media.* Stanford: Stanford University Press.

Schechter, D. 2003 *Embedded: Weapons of Mass Deception: How the Media Failed to Cover the War on Iraq.* New York: Prometheus Books.

Scherer, J. A. and Bevans, S. B. eds 1992 *New Directions in Mission and Evangelisation 1 Basic Documents.* New York: Orbis.

Schleirmarcher, P.1988 *On Religion: Speeches to its cultural Despisers.* Translated by Crouter, R, Cambridge: CUP.

Schramm W. and Lerner D. eds. 1976a, *Communication and Change.* Honolulu: University Press of Hawaii.

Schramm, W & Porter, W. E. 1982, *How Communication developed in Men and Women Messages and Media.* New York: Harper and Row.

Schramm, W. 1964 *Mass Media and National Development.* California: Stanford University Press.

Schulman, M. 1992 Communicating in the Community. In Janet Wasko, Vincent Mosco (eds *Democratic Communications in the*

John Joshva Raja

Information Age. Ablex. Norwood, New Jersey.

Schultze, Q. J. 2000 *Televangelism and American Culture: The Business of Popular Religion.* Eugene: Wipf & Stock Publishers.

Schutz, W. 1958 *Firo: A three-dimensional theory of interpersonal behaviour.* New York: Holt, Rinehart, and Winston.

Seidman, S. 1994 *The Post-modern Turn: New Perspectives on Social Theories.* Cambridge: Cambridge University Press. 1994.

Servaes, J. 1993 Development Communication Approaches in an International Perspective', in Manfred Open ed. *Media Support and Development Communication in a World of Change.* Berlin: Freie Universitat, pp 24-39, 1993.

Shiri, G. 2002, *Saffronisation of Mass Media with Special Reference to Kannada Print Media.* Presented at UTC for the Refresher Course, pp.1-12.

Smith, A. 1991 The Age of Behemoths: The Globalization of Mass Media Firms, New York: Priority Press – pp 21-37.

Soukup, P. A.1991 *Communication and Theology: Introduction and Review of the Literature.* London: WACC.

Sparks, C. 1985 'The Working-class Press: Radical and Revolutionary Alternatives', *Media, Culture and Society 7:133-46.*

Sparks, C.1985. 'The Working-class Press: Radical and Revolutionary Alternatives', *Media, Culture and Society 7:133-46.*

Spenser, F. S. 1984 2 Cronicles 28:5-15 and the parable of the Good Samaritan' *Westminster Theological Journal.* 46, 2, 317-349.

Stein R H 1978 'The interpretation of the parable of the Good Samaritan' pp 278-295, in Gasque WW and Lasor W S (eds Scripture, Tradition and Interpretation. Grand Rapids: Eerdmans.

Stern, D. 1991 Parables in Midrash: Narrative and Exegesis in Rabbinic Literature. Cambridge: Harvard University Press.

Stone, H and Stone, S. W. 1993 *Embracing Your Inner Critic: Turning Self-Criticism Into a Creative Asset.* San Francisco: Harper.

Strobel L and Poole G. 2006, *Exploring the Da Vinci Code.* Michigan: Zondervan.

Tariq, A. 2002, *The Clash of Fundamentalisms: Crusades, Jihads and Modernity.* London: Verso.

Townsley, N. *Forecast and Recommendations: Television and Globalization,* www.matei.org/research/globaltv/forecast.html

Traber, M. 1985 "Alternative Journalism, Alternative Media", *Communication Resource*, October, London: *World Association for Christian Communication.* No.7.

Fraser, N. 1992 'Rethinking the Public Sphere: A Contribution to the Critique of Actually Existing Democracy', in C. Calhoun (ed Habermas and the Public Sphere, 109 142. Cambridge: MIT Press.

Traber, M. 1997, The Ethics of Communication worthy of Human Beings, in Clifford Christians and Michael Traber eds. *Communication Ethics and Universal Values.* Thousand Oaks, CAL. London, New Delhi: Sage, pp.327-343.

Traber, M. *2003 Globalization, Mass Media and Indian Cultural Values.* New Delhi: ISPCK.

289

John Joshva Raja

Tracy, D. 1981 The Analogical Imagination: Christian Theology and the Culture of Pluralism. New York: Cross Road.

Turkle, S. 1997 *Life on the Screen: Identity in the Age of the Internet.* London: Phoenix-Orion Books.

Vallath, C. 2000 "The Technologies of Convergence", in Electronic Communication Convergence: Policy Challenges in Asia, by Mark Hukill, Ryota Ono, Chandrasekhar Vallath, New Delhi: Sage.

Varadhan, M. S. S. 1997 'Opportunities' *The Hindu*, 15th October Supplement.

Via D. O. 1967. The parables: Their Literary and Existential Dimension. Philadelphia: Fortress Press.

Via. D. O. 1974. 'Parable and example Story: A Literary – Structuralist Approach', *Semeia. 1-3,105-133.*

White, R. A. 1982 "Contradictions in Contemporary Policies for Democratic Communication", Paper to an IAMCR Conference, Paris, September.

White, R. A. 1993 The New Order and The Third World, 21-34, in *The Global Media Debate: Its Rise, Fall and Renewal*, edited by George Gerbner, Hamid Mowlana, Kaarle Nordenstreng, Norwood: Ablex Publishing Corporation.

White, R. A.1993 The New Order and The Third World, in *The Global Media Debate: Its Rise, Fall and Renewal*, edited by George Gerbner, Hamid Mowlana, Kaarle Nordenstreng, Norwood: Ablex Publishing Corporation, pp.21-34.

Whitney, C. R. 2005 *The WMD Mirage: Iraq's Decade of Deception and America's False Premise for War*. New York: Public Affairs.

Wilder, A N. 1982 *Jesus Parables and War of Myths; Essays on the Imagination in the Scriptures.* London: SPCK.

Williams, R. 1977 *Marxism and Literature.* Oxford: Oxford University Press.

Williams, R. 1962 *Communications.* England: Penguin Books.

Williams, R. 1977 *Marxism and Literature.* Oxford: Oxford University Press.

Williams, R. 1994 *Television Technology and Cultural Form,* edited by Ederyn Williams London: Routledge.

Williamson, H.A. 1991 The Fogo process: Development support communications in Canada and the developing world. In Casmir, F.L. Ed. *Communication in development,* pp.270-287,. Norwood, NJ: Ablex Publishing Corporation.

Young, B. H. 1989. *Jesus and Jewish Parables, Rediscovering the Roots of Jesus' Teaching,* New York: Paulist Press.

Webliography
Amaladoss. Michael 2004, *Dialogue as Conflict Resolution: Creative Praxis* www.sedos.org/english/amaladoss1.html 2004

An interview with Noam Chomsky, *Third World Network,* July 1, 1996 http://www.corpwatch.org/article.php?id=1809.

Barboza, Francis Dictionary of Indian Christian Theology – Dance. http://www.drbarboza.com/dictionary.htm

Coeyman, Barbara Spirituality of Dance, A Sermon, Oregan: Unitarian church, 2001.
http://www.firstunitarianportland.org/sermons/sermons2001/SpiritualityOfDance.html

Extra ecclesium nulla salus, 2003 'Inter-religious Dialogue is Part of Evangelising mission, Pope says.. It Implies Profound Respect for Culture He tells Indian Bishops', Vatican City, June 26, , http://www.tcrnews2.com/genjp2000.html.

Guidelines on *Nostra Aetate* 1974...
http://www.vatican.va/roman_curia/pontifical_councils/chrstuni/relations-jews-docs/rc_pc_chrstuni_doc_19741201_nostra-aetate_en.html p.2.

Huntington, Samuel P., 1993, The Clash of Civilizations? Foreign Affairs, Summer Issue. http://www.alamut.com/subj/economics/misc/clash.html. 72, n3,pp.22-28.

Lucinda. Coleman, 'Worship God in Dance' *Renewal Journal* #6 (1995:2), Brisbane, Australia, pp. 35-44. http://www.pastornet.net.au/renewal/journal6/coleman.html

No author, Spiritual Significance of Dance, *Theology of Dance*. http://orgs.sa.ucsb.edu/actsone8/Sym_Dance.html

Said, Edward. 2001, *The Clash of Ignorance, Media Monitors Network.* (October, 11, 2001), http://www.mediamonitors.net/edward40.html.

Silvio Waisbord, 2001, Family Tree of Theories, Methodologies and Strategies in Development Communication: Convergences and

Differences, Prepared for The Rockefeller Foundation, http://www.
comminit.com/strategicthinking/stsilviocomm/sld-1774.html

The Following Links are used throughout the book.

Some Christian websites that are often used in this book
http://www.pastornet.net.au/renewal/journal6/coleman.html
http://newark.rutgers.edu/~rtavakol/engineer/clash.htm.
http://ecumene.org/IIS/csss60.htm

Some News paper resources that are used in this book
http://www.alamut.com/subj/economics/misc/clash.html.
http://www.hinduonnet.com/fline/fl1915/19151280.htm
http://www.ee.mu.oz.au/papers/emr/cv.html
http://www.hindustantimes.com/news/specials/emotions2002/
paranoia.html

http://news.bbc.co.uk/1/hi/world/south_asia/2749667.stm

http://www.bbc.co.uk/info/purpose/
http://stream.guardian.co.uk:7080/ramgen/sys-video/
Guardian/Reuters/2003/04/09/various_victims.rm
http://stream.guardian.co.uk:7080/ramgen/sys-video/
Guardian/Reuters/2003/04/06/Basra.rm
http://media.guardian.co.uk/Print/0,3858,4643575,00.html
http://www.hindustantimes.com/news/specials/emotions2002/
paranoia.html
http://news.bbc.co.uk/go/pr/fr/-/2/hi/uk_news/2885179.stm
http://www.worldrevolution.org/projects/webguide/article.
asp?ID=713
http://news.bbc.co.uk/go/pr/fr/-/2/hi/uk_news/2885179.stm

Critical readers of newspapers
http://www.mediamonitors.net/edward40.html.   http://free.
freespeech.org/manushi/98/islam.html
http://journalism.org/resources/research/reports/war/embed/
impressions.asp,
http://www.alternet.org/story.html?StoryID=15507

Website for United Theological College, Bangalore
www.utcbangalore.com

Website for Gurukul Lutheran Theological College, Chennai
http://www.gltc.edu/history.htm

Website on Religion online
http://www.religion-online.org/.
Website for Christian Media Association of India
http://www.cmai.org/memb-mp.htm

Website for Henry Martin Institute for Islamic Studies
http://www.hmiindia.com/academic_04.htm

Website on Interfaith Interaction maintained by the author
www.interfaithinteraction.org

Website for Rastrya Swayam Sevaksangh – A Hindu Nationalist Social Service Organisation
http://www.rss.org/New_RSS/index.jsp

Website of Bharathya Janatha Party – A Political Party Hindu Nationalist
http://www.bjp.org/

Website for Vishwa Hindu Parishad A Hindu Revivalist

Organisation
http://www.vhp.org

Website for ShivSeva – A Hindu Political and Revivalist Movement
http://www.shivsena.org/index.htm

Website on Amnesty resources
http://web.amnesty.org/library/Index/
ENGASA200292003?open&of=ENG-IND

A website for Human Right Reports
http://www.hrw.org/reports/2002/india/India0402-03.
htm#P659_118122
        http://www.pucl.org/Topics/Religion-communalism/2002/
gujarat-media.htm
        http://www.sacw.net/2002/dayal04072003.html
        http://www.sabrang.com/tribunal
        http://www.workingforchange.com/article.cfm?itemid=14813
        http://www.digitaljournalist.org/issue0305/smarkisz.html
        http://www.worldmag.com/world/issue/04-05-03/opening_3.
asp

Websites dealing with Iraq War
http://counterpunch.org/
http://www.zmag.org/content/Iraq/miller_eliminatingtruth.
cfm
        http://www.zmag.org/content/showarticle.
cfm?SectionID=15&ItemID=3484
        http://www.pbs.org/newshour/extra/features/jan-june03/
embed_3-27.html
        http://www.mediaed.org/news/articles/mediairaq
        http://www.fair.org/international/iraq.html

http://www.alternet.org/story.html?StoryID=15507
http://www.defenselink.mil/news/Feb2003/d20030228pag.pdf
www.wsws.org
www.wsws.org

Website resources for embedded media
http://journalism.org/resources/research/reports/war/embed/
impressions.asp
http://journalism.org/resources/research/reports/war/embed/
impressions.asp,
http://journalism.org/resources/research/
reports/war/embed/impressions.asp
http://www.mediaed.org/news/articles/mediairaq
http://www.pbs.org/newshour/extra/features/jan-june03/
embed_3-27.html
http://www.alternet.org/story.html?StoryID=15507
http://www.alternet.org/story.html?StoryID=15507
http://www.alternet.org/story.html?StoryID=15507
http://www.guardian.co.uk/antiwar/story/0,12809,937143,00.
html
http://www.mediaed.org/news/articles/mediairaq
http://www.mediaed.org/news/articles/mediairaq

Websites on Tele-Gurus
http://www.bible.ca/tongues-kundalini-shakers-charismastics.
htm

Websites on Media Awareness
http://www.media awareness.ca/english/teachers/media_
literacy/what_is_media_literacy.cfm
http://www.media awareness.ca/english/teachers/media_
literacy/what_is_media_literacy.cfm
http://www.sacw.net/2002/dayal04072003.html

Websites on Religious communalism

http://www.pucl.org/Topics/Religion-communalism/2002/ gujarat-media.htm

http://www.hrw.org/reports/2002/india/India0402-03. htm#P659_118122. http://web.amnesty.org/library/Index/ ENGASA200292003?open&of=ENG-IND
http://www.pucl.org/Topics/Religion-communalism/2002/ gujarat-media.htm
http://www.sabrang.com/tribunal

Other websites that are used in the book
http://en.wikipedia.org/wiki/The_Passion_of_the_Christ
http://www.sawf.org/newedit/edit02032003/aol.asp
http://www.digitaljournalist.org/issue0305/smarkisz.html
http://www.digitaljournalist.org/issue0305/smarkisz.html
http://news.bbc.co.uk/1/hi/world/south_asia/2749667.stm
www.arabworldbooks.com/Articles/articles51.htm
www.sedos.org/english/amaladoss1.html   http://www. jmcommunications.com/english/DigitalCulture.html
http://www.unrisd.org/engindex/publ/list/dp/dp86/toc. htm#TopOfPage
http://www.unrisd.org/infotech/conferen/castelp1.htm
http://www.ee.mu.oz.au/papers/emr/cv.html
http://www.csisynod.org/
http://www.uelcindia.org/index.html
http://www.csitirunelveli.org/csi_td.asp
http://business.vsnl.com/zion/
http://www.angelfire.com/al3/ipcpallipad/ipc.html
http://www.baptistinfo.com/States/INDIA/INDIA.HTM
http://www.dmpb.org/
www.vishwavani.org & http://www.gospelcom.net/twr/
http://www.radiovoiceofhope.net/
http://www.awr.org/awr-asia/

http://www.indiaevangelical.org/contrib.html
www.utcbangalore.com.
http://hbi.gospelcom.net/home.asp
http://www.wmcarey.edu/carey/serampore/serampore.htm
http://www.otsindia.org/seminary/
http://www.otsindia.org
http://asiapacificuniverse.com/asia_pacific/messages30/358.html
http://www.ayrookuzhiyil.bravepages.com/links.html
http://www.prayertoweronline.org/
http://www.internetworldstats.com/stats.htm
http://www.ecunet.org/
http://home.wizard.org/eocc/eocc1/front.html
http://www.commedia.org.uk/about-community-media/
http://www.commedia.org.uk/about-community-media/community-media-changes-lives/
http://www.drbarboza.com/dictionary.htm
http://www.firstunitarianportland.org/sermons/sermons2001/SpiritualityOfDance.html
http://www.ratzingerfanclub.com/Balthasar/dramatics.html
http://www.brechtforum.org/IPE/boal.htm
http://www.unrisd.org/infotech/conferen/icts/toc.htm.

END NOTES

(Endnotes)

1   Now the word 'God' is used in 420,000,000 WebPages (Google) and receives a billion strikes a week in these websites. The word 'life' is used in 1 050 000 000 websites to be searched.

2   Imagination means image forming power of the mind or the power of the mind that modifies the conceptions, especially the higher form of this power exercised in art and poetry. - Webster's Reference Library, Dictionary and Thesaurus (Concise Edition) 2006, New Lanark: Geddes and Grosset. P.164.

3   Aesthetic means the philosophy of art and beauty - Webster's Reference Library, Dictionary and Thesaurus (Concise Edition) 2006, New Lanark: Geddes and Grosset. P.12-13.

4   http://en.wikipedia.org/wiki/The_Passion_of_the_Christ

5   Leela is the nature of Supreme Consciousness, playful nature. The phenomenal world is manifested Leela. The play is beginningless - as well as endless. Leela is the great adventure and the great discovery. Again, and again, and again, and again - without any loss and without any gain - this endless game is played. Those who realize the "play" in the game are not caught by the game-board, and know it as the Leela (Divine game) of Leela-Dhar (Cosmic Consciousness). Those who identify with the squares and planes of the game-board are played by the game-board; and the game-board becomes maya (illusion), the great veiling power that binds the mind. It is maya which creates the phenomenal world. It is Leela that makes it a great adventure. Tamas brings the player to maya - and boundless love and spiritual devotion to Cosmic Consciousness. Spiritual devotion (bhakti loka) is the great discovery of Leela, created by maya of Supreme Consciousness in order to enjoy Himself - to play hide and seek with Himself. There is no purpose and no responsibility in Leela.

http://www.sanatansociety.org/yoga_and_meditation/hinduism_philosophy_leela_lila_lilla.htm

6   http://news.bbc.co.uk/1/hi/5074578.stm

7   http://news.bbc.co.uk/1/hi/world/south_asia/4759111.stm

8   http://www.asianews.it/index.php?art=6202&l=en&size=

9   http://www.asianews.it/index.php?art=6202&l=en&size=

10   http://www.indcatholicnews.com/news.php?viewStory=874

11   http://www.wsws.org/articles/2006/may2006/dvc-m25.shtml

12   http://www.thetruthaboutdavinci.com/christian-response-to-da-vinci-code.html

13   http://www.asianews.it/index.php?l=en&art=1026&dos=16&size=A

14   http://www.asianews.it/index.php?l=en&art=720&dos=16&size=A

15   http://www.asianews.it/index.php?l=en&art=703&dos=16&size=A

16   http://www.icon-art.info/book_contents.php?lng=en&book_id=32

http://www.asianews.it/index.php?l=en&art=909&dos=16&size=A

17   http://www.icon-art.info/book_contents.php?lng=en&book_id=32

18   Melanie Jane Wright, *Religion and Film: An Introduction.* London: IB, 2007. p.168.

19   http://www.zenit.org/article-8894?l=english

20   Soukup [1991:27-29] points to six communication images that dominate in the relationship between theology and communication

.

- Linguistic image: language with its syntactic, semantic, and pragmatic characteristics, fundamentally defines communication for those who accept this image. People with this view ask about the relationship between language forms and language contents.
- Aesthetic image: communication cannot and must not be restricted to discursive and logical contents nor to their codes. The whole range of art and imagination constitutes

valid communication and provides theological pattern for the analysis of that communication.

• Cultural image: communication cannot be separated from the overall culture - patterns of human thought, manifestations of that thought, and the construction of society. This is an effect model.

• Interpersonal dialogue model: it allows for conversation and sees communication that links people or that builds up community, as the perfection and goal of all communication.

• Sender -message- receiver analogue: this mechanical image originates in 'information theory' and finds application in any broadcast situation in which coding and encoding can defined as relatively value free or neutral.

• Theological terminology: human communication and its media becomes the subject of a re-application of the analogic language applied to divine communication.

•

21   http://www.communiquejournal.org/q4_ryken.html

22   http://feastuponthewordblog.org/2007/11/13/ricoeurs-the-bible-and-imagination-part-1/

23   Dialogue I differ from Habermas because he wants the discussing parties in dialogue to engage through reason and arrive at consensus on enlightenment values. My concept of dialogue is not necessarily arriving at consensus rather establish contact, relationship and agree to coexist (at the point of extreme disagreement). In this way for me different truth narratives though they may be exclusive of each other can coexist alongside without confronting or colliding.

24   For convenient sake only I describe God with exclusive language that describes God in third person as 'him'. I do not assume God either as male or as female.

25   http://www.israelofgod.org/genesis1.htm

26   The Trinity and the kingdom Fortress press, by J. Moltmann http://blakehuggins.com/2009/09/18/moltmann-reflections-a-trinitarian-eccelsiology/

27   http://www.inplainsite.org/html/tele-evangelist_lifestyles.
html

28   http://www.geocities.com/CapitolHill/7027/quotes.html

29   Kraemer argues that under the search light of Christ all
religious life, the lofty and degraded, appear to lie under the divine
judgement, because it is misdirected [Kraemer 1938: 136]. For him
undeniably God works and has worked in man outside the sphere
of Biblical revelation and so even in this fallen world God shines
through in a broken troubled way: in reason, in nature and in history.

30   http://www.irf.net/irf/drzakirnaik/index.htm

31   Sri Sri Sri Ravi Sankar of Art of Living has described Jesus
in his own ways - Another way to look at these "I am the only way"
statements is that Jesus, Krishna and Buddha were saying the abstract
cannot be approached directly, but only though the personal. The
teacher, the enlightened one, comes to be a bridge for you so that
you can move from that which you can see and know to that which is
invisible and unknown, from that which is changing and impermanent
to that which is imperishable. Saying "I am the only way" is also a
means of focusing attention. In every religion, there are words offered
which bring this focus. Jesus said, "Those who have come before
me are robbers and thieves." He meant, you are thinking about the
prophets who came before me and ignoring what is present. The
prophets are stealing your minds and attention. I am here and now.
Come to me and me alone. Don't look anywhere else. Krishna has
spoken in this way also: Look only here. I and the only one. And
Buddha said, "I am the past, the present and the future. I come again
and again in every age." The eternal son of God has come more than
once—He has manifested many times. In the guru's great generosity
he returns again and again, bringing wisdom from age to age. Sri Sri
Sri Ravi Sankar 2003, One God, One truth, One World, *Connect,*
http://www.sawf.org/newedit/edit02032003/aol.asp

32   He outlines four theses in favour of this approach – first, he
writes,   that Christianity understands itself as the absolute religion,
intended for all men, which cannot recognise any other religion

besides itself as of equal right (Vol 5, p.118, 1966); secondly, he emphasises on the universal salvific will of God revealed in Christ. Thus for him a non-Christian religion can be recognised as a lawful religion (although only in different degrees) without thereby denying the error and depravity contained in it (Vol 5, p.121); thirdly he argues that a non- Christian cannot be considered as a person deprived of salvific grace, living totally sinful and depraved condition, untouched in any way by God's grace and truth. Those non-Christians who have accepted God's grace in the depths of their hearts are called by Rahner as 'anonymous Christians' (vol 5 p.132); fourthly for him the church is the tangible sign of the faith, hope and love made visible, present and irreversible in Christ.

33   An interesting and critical analysis of the Charismatic groups in television and of tele-gurus is carried out from a Biblical perspective. Even such a critical study can be biased. http://www. bible.ca/tongues-kundalini-shakers-charismastics.htm

34   For Hick the Incarnation should be understood mythological rather than literally. His intention is not to destroy religious particularity, but to view different types of religious experience as complementary and not mutually exclusive. It is the question of the relative validity or adequacy of the images of God which are alive in the different traditions.

35   Also see http://www.mediaawareness.ca/english/teachers/ media_literacy/what_is_media_literacy.cfm

36   Wally Bowen, Citizens for Media Literacy, Asheville, NC, U.S.A, 1996. http://www.media awareness.ca/english/teachers/ media_literacy/what_is_media_literacy.cfm

37   The media do not present simple reflections of external reality. Rather, they present carefully crafted constructions that reflect many decisions and result from many determining factors. The media are constructions. They play the role of a gatekeeper (allowing us to see only part of the reality), mirror (reflecting the society) and screen (blocking our views on certain realities). Media Education works towards deconstructing these constructions, taking them apart to

John Joshva Raja

show how they are made.

38   The media are responsible for the majority of the observations and experiences from which we build up our personal understandings of the world and how it works. Much of our view of reality is based on media messages that have been pre-constructed and have attitudes, interpretations and conclusions already built in. We know about many countries and people because we see them through the media. But they may not exactly represent the countries or the people there. The media, to a great extent, give us our sense of reality.

39   The media provide us with much of the material upon which we build our picture of reality, and we all "negotiate" meaning according to individual factors: personal needs and anxieties, the pleasures or troubles of the day, racial and sexual attitudes, family and cultural background, and so forth. The audiences decode the communicated message in three ways. At times some of them may agree, some may disagree and some may negotiate meanings that are embedded in the media texts.

40   Gesa Elsbeth Thiessen (2004). *Theological Aesthetics: A Reader*. Eerdmans. p. 1.

41   Kierkegaard states: If someone says directly 'I am God; the father and I are one, this is direct communication. But if the person who says it, the communicator, is this individual human being... just like others, then this communication is not quite entirely direct. ...an individual human being should be God - whereas what he says is entirely direct. Because of the communicator, communication contains a contradiction, it becomes indirect communication [(1850) 1991:134].

42   For Kierkegaard Christ places before individuals a choice, and while they choose, Christ himself is revealed to them [1941A:98]. Kierkegaard points out that Christ called on people to accept him as Lord by accepting rejection and by allowing himself to be crucified. It

304

is in the form of an irony that attempts to persuade a learner to choose to believe that Jesus is God.

The second point that Kierkegaard makes in defence of indirect communication is that it exists only for faith. He argues: He (Christ) is the paradox, the object of faith, existing only for faith. But all historical communication is communication of 'knowledge'; hence from history one can learn nothing about Christ. History makes out Christ to be other than He truly is [1941A:28]. For Kierkegaard faith is thus the response to a communication that is indirect and direct communication of Christ is an impossibility26. He argues that the 'proofs' in Scripture for Christ's divinity, such as his miracles and his resurrection from the dead, are recognised through faith. The miracle stories prove that all these conflict with reason and therefore are objects of faith [1941A:29].

In Kierkegaard's theological understanding God is seen as one who has given freedom of choice to human beings; the choice whether or not to believe in him. In Kierkegaard's argument God chooses to participate in communication with his people through indirect communication. It is God who wants to communicate indirectly27. It brings a new understanding to the relationship between God and human beings, as communication does not simply flow from God to people. God enters the human level of understanding and uses the form through which he attempts to share his love and care for his people.

43   In his *Training in Christianity,* he identified the learner as being in the age of aesthetics. The teacher has to go to the place where the learner is in order to communicate with him or her indirectly [Kierkegaard 1941]. The age in which the clergy of the established churches are derided as 'poets' and in which the sort of character portrayed in Heiberg's *A Soul After Death,* is also considered as aesthetic [Pattison 1992:62]. The aesthetic age means the age in which the audience engages often in the cultural practices that give them pleasure and entertainment. To make communication effective,

there is a need to recognise and share their audience's medium and aesthetic interests. The primary task of the Christian communicator must be to find and to start from the place where the audience is.

44   In Christian communication it is essential to recognise the fact that the task is to help audiences to realise their capability and to persuade them to see in themselves these virtues. Pattison argues that the ethical teacher is not concerned to put knowledge into the learner but to draw out from him his own capability or potentiality [1992:74]. Kierkegaard notes, "It may be that science can be pounded into a person, as far as aesthetic capability is concerned and even more so with the ethical, one has to pound out of him" [1967 (4): 285]. He explains this using an analogy in which he illustrates the difference between pounding the soldier out of the farm boy by recognising the capability in him and the soldier studying a manual of field tactics in order to become a farm boy. It means that ethical communication does not require any kind of knowledge [1967(1):285]. This argument
supports the fact that the audience shares certain ethical and social values even before they
89 are communicated to them. The task of the communicator is to make them to realise these values in them.

It is important to note that in Kierkegaard's argument about indirect communication, the communicator should make it clear that he is not the teacher since only God bestows eternal truth on each individual. It leads to an act of recognition on the part of the communicator that the learner somehow already possesses the truth. He must acknowledge that everyone stands absolutely alone in his relationship to God.
45   (Lk 14:15-24; Mt 22:1-14 and G Th 64.)
46   In the Old Testament some of the prophets used similar genre and forms [2Sm 12:1ff, Is 5:1-3 and Ecc 9:13-16]. Jesus' hearers might have been familiar with the characters and form of the stories in the Old Testament which were interwoven with aesthetic elements. In the earlier prophets the story of a king and the woman of Teko'a is a good example of using aesthetic elements in communication (2 Sm

14:1-7). This woman tells him a story which uses familiar characters, genre that can bring the listener into its context and mediates the contemporary social issues. The later prophets (e.g. Is 28:23-25 and Jar 18:1-6) use such aspects of communication. This is primarily to show that people were accustomed to this style of storytelling and its mediating role between their beliefs and their contexts. In the Old Testament many narratives that described historical events contained aesthetic elements [e.g. the narratives in the book of Esther and in the book of Job].

In the Inter-Testamental writings there are references to parabolic forms and comparisons during this period. During the Inter Testamental period, the Old Testament narratives were interpreted by using aesthetic elements and with additional descriptions. Vander Kam [1981:70] concludes that the synoptic stories drew their inspiration from the Inter Testamental pronouncement stories which share common traits among them. The practice of using aesthetic elements that mediated people's beliefs and context was already known to the Jewish interpreters and to the people. Greenspoon [1981:76] argues that Philo included the pronouncement stories that were circulating through the Greek world (e.g. Cher 63; Plant 65). Josephus composed these stories by himself, related them to the historical narratives and interpreted them from his religious viewpoint (BJ 4.460-65 – Elisha's story & 6.409-411). Greeenspoon [1981:77] comments: Titus entering the defeated city of Jerusalem commends the strength of that city's towers and especially the God of Israel, who indeed 'has been with us in the war'.

It was God who brought down the Jews from these strongholds; for what power have human hands or machines against these towers. He referred to another story in which a Jewish soldier corrected the view of Alexandrian soldiers in shooting the bird (Ap 1.201-204). This clearly shows the use of aesthetic elements by Josephus not only in narrating the events but also in interpreting them in order to share certain meanings with his audience.

47   The Qumran texts contain one parable - the parable of the Tree (4Q 302a). Philo has a few parables in Ebr 35,155 and Conf Ling 99. Josephus retells Nathan's story in Ant 7.147-150; 8.44. Josephus writings are dated after 70 CE, but they are used to show the possible use of the parabolic forms among the Jewish interpreters.

48   It was not till after 200 CE the rabbinical writings recorded parables, but some scholars argue that the oral tradition of the Tannaitic period could be attributed to the time of Jesus or even earlier. Young [1989:55] argues that parables took shape as artistic creations in oral teachings before they became a literary genre and that they arose from Haggadic teachings. He recognises that the parables preserved from Hillel and Shammai were fragmentary and that R. Johanan b. Zakkai (90 CE) employed the parable as a teaching device [1989:107]. He also points out that illustrations and parables appear frequently in Midrashic texts which deal with Halakhic matters [Young 1989:60].

49   The parable of the sower portrays a familiar event in the life of the sower (Mt 13:1-9; Mk
    4:1-9 and Lk 8:4-8).

50   A familiar scene is shown in the parable of the net where an action of throwing the net into
    the sea is compared with the kingdom (Mt 13: 47-50).

51   The problem with the study of the parable of the Good Samaritan is that many of the texts including Inter Testamental books, the writings of Philo, Qumran texts, and the writings of Josephus do not contain similar forms of stories. The lawyer is not presented with a role model but with an unexpected character (Samaritan) that might enable him to interpret his beliefs. For reasons already given this study considers this parable to be more than a straightforward example story82. Example stories were less used in the texts that

were contemporary to Jesus83. Stern [1991:197f] claims that parables were popular at the time of Jesus among the Jewish audience. His hypothetical argument that the scribes did not consider them worthy to be recorded until late antiquity does not hold good except in a single reference to Bar Kappara (late rabbinical writings).

I recognise the fact that there is an absence of the use of the example stories just before the time of Jesus. Some of them used 'parables' in a shorter form (the prophets, the Qumran texts and Philo's writings). In this section it is argued that Jesus' contemporaries made use of aesthetic elements and plots in their teachings. This is supported by the fact that such characteristics of communication occur in both the Old Testament and in the Inter Testamental books. Old Testament references show that some of the early prophets used such forms and genre in their parabolic communication (e.g. Nathan's story in 2Sm 12:1-4, Jehoash's fable in 2Ki 14:8-10). My study argues that Jesus could have brought the Haggadic practice of interpretation with the Mashal type of communication together to result in this story form. It points out the use of Haggadic method of interpretation by the Old Testament prophets and by other Inter Testamental writers.

52 'Using Aesthetic Elements in Haggadic Exegesis'

The aesthetic elements were displayed in the parables in order to enable the audience to participate in the process along with Jesus. By comparing other texts, it may be possible to identify whether Jesus interacted with the existing practice of using aesthetic elements. Jesus' use of aesthetic elements in the parable differed from their use in fantasy stories and myths. The parable of the Good Samaritan displayed those characters and plots that were part of everyday human life [Jones 1964:113-6].

It is essential to recognise that Jesus engaged in the people's process of communication by interacting with the aesthetic elements. In the parable of the Good Samaritan, an unidentified traveller was brought into the scene and the background was the road between Jerusalem and Jericho. This setting on the road between Jerusalem and Jericho brought the context of the story closer to the audience's place. Nolland [1993:593] points out that the Jericho of New Testament times is to be distinguished from ancient Jericho.

Marshall [1978:447] gives a picture of this road which descends some 3,300 ft in the course of 17 miles. Jericho was rebuilt by Herod the Great about a mile and a half to the south, on the western edge of the Jordan plain (BJ 4.451-4 & 4.473-5). Josephus refers to an incident in which Pompey, the Roman Emperor destroyed brigands here (BJ 4.478 cf. Strabo 16. 2.41). The arrival of bandits in the story raised a sympathetic attitude towards this traveller which was further increased by the attack and by the description of his condition. Jesus used these elements in order to enable his audience to feel the reality which he displayed in the story and thus allow them to participate in the search for meanings relevant to them.

Such use of aesthetic elements in the parables was a common practice among Jewish interpreters. It was an ongoing process of communication in which his contemporaries used these elements as a way of capturing and maintaining the attention of their audience in order to interact with them. These aspects of communication could be found in the Haggadic exegesis which was a common practice during the later rabbinical period. The Haggadic exegesis on the texts had stories which displayed such elements. Schwartz [1983:87-93] notes the development in the Haggadic process of the story of Cain in which different aesthetic elements (such as embellishment) and popular forms (such as fantasies and dreams) were added at different historical stages. Jesus participates in such exegetical practice in order to maintain the attention of the lawyer and of the audience86 in general.

53   http://in.reuters.com/article/idINIndia-32129120080225
54   Myth is also defined as a traditional story, either wholly or

partially fictitious, providing a popular idea concerning some natural or social phenomenon or some religious belief or ritual (The New Shorter Oxford English Dictionary –first definition).

55   Fundamentalism is understood as the strict maintenance of traditional orthodox religious beliefs or doctrines especially belief in the inerrancy of scripture and literal acceptance of the creeds as fundamentals of one's own religion (The New Shorter Oxford Dictionary). Fundamentalism in simple words can be explained as an act of return to the fundamentals of a particular religion which people believe to be literally true.

56

57   Ignorance does not refer to 'not-knowing the other' rather it means to 'knowing more or only the negative side of the other'. It is often articulated by the vested groups and so can be identified as 'articulated ignorance' of the other. This makes it clear that it is not only the media but also the intellectual as well as political forces that are creating myth about the other which in turn creates ignorance (intentionally as well as unintentionally).

58   The news about north-eastern states is often reported when there are problems or disasters in those areas except the peace process in Nagaland. This is commonly practised by the news media as an accepted practice. During a one-year period   in magazines such as India Today and Frontline, nearly 90% of the articles about the North Eastern states are related to violent incidents or insurgency.

59   I classify this under negative because there are a number of grand, positive events and social services among the churches which were never noticed by the news reporters. Even popular events among Christians were not reported.

60   e.g. *India Today* January, 7, 2002 p.33 – Islamism; The New Enemy; *Frontline* July 5, 2002 Freelance Jihads.

61   *India Today* June 3, 2002

62   (e.g.' Bloodied Brothers' – statement by Hindutva leaders, in *India Today*, August 5, 2002; Prime minister's statement 'Wherever Muslims are, they don't want peace. They don't want to mix with

others. They use terror as a weapon', quoted by P Chidambram, in *India Today*, April 29, 2002).

63 It means, for the magazines, men could divorce their wives without their consent even through email, post or telephone (in *India Today*, May 20, 2002); women should cover their head; the full application of Sharia Law wherever they are in a majority (*Frontline*, September 14–27, 2002) and so on. They are seen as fanatics and fundamentalists in promoting their faith whereas many of us have not heard anything about Red Crescent (e.g. *Frontline* 2002 July 5: 116, – Muslims will hoist their flag in the Red Fort). These are examples of myths that are popularly believed by other religious communities in India.

64 They illtreat women, yet they have accepted a number of rulings by Indian courts in relation to Talaq and women's rights (e.g. *India Today* 2002, April 29, Honour killings of Women; Male Dominated Society to refer to Muslim communities. *India Today* 2002 May 20, Talaq is one of the most feared words in the lives of Muslim women). They are exploiting Hindu's hospitality and patience. (e.g. *India Today*, May 13, 2002, News about RSS' Prahnidhi Sabha in Bangalore – their statement is reported – Muslims to understand that their safety lay in the goodwill of the majority. No good will and no safety, the RSS explains, unless Muslims respect, tolerate and co-operate with the Hindus.)

65 http://www.sacw.net/2002/dayal04072003.html

66 http:\\www.Documents and Settings\Administrator\Desktop\Taiwan\pluralism\Coping with the fallout.htm

67 *Sandesh (a Gujarathi* Newspaper) quoted in *India Today Magazine*, "ten to fifteen women were kidnapped and raped by religious (Islamic) fanatics from the Godra Train" (p.13, Aug 2, 2002) and "70 HINDUS ARE BURNT ALIVE" as Headlines. A quote from a statement issued by a VHP leader Ashok Singhal, of the Vishva Hindu Parisad -VHP (World Hindu Council) says, 'AVENGE BLOOD WITH BLOOD'. The communal violence in Gujarat symbolizes the first positive response of Hindus to Muslim fundamentalism in a

thousand years'

68 'Gujarat Violence as natural and spontaneous response' - RSS, May 13, 2002. The Chief Minister of Gujarat Modi said, "If they cannot shout 'Jai Shri Ram' in India, will they go to Italy and raise the slogan? - November 25, 2002. Inter-Services Intelligence (ISI – Pakistan) agents were in every corner of the country and they were all Muslims. ... Gujarat is just like Kashmir, is just another example of "cross border terrorism" in which Indian Muslims routinely take part. (July 5, 2002, p.117).

69 http://www.hrw.org/reports/2002/india/India0402-03. htm#P659_118122 "We Have No Orders To Save You" State Participation and Complicity in Communal Violence in Gujarat, Human Rights Watch Report. April 2002. **http://web.amnesty.org/ library/Index/ENGASA200292003?open&of=ENG-IND** This is an Amnesty International Report on the Godhra incident and the role of Media during and after such incidents.

70 1. THE VICTIMS MASS MURDERS: 10-15 GIRLS WERE PULLED OUT BY RELIGIOUS FANATICS: 10-The report says: 15 girls were dragged out of the Sabarmati Express; this is being hotly discussed in Godhra. As a result there is tension. The survivors of this incident also said this. The police are also trying to look for this. These girls were trying to escape from the train, police has denied it, but Kaushik Patel of VHP has accused. 2. MUSLIM LEADER PREVENTED THE FIRE ENGINE BY BRANDISHING AN OPEN SWORD. The fire brigade learnt of the fire at nine o'clock and rushed to the spot soon after. But at that very moment a local Muslim leader armed with an open sword appeared and prevented the fire brigade from putting out the fire. Other religious fanatics joined them and an atmosphere of communal tension/discord spread in the entire Godhra city.

3. ABOUT 10 YOUNG GIRLS WERE PULLED OUT FROM THE RAILWAY CARRIAGE BY A GROUP OF RELIGIOUS FANATICS. The news item goes on to refute the headline.

Analysis: What is the intention in having such headlines if not to provoke? On 2nd March Gujarat Samachar another Gujarati newspaper said that this report was false.
http://www.pucl.org/Topics/Religion-communalism/2002/gujarat-media.htm

71   http://www.sabrang.com/tribunal
The former Indian Prime Minister made a few statements such as 'Muslims not repentant enough for Godhra, December 17, New Delhi. The pamphlets were circulated in large numbers in Gujarat containing a number of calls for Hindus to boycott Muslims saying 'Hindus and Sikhs Beware!'" dated 13 April, 2001, and 'Rise! Awaken!' More than 2000 Muslims were killed after the Godhra incident in Gujarat and many thousands were internally displaced and cannot return to their native place.

72   17 December 2001, New Delhi Sample this statement by VHP's Pravin Togadia, made soon after the Gujarat election results were announced, 'India will be a Hindu Rashtra in two years... the status of Muslims here will be similar to that of Hindus in Pakistan or slightly better.'
http://www.hindustantimes.com/news/specials/emotions2002/paranoia.html
http://www.sabrang.com/camp/hatespeechtogadia.pdf

73   India has the population of 133 millions.
http://www.milligazette.com/Archives/15092001/29.htm
http://ibnlive.in.com/news/indian-muslims-unite-against-terror-hold-peace-march/80002-3.html

74   http://www.asiamedia.ucla.edu/article.asp?parentid=51223

75   He defined civilization as the largest units of identity to which people adhere – each unit consisting of groups of culturally compatible countries. Civilization is the highest cultural grouping of people and the broadest level of cultural identify people have short of that which distinguishes from other species. [Huntington 1993: p. 2].

76   Huntington adds the Russian orthodox as a separate civilization.

77   Sinic describes the common culture of China and the Chinese communities in Southeast Asia and elsewhere.

78   He refers to Saudi Arabian country as the most extreme fundamentalists in extreme. For him Saudi Arabian leaders treat women as awfully as they want and direct the money to US.

79   http://news.bbc.co.uk/go/pr/fr/-/2/hi/uk_news/2885179.stm 2003/03/25

80   http://www.defenselink.mil/news/Feb2003/d20030228pag. pdf

81   www.wsws.org

"The Department of Defence issued invites for more than 800 embedded media positions, of which more than 600 were deployed from 220 media organizations," she said. "70% of media allocations were slated for domestic national print and electronic media, 20% for international media representing more than 60 countries in Europe, Asia and South America, including news agencies such as Sky News and Al Jazeera, and the remaining 10% of the embedded positions were allocated to local and regional media." http://www.defenselink. mil/news/Feb2003/d20030228pag.pdf

82   www.wsws.org,   http://www.wsws.org/articles/2003/ mar2003/med-m05.shtml,
      http://www.defenselink.mil/news/Feb2003/d20030228pag.pdf

83   http://www.worldrevolution.org/projects/webguide/article. asp?ID=713

84   http://mtprof.msun.edu/Fall1997/Blevins.html

85   http://news.bbc.co.uk/go/pr/fr/-/2/hi/uk_news/2885179.stm

86   http://ics.leeds.ac.uk/papers/vp01.cfm?outfit=pmt&folder=34 &paper=461
      http://www.journalism.org/node/1536
      http://journalism.org/resources/research/reports/war/embed/ impressions.asp, p. 6,7

87   http://www.journalism.org/node/1536

88   http://journalism.org/resources/research/reports/war/embed/ impressions.asp,

89   http://journalism.org/resources/research/reports/war/embed/impressions.asp, p.8
http://www.mediaed.org/news/articles/mediairaq
90   http://www.pbs.org/newshour/extra/features/jan-june03/embed_3-27.html
http://www.poynter.org/
91   http://www.pbs.org/newshour/extra/features/jan-june03/embed_3-27.html
92   http://www.alternet.org/story.html?StoryID=15507
93   http://www.alternet.org/story.html?StoryID=15507
94   http://www.alternet.org/story.html?StoryID=15507
95   http://www.guardian.co.uk/antiwar/story/0,12809,937143,00.html
96   http://www.mediaed.org/news/articles/mediairaq
97   http://www.mediaed.org/news/articles/mediairaq
98   http://www.digitaljournalist.org/issue0305/smarkisz.html
99   http://www.digitaljournalist.org/issue0305/smarkisz.html
100 http://www.digitaljournalist.org/issue0305/smarkisz.html
101 We need to bring the journalists and media practitioners together to discuss about these issues along with religious scholars (e.g. the conference on the 'Perception of Islam in the News Media). We should also realise the fact that mass media are not the only means of communication to know about the other religious communities.
102 Def: A culture of dialogue is one in which people habitually gather together to explore their lives, their dreams and their differences. (Tom Atlee - Building a Culture of Dialogue) Every facet of such culture would contribute to people learning together, building healthy relationships with each other and the natural world and co-creating better prospects for their shared future.
103 John Joshva Raja *Facing the Reality of Communication: Culture, Church and Communication.* 2001 Delhi: ISPCK.
104 Avery Dulles, Christ Among the Religions, *The National Catholic Weekly,* February, 4, 2002, Vol 186, No 3,p 1-12).
105 R Panikkar, *The Intrareligious Dialogue.* Paulist Press New

York, 1978.

106 Francis, D 1983, 'Christianity, Culture and Communication', The South India Churchman (now CSI Life), July, 10-11.

107 (Quoted in the book, *What Religion is in the Worlds of Swami Vivekananda*, S Vidyatmananda (ed) Calcutta 1972, p.235)

108 Maulana Wahiduddin Khan, *Progress in Inter-Religious Dialogue*. http://www.alrisala.org/Articles/papers/progress.htm

109 M Fethullah Gulen, 'The Necessity of Interfaith Dialogue: A Muslim Perspective', *Fountain,* Vol. 3, Issue 31, 2000, pp.4-9.

110 D G Moses, Evangelism – 'The Mission of the Church to those outside her life', *The South India Churchman.* 1954, June 4-5.

111 Among many television channels broadcast from 4.30.a.m. to 7.30.p.m. a number of Christian, Hindu, Sikh, Islamic and other religious programmes are broadcast every morning. These programmes focus mainly on healing, spiritual advice, miracles, fortune telling, prosperity gospel, astrology, numerology, nameology or religious teachings. For evangelical preachers masses come together to listen to television preachers such as D G S Dhinakaran (in India), Mr Benny Hynn (in US) or others.

112 For this one needs to understand why lay Christians are not taking lead in the dialogue? The lay Christians in India (may be to some extent in South Asia) are interested in evangelising other communities and are often suspicious about the native culture and faith. Many of them support missionaries and evangelists who are trying to convert people from other religions to Christianity. They have a fear about exclusive **pluralism** by which I mean a stand point where everyone is supposed to agree that all the religions lead people towards the ultimate truth that is God. Some fundamentalist Christian preachers share common concerns with other religious fundamentalists. For example some ultra evangelical speakers speak against the Valentine's Day just like the Shiv Sena (a Hindu Fundamentalist and regionalist group) had attacked the shops that were selling Valentine's Day cards. http://www.shivsena.org/index.htm   http://news.bbc.co.uk/1/hi/

world/south_asia/2749667.stm

113 Doing theology of dialogue at grassroots seriously needs to radically address the three issues given below: 1. Too much emphasis of 'evil' outside the 'self' and seeing it in the social structure or institution or religion (evil as an outside force rather than part of each one's self); 2. Identifying the other community as one monolithic community and linking them with evil and darkness, blackness, uncivilised, ugly and lower strata (poverty as a curse or punishment); 3. Fixing 'narratives' into a static packaged narrative in order to play god. These three elements need to be addressed in doing theology in a pluralistic context.

114 Gadamer [1979:347] uses the word 'conversation' that he describes as a process of two people understanding each other. It is a process in which each opens himself/herself to the other person, accepts the other's point of view as worthy of consideration and gets inside the other to the extent that he understands not the individual but what the other says. For him the horizons for the present (interaction with the other) merge with the horizons of the past (prejudices and traditional thinking) and thus continually grow together in order to make living value without being explicitly distinguished from the other. One has to put one's own prejudices and understandings to the test. By seeking to discover other people's standpoint and horizon their ideas become intelligible without one necessarily having to agree with them [Gadamer 1979:270]. The dialogue for Gadamer is 'conversation' between people as individuals.

115 Bakhtin explains dialogue in terms of human life. For him life by its very nature is dialogic. To live means to participate in dialogue. He says, "To live means to participate in dialogue: to ask questions, to heed, to respond, to agree and so forth. In this dialogue a person participates wholly and throughout his whole life; with his eyes, lips, hands, soul, spirit, with his whole body and deeds. He invests his entire self in discourse and this discourse enters into the dialogic fabric of human life, into the world symposium [Bakhtin 1984:293].

Bakhtin is concerned about the language and its meanings. He uses the term 'Heteroglossia' to describe the inscription of multiple voices engage in dialogue within the text. For him dialogue is the dialectical relationship between self and other where self occupies a relative center, and thus requires the other for existence.

116 In Bohm's view: "the general tacit assumption in thought is that it's just telling you the way things are and that its not doing anything - that 'you' are inside there, deciding what to do with the info. But you don't decide what to do with the info. Thought runs you. Thought, however, gives false info that you are running it, that you are the one who controls thought. Whereas actually thought is the one which controls each one of us." *Thought is creating divisions out of itself and then saying that they are there naturally. This is another major feature of thought: Thought doesn't know it is doing something and then it struggles against it is doing. It doesn't want to know that it is doing it. And thought struggles against the results, trying to avoid those unpleasant results while keeping on with that way of thinking. That is what I call 'sustained incoherence.*

117 Walid Abdelnasser, *The Media and Dialogue among Civilizations.*
www.arabworldbooks.com/Articles/articles51.htm
118 Interfaith Search refers to a participation in the search for the ultimate reality through intellectual discussions and exercises. There should be a space for dialogue that leads to an intellectual exchange between different religious communities. Such an exchange would continue to nourish each other's faith and enable them to listen together with people of science, people without any faith and people with different ideologies.
119 In this path three stages of communication are essential to follow that are contact (*thodarbu* – in Tamil – Rev Thomas Thangaraj uses this term), relationship (*uravu*), understanding (arivu). Through this dialogue we need to establish these three stages of communication.

It is also reflected in the present Pope's statement to the Indian Bishops on 26th June 2003, Inter-religious dialogue will not only increase mutual understanding and respect for one another but will also help to develop society in harmony with the rights and dignity for all. This clearly shows that at leadership level the churches wanted to encourage the people to engage in dialogue and thus coexist with other religious communities in harmony and peace with justice and human dignity.

120 http://www.vatican.va/roman_curia/pontifical_councils/pccs/documents/rc_pc_pccs_doc_04101989_criteria_en.html

121 http://watkins.gospelcom.net/bible.htm

122 S M Hoover, L S Clark, L Rinie, 64% of wired Americans have used the Internet for Spiritual or Religious purposes, Faith Online, Internet and American Life a research, Washington: Pew Internet and American Life Project. http://www.pewinternet.org/pdfs/PIP_Faith_Online_2004.pdf

123 http://www.ekiba.de/editorial_4109.htm

124 Interfaith Action involves a process of acting together in social processes such as eliminating poverty, exploitation and corruption in our society. This effort is to work together towards the betterment of human beings and human society in general.

125 Michael Amaladoss, *Dialogue as Conflict Resolution: Creative Praxis*

www.sedos.org/english/amaladoss1.html 2004

126 Inter-religious Experience involves engaging in each other's search for meanings of life and of God and thus making a search for ultimate reality and take all together towards God. It also involves in participating in each other's religious activities to test and find whether some of them are meaningful, relevant, nourishing and useful to all. This effort is basically to learn more about each other's spirituality and faith.

127 Fabio Pasqualetti, Characteristics of Digital Culture - A Challenge For Education

http://www.jmcommunications.com/english/DigitalCulture.html

128   http://www.blogcatalog.com/blogs/ezine-blog/posts/tag/goo gle%27s+most+searched+words/

129   This new technology is directing communities towards a new type of society where they become principle organisers [Kellner 1995:2]. The Multi-User Dungeons (MUDs) provide unlimited access to anything on the Net by converging the texts into audio-visual-written- graphic multimedia texts. There is an open access to anyone to create his or her own website. Information is fragmented [Heather Campbell, Cultural Implications of the Internet & Postmodernity, pp39-47, in *Interactions: Theology Meets Film, TV and the Internet.* Edited by Heidi Campbell and Jolyon Mitchell Edinburgh: CTPI, 1999].

130   "We are seeing a revitalization of society. The frameworks are being redesigned from the bottom up. A new more democratic world is becoming possible. ... The Net seems to open a new lease on life for people. Social connections which were never before possible, or which were relatively hard to achieve, are now facilitated by the Net. Geography and time are no longer boundaries. Social limitations and conventions no longer prevent potential friendships or partnerships. In this manner netizens are meeting other netizens from far-away and close by that they might never have met without the Net." Stanely Hauerwas, A Community of Character, (Notre Dame, IN: University of Notre Dame, 1981), 44.

131   European Union Green paper on Convergence of telecommunication, Media and IT sectors -1997 - a policy paper.

132   Hamelink [1997] notes "As a result digital technologies are instrumental in the convergence of electronics, telecommunication and data processing technologies. They bring the formerly separated and different worlds of broadcasters, cable manufacturers, publishers and Internet users together... The personal computer, the television set and the telephone begin to be integrated into real multimedia stations". Cees J. Hamelink "New Information and Communication Technologies, Social Development and Cultural Change". Discussion Paper No. 86, June 1997, United Nations Research Institute for Social

Development, Geneva, Switzerland 1997,
        http://www.unrisd.org/engindex/publ/list/dp/dp86/toc.
htm#TopOfPage
The Nature and Advantages of Digitalisation, 1997.

133 Manuel Castells, Information Technology, Globalization and
Social Development, Papers presented at the UNRISD Conference on
Information Technologies and Social Development. Geneva, 22-23
June 1998, http://www.unrisd.org/infotech/conferen/castelp1.htm

134 . For more valuable reading on cultural issues in cyberspace,
see Elizabeth M. Reid, Cultural Formations in Text-Based Virtual
Realities, M.A. Thesis at University of Melbourne, Australia,
Department of History, 1994. Available from http://www.ee.mu.
oz.au/papers/emr/cv.html.

135 I have given a few examples from the Indian Context. The
Church of South India provides basic information about the churches
and their activities. http://www.csisynod.org/

In the same way the United Evangelical Churches in India provide
a good website with a lot of information about their activities.
        http://www.uelcindia.org/index.html

To see a specific diocese please visit http://www.csitirunelveli.org/
csi_td.asp

136   Marthoma   Church   http://www.marthomachurch.com/
Heritage-Mission/15thcentury-story.htm

The Assemblies of God church - http://business.vsnl.com/zion/

Indian   Pentecostal   church   -   http://www.angelfire.com/al3/
ipcpallipad/ipc.html

Independent Baptist Churches' directory - http://www.baptistinfo.
com/States/INDIA/INDIA.HTM

A bit about CBCNEI http://www.wfn.org/2000/04/msg00025.html

137 There are number of missionary organisations that send
missionaries but do have websites - Diocesan Missionary Band
-http://www.dmpb.org/

Radio Viswavani - www.vishwavani.org & http://www.gospelcom.
net/twr/

Voice of Hope - http://www.radiovoiceofhope.net/

Adventist Radio asia - http://www.awr.org/awr-asia/

Other organisations are Friends Missionary Prayer Band, Indian Missionary Society, National Missionary Society, GEMS, Indian Church Growth Mission (an Indigenous one)

138 http://www.indiaevangelical.org/contrib.html

139 www.utcbangalore.com.

140 http://hbi.gospelcom.net/home.asp

This is Hindustan Bible Institute's website.

Serampore College - http://www.wmcarey.edu/carey/serampore/serampore.htm

Orthodox Seminary - http://www.otsindia.org/seminary/

http://www.otsindia.org

Gurukul http://www.gltc.edu/history.htm

UTC – www.utcbangalore.com

141 http://www.religion-online.org/.

142 http://www.cmai.org/memb-mp.htm

This is a website of Christian Medical Association of India. This website has lots of information about medical work in India. Who is the audience? In what way does it attract the audience? What are the ways of interaction with their promotional work on awareness and networking? These are a few questions that one needs to ask about this website. More people from abroad would have visited this page than many Indians.

http://www.hmiindia.com/academic_04.htm

This is the website of Henry Martin Institute which also provides information about their programmes and activities.

143 www.interfaithinteraction.org

144 Some examples of other groups can be seen in these websites which are mainly for Indian Christians http://asiapacificuniverse.com/asia_pacific/messages30/358.html

http://www.ayrookuzhiyil.bravepages.com/links.html

145 One of the examples is Jesus Calls ministries where you find a kind of tele-evangelism and internet evangelism with much emphasis

on prosperity and promises of blessings.

http://www.prayertoweronline.org/

146 http://www.internetworldstats.com/stats.htm

147 Ecumenical Net can be seen in the website - http://www. ecunet.org/

another ecumenical site - http://home.wizard.org/eocc/eocc1/front. html

148 http://reconstruction.eserver.org/052/rheindorfintro.shtml

149 Markus Raindorf, An Editorial Introduction to "Reconstructing Media" *Reconstruction: Studies in Contemporary Culture.* 5.2, Spring 2005.

150 I quote the text from Silvio Waisbord [2001:10-16] "The value of participatory media is not in being instruments of transmission but of communication, that is, for exchanging views and involving members. Community media dealt with various subjects: literacy, health, safety, agricultural productivity, land ownership, gender, and religion. There have been a number of paradigmatic examples. In Latin America, miners' and peasants' radio in Bolivia, grassroots video in peasant and indigenous movements in Brazil, tape recorders in Guatemala, small-scale multimedia in Peru and other cases of low-powered media based in unions and churches were offered as concrete examples of participatory communication development (Beltrán 1993). Canada's "Fogo process" was another experience informed by similar principles in which populations living in remote areas actively produced videos to discuss community issues of people living in remote areas and to communicate with outsiders about their concerns and expectations (Williamson 1991). In Africa, popular theatre has been successfully used to increase women's participation and ability to deal with primary care problems. Through songs and storytelling, women were able to raise awareness and attention to issues and address problems, something that had not been achieved through "modern" media such as television and newspapers (Mlama 1991). Community participation through popular theatre motivated rural communities to become involved in health care. Participation

was credited for the reduction of preventable diseases such as cholera and severe diarrhoea after communities constructed infrastructure that helped to improve sanitary conditions situation (Kalipeni and Kamlongera 1996).

151 Lucinda. Coleman, 'Worship God in Dance' Renewal *Journal* #6 (1995:2), Brisbane, Australia, pp. 35-44. http://www.pastornet.net. au/renewal/journal6/coleman.html

152 No author, Spiritual Significance of Dance, *Theology of Dance*.

http://orgs.sa.ucsb.edu/actsone8/Sym_Dance.html

153 Francis Barboza, Dictionary of Indian Christian Theology – Dance.

http://www.drbarboza.com/dictionary.htm

154 Barbara Coeyman, Spirituality of Dance, A Sermon, Oregan: Unitarian church, 2001.

http://www.firstunitarianportland.org/sermons/sermons2001/ SpiritualityOfDance.html

155 http://www.ratzingerfanclub.com/Balthasar/dramatics.html

156 http://www.brechtforum.org/IPE/boal.htm

157 Cees Hamelink, "ICTs AND SOCIAL DEVELOPMENT: THE GLOBAL POLICY CONTEXT", Papers presented at the UNRISD Conference on Information Technologies and Social Development. Geneva, 22-23 June 1998, http://www.unrisd.org/infotech/conferen/ icts/toc.htm.

158 In this techno centric perspective the imperatives of technological development determine social arrangements: technological potential drives history (e.g. Zuboff 1988). It holds that the digital revolution definitively marks the passage of world history into a post-industrial age. Those who support this perspective argue that the emerging global information society is characterised by positive features: there will be more effective health care, better education, more information and diversity of culture. New digital technologies create more choice for people in education, shopping, entertainment, news media and travel.

159 It is based upon the notion that a technological discontinuity (the "digital revolution") causes a social discontinuity (a "Third Wave civilisation - Toffler 1980).

160 In the economy, ICTs will expand productivity and improve employment opportunities; will upgrade the quality of work in many occupations and will offer great many opportunities for small-scale, independent and decentralised forms of production.

161 In politics, decentralised and increased access to unprecedented volumes of information will improve the democratic process, and all people will ultimately be empowered to participate in public decision-making.

162 New and creative lifestyles will emerge, as well as increased opportunities for different cultures to meet and understand each other. New virtual communities will be created that easily transcend all the traditional borderlines and barriers of age, gender, race and religion.

163 A perpetuation of the capitalist mode of production, with a further refinement of managerial control over the production processes which results in massive job displacement and de-skilling.

164 A pseudo-democracy will emerge, allowing people to participate in marginal decisions only. ICTs will enable the exercise of surveillance over their citizens more effectively than before. The proliferation of ICTs in the home will individualise information consumption to a degree that makes the formation of a democratic, public opinion no more than an illusion.

165 There are tendencies of forceful cultural "globalization" - e.g. Macdonaldization and aggressive cultural tribalization - fragmentation of cultural communities into fundamentalist cells with little or no understanding of different tribes.

166 Among the factors shaping ICTs are socio-economic, political, cultural, and gender variables, geography and market forces. [Hamelink 1998]

167 My understanding of communication is developed from James Carey's ritual view of communication. Communication is defined as an ongoing process in which people participate and interact

in sharing, negotiating and constructing meanings (social, cultural and religious).

168   Web-cafes are popular in urban areas of India. Such web-cafes could be made available in rural areas. One of the major constraints is that servers are in city areas and so the phone lines often happen to work through STDs. But most of the village areas are brought under local network and so such problems in many places do not exist anymore. Some computer literate person can help people to have access to those pages that would be useful to them such as market prices for their vegetables or for any other goods, train or bus ticket booking, weather information for fishermen and online medical advice. For all these people can pay a small amount for their use of computers and thereby maintain the system.

169   Internet Radio stations could be made available from anywhere in the world except in India. By buying space in the Web and by providing the content from India, NGOs will be able to operate such stations from rural India. To do this one or two room broadcasting centres could be developed in villages from where they can communicate to different parts of the world. Only by networking and popularising such radio stations will the project be successful. Such type of webcasting should consider entertainment, educational, informative and development oriented programmes. This could operate like some of the community radio centres that are already doing some narrowcasting in India. Here the investment and operational costs are comparatively cheap. There is no clear-cut policy by the Indian Government about webcasting. Development oriented information can be made available to the public through such internet radio casting.

170   In rural villages local Panchayat buildings have loud speakers and display notice boards. Local village radio stations are given a licence by the government if they are used for educational and developmental purposes. These means could be networked with the Internet and Computer system in such a way that the selected useful message could reach people, who in turn can also respond to certain

messages among themselves. If the people can meet together at the computer centre, they can also communicate to other villages through the net. I identified this as a multicasting model because ICT and other media could be used together with a different use of ICT in different areas. This would be cheaper than other broadcasting or narrowcasting practices. This would be a participatory event and could be modified to suit the needs of the people.

171 MS Swaminathan Project in Pondicherry uses computers to supply useful information to the fisher folk. The NGOs encourage people to participate in using the net. People from marginalised communities think that having access to computers means a step up in their status. Having computers in a Dalit's village brings non-dalits to their place. It also allows the Dalits to communicate to others. They provide information about weather, pesticides, market prices, cost of seeds and fertilizer. Other government schemes are also announced such as Women Public Welfare Schemes, low cost insurance and health issues, Government provisions and applications online for benefits. Mailing complaints to officials and to political leaders is also made easy in this process.

172 Subhash Bhatnagar, "Information Technology and Development: Foundation and Key Issues" in *Information and Communication Technology in Development - Cases from India, et al by Subhash Bhatagar and Robert Schware, New Delhi:* Sage, 2000, pp.17-32.

173 http://www.lycos.com/info/tiananmen-square-massacre--students.html?page=2

http://www.rfa.org/english/internet-censorship/netizenstiananmen-04212009175648.html

174 **John Roxborogh** Persecution: Interpreting the information on the Internet, Evangelical Review of Theology, 24:1, 31-40, 2000. - The advent of email, the internet and then the development of the World Wide Web have enabled minority groups to tell their stories to a global audience. He raises questions about quality in what is reported and asks us to exercise discretion in making information

public. Judgement in analysis and wisdom is essential in determining strategies to ameliorate suffering.

175 A.K Gupta, Brij Kothari and Krit Patel, Knowledge, Network for Recognising, Respecting and Rewarding Grassroots Innovation! – in *Information and Communication Technology in Development - Cases from India, et al by Subhash Bhatagar and Robert Schware, New Delhi:* Sage, 2000, pp.117-131.

176 We need to follow some of the examples already set before us – such as Reformed Online where virtual library of Reformed Protestantism.... Question of understanding of community... Bibliography, Libraries, Full Text Resources, Original Documents/ Texts from the 16th Century, Links... Making it free for those who are not able to access this at the cost of those who can access these page. http://www.reformiert-online.net:8080/t/eng/bibliothek/inedx. jsp Reformed Online Library Homepage. I appreciate the team that worked on this very useful website.

177 Long back the churches, temples and mosques played a major role as the centre of the community. They provided values, worldviews and attitude to her members – particularly to the children. Nowadays it is the mass media particularly television that has taken over this role in providing values and worldviews to the children and even to the adults. Interestingly it is not merely the local media but the global media which is playing this role of a teacher, priest and parent argues Gregor Goethals. Due to economic interests and the concentration of global media in a few rich Mughals, they happen to promote a neo-liberal ideology that suits their business of competition, survival and successful stories. This has led to the commoditisation of values, people's lives, service, faith and religion. Even the public sphere is shrinking into a private and personal space where everything can be bought and sold. Only those things that are saleable can be transmitted through mass media. In such context there is often no public sphere where the basic human values are often neglected or rejected for the churches.

John Joshva Raja

178 First of all there are many definitions of globalization. I give one or two for simplicity in defining the word. Mowlana [1996:198] defines globalization "as a process of structuration that encompasses homogenization and heterogenization – process in which agencies operation under different temporal sequences interact to connect and alter varying structures of social existence to create a structurally oligarchic, but interconnected, world". Mohammadi [1997:3] also identifies globalization "as the way in which, under contemporary conditions especially, relations of power and communication are stretched across the globe, involving compressions of time and space and a recomposition of social relationships" From different perspectives the word is critically defined. For Traber [2003] globalization is undoubtedly a continuation of Western Imperialism whether economic, political or technological or broadly cultural. The globalization of the mass media in terms of professional techniques is an accomplished fact. Globalization of the media for Chomsky [1996] means huge increases in advertising, especially foreign commodities. It also means a much narrower concentration of media sources. It will reflect the points of view of those who can amass the huge capital to run international media. Diversity and information will decline; media will get more and more advertiser-oriented.

179 The Hindu, 15th October 1997, Supplement Opportunities.

180 Nikki Townsley, Forecast and Recommendations: Television and Globalization, www.matei.org/research/globaltv/forecast.html

181 Tissa Balasuriya, Recolonization and Debt Crisis, p8-12, in Globalization: A Challenge to the Church edited by Jagadish Gandhi and George Cheriyan, Chennai, Association of Christian institutes for Social Concern in Asia.

182 In 1960s Alternative media was understood in Latin American region as indispensable weapon of political communication to combat disinformation and misinformation to connect members, and to spread political ideology [WACC, 2001:1]. Such media were basically inspired by the Leninist and Gramscian writings about the

role of intellectuals in revolutionary action and thus were identified as revolutionary media. Taking Paulo Freire's concept of alternative communication some of the catholic churches have supported and developed grassroots communication among poor communities (Heresca 1995; O'connor 1989). In 1970s the oppressive regimes that tended to asphyxiate the public sphere and to let the state and the market rule made the people at the margins to find their own alternative means of communication (Kucinski 1991: xiii). The alternative media operated as a corrective mechanism to the main stream media and became the expression of the public (Rodrigues 1986: 55-56). It brought the alternatives and the oppositional groups together (Raymond Williams 1977:55-56).

Would you like to see your manuscript become a book?

Lightning Source UK Ltd.
Milton Keynes UK
UKOW050700191011

180571UK00001B/60/P